SO-AZP-442

Fire Services Today

International City/County Management Association

Fire Services Today:
Managing a Changing
Role and Mission

The International City/County Management Association is the professional and educational organization for appointed administrators and assistant administrators in local government. The purposes of ICMA are to enhance the quality of local government and to nurture and assist professional local government administrators in the United States and other countries. To further its mission, ICMA develops and disseminates new approaches to management through training programs, information services, and publications.

Local government managers—carrying a wide range of titles—serve cities, towns, counties, councils of governments, and state/provincial associations of local governments. They serve at the direction of elected councils and governing boards. ICMA serves these managers and local governments through many programs that aim at improving the manager's professional competence and strengthening the quality of all local governments.

The International City/County Management Association was founded in 1914; adopted its City Management Code of Ethics in 1924; and established its Institute for Training in Municipal Administration in 1934. The institute, in turn, provided the basis for the Municipal Management Series, generally termed the "ICMA Green Books."

ICMA's interests and activities include public management education; standards of ethics for members; the *Municipal Year Book* and other data services; urban research; and newsletters, a monthly magazine, *Public Management,* and other publications. ICMA's efforts toward the improvement of local government management—as represented by this book—are offered for all local governments and educational institutions.

Fire Services Today

Managing a Changing Role and Mission

Edited by
Gerard J. Hoetmer

International
City/County
ICMA
Management
Association

PRACTICAL MANAGEMENT SERIES
Barbara H. Moore, Editor

Fire Services Today
Accountability for Performance
Balanced Growth
Capital Financing Strategies for Local Governments
Capital Projects
Current Issues in Leisure Services
The Entrepreneur in Local Government
Ethical Insight, Ethical Action
Hazardous Materials, Hazardous Waste
Local Economic Development
Long-Term Financial Planning
Managing for Tomorrow
Pay and Benefits
Performance Evaluation
Personnel Practices for the '90s
Police Practice in the '90s
Practical Financial Management
Productivity Improvement Techniques
Quality Management Today
Resolving Conflict
Shaping the Local Economy
Strategic Planning for Local Government
Successful Negotiating in Local Government

The Practical Management Series is devoted to the
presentation of information and ideas from diverse
sources. The views expressed in this book are those of
the contributors and are not necessarily those of ICMA.

Library of Congress Cataloging-in-Publication Data

Fire services today : managing a changing role and mission / edited by
  Gerard J. Hoetmer.
      p. cm. -- (Practical management series)
    ISBN 0-87326-109-7
    1. Fire departments--Management. I. Hoetmer, Gerard J.
  II. Series.
  TH9158.F56   1996
  363.37'068—dc20   96-3668
                                                          CIP

Copyright © 1996 by the International City/County Management
Association, 777 North Capitol Street, N.E., Washington, D.C.
20002. All rights reserved, including rights of
reproduction and use in any form or by any means,
including the making of copies by any photographic
process, or by any electronic or mechanical device,
printed or written or oral, or recording for sound or
visual reproduction, or for use in any knowledge or
retrieval system or device, unless permission in writing
is obtained from the copyright proprietor.

Printed in the United States of America.
2000
5 4 3

Foreword

Over the past twenty years, the number of fires in the United States has steadily decreased, creating an entirely new set of responsibilities for today's fire service. Faced with a changing environment, fire managers now must look far beyond their traditional mission as they carve out a new role in prevention, code services, EMS, and other emergency services.

Fire Services Today: Managing a Changing Role and Mission brings today's fire chief, fire service manager, local government administrator, and assistant administrator up to date on the revolutionary changes affecting this critical function—from new research in fire science to new training paradigms; from funding questions to regulatory compliance; from hoses and ladders to computers and "virtual environments."

This book is part of ICMA's Practical Management Series, which is devoted to serving local officials' needs for timely information on current issues and problems.

ICMA is grateful to staff member Gerard J. Hoetmer, who made time in his busy schedule to compile the book; to Gary B. Marrs, fire chief in Oklahoma City, who shared his experiences with the federal building bombing in that city; to former ICMA staff member Greg Gorden, who prepared the article summarizing a research project on residential sprinklers; and to the organizations that cooperated with the editor and granted permission to reprint the articles contained in the book.

William H. Hansell, Jr.
Executive Director
International City/County
Management Association

About the Editor

Gerard J. Hoetmer has been the assistant executive director for research and development and public policy for the International City/County Management Association since 1989, prior to which he was ICMA's director of public safety programs. A former assistant to the fire chief in Aurora, Colorado, he holds a master's degree in public administration and finance. Mr. Hoetmer represents ICMA to the Federal Emergency Management Agency, the International Association of Fire Chiefs, and the United States Environmental Protection Agency and has served on the 1201 and 1500 Committees of the National Fire Protection Association. He is co-editor of *Emergency Management: Principles and Practice for Local Government.*

About the Authors

Unless otherwise noted, contributors are listed with their affiliations at the time of writing:

Jack Abraham, chief, Clemson University Fire Department/ Emergency Medical Service, Clemson, South Carolina, and adjunct faculty member, Clemson University.

Randy R. Bruegman, chief, Hoffman Estates (Illinois) Fire Department.

Ron Coleman, California state fire marshal and chairman of the IAFC Accreditation Task Force.

Brian Crandell, assistant chief, Rae Fire Department, Bozeman, Montana, and coach, Operations and Planning Sections, Montana Fire Training School, Great Falls, Montana.

Mary Jane Dittmar, associate editor, *Fire Engineering* and *Industrial Fire Safety*.

Karin L. Foster, attorney, Seattle (Washington) Labor Department.

Jessica Gaynor, assistant clinical professor of psychiatry, University of California at San Francisco, and clinical psychologist.

Greg Gorden, assistant parish manager, St. Tammany Parish, Covington, Louisiana

John A. Granito, consulting editor, *NFPA Journal*.

Gerald F. Grover, chief, Bridgeport (Connecticut) Fire Department.

John R. Hall, Jr., assistant vice-president, Fire Analysis and Research Division, National Fire Protection Association.

Ken Lavoie, chief, Covina (California) Fire Department.

John Lawton, city manager, Great Falls, Montana.

John LeCuyer, health and safety coordinator, Training Division, and firefighter, city of Aurora, Colorado.

Murrey E. Loflin, captain, Virginia Beach (Virginia) Fire Department and adjuct instructor and course developer, National Fire Academy.

Gary B. Marrs, chief, Oklahoma City Fire Department.

George Oster, executive officer, Fire Service Institute, Iowa State University, Ames.

Michael T. Reynvaan, partner, Seattle (Washington) Labor Department.

Robert R. Rielage, assistant chief, Colerain Township (Ohio) Fire Department.

Joe Schumacher, district manager and chief budget officer, Arvada (Colorado) Fire Protection District.

James H. Shanley, Jr., fire protection engineer, John A. Kennedy and Associates, Hoffman Estates, Illinois.

Bob D. Simpson, member of the city council, Anaheim, California.

Daniel Stern, clinical psychologist, USAF model juvenile firesetting project for the Police Executive Research Forum (PERF), Washington, D.C.

Harold (Gene) Stofer, member of the board, National Association of Towns and Townships; trustee, Wayne Township, Indiana.

Contents

PART 4
Improving Productivity

Introduction

Gerard J. Hoetmer

Change is inevitable. It is also difficult—for virtually everyone and every organization. Organizations require agreement about their mission and the procedures for achieving that mission. This requires at least the acquiescence, if not the full commitment, of the employees who make up the organization. Positive change therefore requires time. It takes time to plan how to change operating procedures, set new goals and objectives, explain the reasons for change to employees, and obtain their commitment.

Life without change is impossible. Organizations, professions, or individuals that avoid or resist change become irrelevant or ineffectual. Yet radical change—from genetic mutation to political revolution—is almost always destructive. Resistance to gradual change makes organizations susceptible to destructive radical change.

The American fire service today finds itself in such a position. Taken as a whole, it has only grudgingly accepted change, and some sectors have actively resisted it. The U.S. fire service is not a monolithic institution; it consists of all types of organizations and departments—some progressive and some reactionary. But many organizations in the fire service have been reluctant to embrace the change that is needed to prepare for, and keep pace with, the rapidly changing world in which they find themselves. At the same time, there is a growing uneasiness among fire service leaders, leading to calls for more introspection and open dialogue on crucial questions about how to improve services, become more efficient, and bring more value to the customer.

A number of critical issues face today's fire service. Those issues must be addressed if fire departments and fire service organizations are to minimize the threats and capitalize on the opportunities that result from the changing context in which they operate. *Fire Services Today: Managing a Changing Role and Mission* discusses these issues from a variety of perspectives.

The U.S. fire service has made significant strides in the last two decades to reduce the number fires and consequently the injuries and loss of life associated with fire. Yet the United States still has a higher incidence of death, injury, and property destruction from fire than any other nation in the developed world.

The U.S. fire service has also significantly reduced the severity of fires by strengthening its suppression capability via improved fire apparatus and equipment and improvements in training. Yet for the service to continue to improve, it must put an equal emphasis on fire prevention, including fire safety education and the enforcement of building codes and ordinances.

The use of residential fire sprinklers, for example, has vast potential for reducing injuries and loss of life from fire. Yet their use remains limited. The fire service needs to actively promote adoption of residential sprinkler codes and measures to reduce the costs of sprinkler installation. Smoke detectors, which have been proven effective in preventing loss of life due to fire, are installed in over 80 percent of homes, but most homes have no more than one, and in too many homes the smoke detectors are inoperable because of dead or missing batteries.

Another challenge facing today's fire service is the growing demand for emergency medical services (EMS), which in many communities has become the responsibility of local fire departments. The cost of EMS is outpacing the ability of jurisdictions to pay for it, and the number of emergency medical calls as a percentage of total calls is on the rise—often amounting to 70 to 90 percent. Furthermore, unnecessary or nonemergency calls to 911 systems are straining many local government emergency systems. Many fire departments have responded by cross-training firefighters, but the volume of EMS calls is forcing many departments to reevaluate their structure and operations.

The private sector is not shy about seizing opportunities for providing these traditional public services. Rural/Metro and AMR Corporation are aggressively bidding to provide fire and EMS services to local governments. There is no doubt that fire departments will need to find new ways to cope with the increasing demand for EMS.

While the fire service emphasizes the dangers involved in fighting fires, statistics demonstrate that the two primary causes of death for firefighters are heart attacks and vehicle accidents on the way to and from the scene of an incident. More needs to be done to reduce these causes of death in the fire service. Firefighter safety on the fireground depends on good training and proper use of equipment. The fact that firefighter injuries represent 50 percent of all injuries due to fire suggests that greater emphasis needs to be placed on training and the proper use of equipment.

The nature of the fire service makes managing change a challenge in itself. Fire chiefs and management need more and better training in planning, organizing, and leading the fire department. The fire labor union regularly issues votes of no confidence in progressive fire chiefs—a fact surely likely to inhibit the initiation of new approaches or techniques. Fire chiefs frequently stand alone when representing management. To restructure fire services to deal with changing circumstances and demands, management and labor will need to come together to develop a common definition of problems and identify realistic solutions. A significant step toward fostering more positive dialogue is the creation of the IAFC National Fire Service Accreditation Program. This voluntary assessment system should go a long way toward setting nationally accepted standards on which both management and labor can agree.

Each article included in this book was carefully selected from hundreds of articles that have appeared in fire service magazines and journals over the past several years. They represent areas of priority and provide insight into how the fire service is meeting the challenges it faces today.

Managing in a changing environment

The bombing of the federal building in Oklahoma City was a chilling reminder of the broadening role of the fire service. In the opening article, Chief Gary Marrs shares insights he gained from the experience. Suddenly, fighting fire took a back seat to interagency coordination, strategic decision making, and communication with the media and elected officials—and to the realization that in the future local fire departments may find themselves dealing with more acts of urban terrorism.

Next, a panel of fire service experts and observers discuss the variety of different ways that local fire departments are dealing with reductions in funding and increases in service delivery requirements, especially in EMS. They detail how departments are employing user fees and other cost-sharing and revenue-enhancing measures, including fees for service and charges for reinspections for code violations. The article also discusses the impact of unfunded state and federal mandates, the possibilities of regional consolidation and functional consolidation of certain fire department functions such as training, communications, and computer services.

In "EMS: An Overview," Mary Jane Dittmar discusses EMS and its relationship to the fire service, which is often that of a "stepchild" within the department. She discusses several EMS myths as well as the future of combined fire and EMS services.

Another area of rapid change is fire investigation. James H. Shanley, Jr., reports recent fire research that has provided fire investigators with scientifically sound explanations for phenomena fire investigators have observed for years at fire scenes. He also reveals myths based on anecdotal fire investigator observations.

Among the other changes fire managers have faced in recent years are the provisions of the Americans with Disabilities Act (ADA). Karin L. Foster and Michael T. Reynvaan provide an overview of the ADA's employment provisions and illustrate how to analyze their application. They discuss how an employer must carefully look at hiring standards, the interview process, medical examinations, fitness tests, and other factors to ensure that they do not violate ADA requirements. The article also discusses employer defenses to ADA claims.

Dr. John R. Hall, Jr., then provides an overview of home smoke detector use, showing clear evidence of the life-saving effectiveness of detectors. Smoke detectors cut the risk of dying in a home fire by roughly 40 percent, and smoke detectors are able to discover fires so quickly that they can be extinguished by occupants, cutting the number of fires reported to fire departments by 75 to 80 percent. Still, many homeowners fail to refresh their batteries, or they deactivate their smoke detectors out of frustration with nuisance alarms.

Residential sprinklers are another emerging factor in early suppression, and Greg Gorden summarizes a study of barriers to residential sprinkler adoption.

New insights into critical operations

Mary Jane Dittmar opens a discussion of change in critical operations with a discussion of what it takes for a jurisdiction to have an effective EMS system. There are a number of troublesome factors that can interfere with an effective EMS service, including accountability, burnout, stress, recruiting and training, EMS personnel/fire officer interaction in the field, staffing, and wages. The article suggests approaches for each of these areas and discusses some common configurations for providing EMS services, such as using private ambulances and cross-training firefighter paramedics. Finally, the article shows how EMS services are delivered in Atlanta, Georgia; Austin, Texas; Fayetteville, North Carolina; Haines County, Illinois; Phoenix, Arizona; Plano, Texas; and San Jose, California.

James H. Shanley, Jr., continues his discussion of changes in investigation, discussing fire dynamics as one of the most useful tools for determining fire origin. He describes the technical terms and techniques for uncovering both the origin and the cause of a fire, then goes on to describe new tools that are being applied to fire investigation—computer models, dogs, electronic sniffers, and portable gas chromatographs.

Next, Jessica Gaynor and Daniel Stern discuss the psychological profile of juveniles who set fires and effective intervention strategies used to reduce the number of juveniles involved in firesetting.

Improving firefighter safety and training

In the next article, George Oster underscores the point that physical conditioning and fireground training are the keys to reducing firefighter fatalities and injuries. He refers to the Montana State University Fire Training School "training in context" (TIC) concept, which is more fully discussed by Brian Crandell in the article that follows. TIC teaches fundamental skills—not in isolation, but as part of a structured process that simulates the experience of firefighters during an incident.

Another aspect of training is the proper use of hoses, ladders, and other equipment, given that the rate of job-related injuries for firefighters is 4.3 times that for the average worker in private industry. John LeCuyer discusses the application of ergonomics, or the science of human performance and wellness, in relation to jobs in the fire service. He also notes the National Institute for Occupational Safety and Health alert on preventing death and injury among firefighters.

Next, Jack Abraham reminds the reader that the fire department is no different from any private place of business when it comes to complying with regulations of the Occupational Safety and Health Administration (OSHA). He relates what happens during an inspection by OSHA and reviews the administrative options a fire department has if it receives a citation and notification of penalty.

Occupational exposure to bloodborne pathogens is one of the areas in which OSHA provides guidance to fire departments, through standard 29 CFR 1910.1030. Murrey E. Loflin explains how infection control procedures should be instituted in a department.

Improving productivity

Although it was written in 1989, "Lessons in Productivity" by Joe Schumacher still contains sound suggestions for improving productivity in a fire department. Many of them involve using citizen volunteers as well as getting local businesses to assist with code inspection as a community-wide productivity improvement program.

A major tool for productivity in the fire service is the computer. In "From Hoselines to Online," John A. Granito examines the impact of computers on fire services. He reviews the use of PCs for training simulations, including virtual reality environments that simulate the sight, sound, and smell and other sensations of a fire. He also explains how computers have made inspections easier by allowing a single inspector with a pen-based computer to inspect numerous types of businesses and automatically input text put into a computer. Computers are also helping fire departments update their master plans and assist with station location and relocation calculations. The use of advanced computer software also allows a fire department to analyze and understand the productivity of its various program areas.

Finally, the book provides a revealing look at the relationship between fire chiefs and chief administrative officers. Ron Coleman and Randy R. Bruegman report on a survey they gave to city and county managers asking their perceptions of their fire service, the issues that the fire service and chiefs will be facing over the next five years, and their ability to deal with those issues. The results are thought-provoking.

Taken as a whole, the articles in this book present a picture of a service area in evolution. Although change may be difficult, it is heartening to realize that the challenges facing the fire service are least being discussed and alternative strategies and solutions are being tried by those who recognize the imperative of change.

PART 1

Managing in a Changing Environment

It's Not Just a Fire Department Anymore

Gary B. Marrs

If you're a fire chief now or would like to be one someday, have you given much thought to the fact that your department isn't just a fire department anymore? You might say that this is nothing new. We've realized for some time that our fire calls have been dwindling and our other calls have been increasing. But how many of you have really analyzed where we're heading in the fire service? And how many of you have started to prepare your department for whatever the new look is going to be?

We are being challenged to provide the greatest possible level of service to our communities for the tax dollars spent, and I believe the days when citizens never questioned the services provided, or the lack of services provided, are gone for most departments today.

We've known for a long time that our departments are dealing with issues and technologies that change daily. Not only do we encounter new hazards from new technologies, but we also have to deal with new hazards from the political world we live in. How many of you would have thought five or ten years ago that the fire service would need extensive training on how to handle terrorist attacks? I can tell you from first-hand experience that *we do.*

The Oklahoma City bombing

The explosion on April 19, 1995, at the Alfred P. Murrah Federal Building in Oklahoma City showed that no place is immune to these hazards. And it provided plenty of evidence that we are not just a "fire" department anymore.

Early in the first hour of the incident at the federal building, it hit me that we in the fire service haven't had much exposure to urban terrorism. I was standing in front of the building talking to Police Chief Sam Gonzales when he made a comment that really brought that fact home. I said that I couldn't figure out what kind of accidental explosion in the building could have caused that much destruction. He immediately replied that he was fairly certain that it was caused by a car bomb. He had spotted a crater in front of the building and identified what he thought were the remains of the bomb vehicle.

His assessment was based on his training and experience in law enforcement today. Because of my training and experience, I assumed that an accidental explosion of some kind was the cause. You might ask what difference the cause makes in how we handle things from a fire service perspective. It makes a world of difference. It affected how this incident was handled and affects how future incidents should be handled. The following paragraphs will, I hope, provide some insight into the changing world of the fire service and into why it's important for the leaders of the service to realize that "firefighting is all we do" is an outdated attitude.

We responded to the explosion on April 19 as the Oklahoma City *Fire* Department. As it turned out, the only fires to be fought were automobile fires in the parking lot across the street. No fires occurred in the buildings. One pumper company with a crew of four handled the automobile fires within the first few minutes, and for the rest of seventeen days, the fire department engaged in activities other than fighting fire.

Working with other agencies

One of the first things that became obvious was that the site of the bombing was going to be a major crime scene area, creating a completely new set of considerations to deal with. While the fire department was focusing on rescue and recovery, the local, state, and federal law enforcement agencies were focusing on the detailed investigation of the crime required by the legal system.

Are you prepared to coordinate with law enforcement agencies in a manner that achieves the goals of both services? Evidence recovery and documentation has to proceed at the same time as victim rescue and recovery and building stabilization. Procedures need to be established that allow those tasks to be done simultaneously, and relationships need to be in place that allow them to be done in the most efficient way possible.

Building relationships Today's fire chiefs need to develop, or participate in, open communication with the various levels of law enforcement they may have to interact with. We can no longer afford to let personalities or politics determine the course of action when an incident occurs. The communities we serve deserve the best service possible, and they will raise questions—and demand answers—if they don't get it.

Prior to the incident in Oklahoma City, Police Chief Gonzales, FBI Special Agent Bob Ricks (who is in charge of the local office of the FBI), and I had become friends, communicating frequently on both a professional and social level. That proved invaluable in handling the incident. Very early that first morning, we met to discuss long-range plans and goals for what we knew would be a significant undertaking. We agreed that the fire department would be in charge of rescue and recovery efforts for the building and surrounding areas, the police department would be in charge of security and perimeter control, and the FBI would be in charge of crime scene activities. They understood that I had to have ultimate authority for the activities in and around the building for safety reasons. I understood that they had ultimate authority for security and the criminal investigation, and I would support them every way possible. For example, we made sure the FBI had access to heavy equipment for their activities, but we monitored those activities to ensure that they would not hamper the rescue and recovery efforts. It was a relationship that worked very well, made possible by the communication network established beforehand.

Accepting help   We in the fire service are quick to say that we can handle anything in our jurisdictions, that we don't need outside help. Not only is this dated thinking, but it puts departments at a disadvantage when they need, or are forced to use, help from the outside. How much training or research have you done to prepare your department for a large influx of outside agencies, all looking to you for guidance and leadership? If you're unable or unwilling to offer it, they'll work without you. Once again, the community won't get the service it deserves.

We must accept the fact that we're not equipped or trained to handle every type of incident without the involvement of other agencies. The Urban Search and Rescue (USAR) teams from the Federal Emergency Management Agency (FEMA) are an invaluable resource for departments that are willing to use them. They bring experience, training, and equipment to an incident that most departments don't have and can't afford. They arrive on the scene ready to support, and follow the directions of, the local department in its activities. Are you willing, and ready, to accept the fact that they can help you, again without personalities and politics getting in the way?

Making good decisions

Hazards today can take many forms, including terrorist activities. The Japanese experience with poisonous gas shows that bombings are not the only things you have to prepare for. Of course, we've been dealing with hazardous materials for some time now. But what if an incident affects the entire community, or if your entire department is trying to rescue some part of the community? Will you know what to do if you have to decide whether to expose your entire department making a quick rescue attempt or hold back and make rescues only with your available haz-mat equipment and trained personnel?

Fire chiefs in the future must seek out information that allows them to make intelligent decisions that affect large numbers of people. For example, statistics show that in a large percentage of terrorist bombing incidents a secondary device is also placed, designed to take out the rescuers. I learned this a few days after the incident. But in the first few minutes after the explosion, an extremely large number of people were allowed to enter the building to help with the rescue. These people, from citizens in nearby buildings to off-duty public safety personnel, had not been systematically accounted for by anyone—and were not accountable to anyone—and they would have greatly increased the problems had a second collapse occurred. In retrospect, those people should have not been allowed to enter the structure. Are you prepared, with training and information, to make that kind of decision in your community?

Working with the media

When tough decisions are necessary, a good relationship with the media is invaluable. During the incident in Oklahoma City, the media worked very well with the fire department's public information officer because, even before the bombing, we enjoyed a good relationship with the local media. They knew we would work with them to meet deadlines, live broadcasts, scheduled newsbreaks, and so on. We continually updated them, even when activity was slow, and we were available for interviews at any time. We understood their need for information to keep their readers and viewers (who are also our citizens) informed, and in turn we asked them to understand that there were things we could not, or would not, discuss.

When it became apparent that the media were starting to question our progress, we put together a pool of reporters from print, radio, and television media and took them on site and into the building. We allowed them to go anywhere they wanted, within safety restrictions, and allowed them to photograph anything they wanted, with the exception of visible victims. The emotional impact of their experience had a profound effect on the rest of the media people. We were no longer asked questions regarding the speed of our work. Again, working with them was positive, when trying to explain away the issue would have been negative.

This type of relationship does not get built overnight. We have been upfront and honest with our local media and have taken the initiative to discuss fire department actions and issues with them for a long time. We have encouraged media representatives to ride with us and see what we do, live in the station and see how we work, and help us reach the public with our programs to better serve our citizens. This relationship has proven to be an asset for us, and it was a significant factor during the bombing incident in the way the nation saw our activities. If you are second-guessing or avoiding the media, you are not using one of the best tools you have, especially today, in a world of instant communication.

Relationships with elected officials

Another area in which the groundwork must be laid ahead of time is the fire chief's relationship with elected officials. One of the most important factors in my command of this incident was that the mayor, city council, and city manager did not try to micromanage the operation. They allowed me, the police chief, and all other department heads to operate freely without orders, suggestions, or questions. They were at the scene of the incident almost daily, but only to see whether we needed anything they could help us with.

Elected officials at the state level were just as supportive and concerned. Our governor, state senators and representatives, and department heads of state agencies were eager to make sure we had all we needed. These relationships were well established before the incident, because we'd all talked to each other to learn what support we could give each other to best serve our citizens. When was the last time you set out to determine the best way to coordinate an effort without egos and turf battles getting in the way? You can't wait until you're standing in front of a bombed out building to try to settle differences.

Staffing for the future

All the things I've discussed so far should raise some questions in your mind about your department in the future. I'll throw out one last thing for you to think about: if your department is going to have a new look in the future, you need to think about your employees.

We used our internal training, equipment, and operations to handle this incident, but the need to work with so many other agencies, at all levels of government and private industry, put a premium on customer service and communication skills. Most of our work during this incident involved heavy manual labor operations, but it took people of great compassion and concern to understand what the victims' families, and the community as a whole, were going through while awaiting word of our recovery efforts.

We used our entire department during this incident, but only limited numbers could work at the building itself at one time. Many people were doing very mundane or boring jobs when they really wanted to be involved in the efforts on site. To do this, they had to be the kind of people who understand that if we're going to provide the best service we can, all jobs are important.

We should decide what attributes will be needed by departments of the future. Are we really looking for the kind of people who can best serve the community today and in the future, or are we still hiring people because they fit the stereotype of the fire service many years ago? Think about it—we're not just a fire department anymore.

Funding Fire Protection: A Roundtable

Note from Scott Baltic, editor of **Fire Chief:** *One of our regular contributors, A.K. Rosenhan, of Starkville, Miss., is fond of saying that fires aren't put out with water, they're put out with money. If that isn't a truism within the fire service, it probably should be.*

Whether a department pays its personnel or not, whether its funding comes from local taxes or from pancake breakfasts, money is an indispensable resource for fire suppression, fire prevention, EMS, hazmat and anything else a department might include among its reasons for existence.

What's more, for many departments, their usual sources of funding are no longer adequate for traditional missions (or at least for traditional missions approached in traditional ways), much less for additional responsibilities.

That's why we pulled out the stops on this one. Three paid fire departments, a combination department, a volunteer department, the International City/County Management Association and the National Association of Towns and Townships are all represented among our eight panelists: Randy R. Bruegman, chief, Hoffman Estates (Illinois) Fire Department; Gerald F. Grover, chief, Bridgeport (Connecticut) Fire Department; Gerard J. Hoetmer, assistant executive director, Research and Development, International City/County Management Association; Ken Lavoie, chief, Covina (California) Fire Department; John

Abridged and adapted from "Funding Fire Protection," *Fire Chief* (August 1994) and "Funding Fire Protection, Part 2," *Fire Chief* (September 1994). Reprinted with permission of *Fire Chief* magazine.

Lawton, city manager, Great Falls, Montana; Robert R. Rielage, assistant chief, Colerain Township (Ohio) Fire Department; Bob D. Simpson, member of the city council, Anaheim, California; Harold (Gene) Stofer, member of the board, National Association of Towns and Townships.

After selecting these contributors, FIRE CHIEF asked them to suggest questions for the panel as a whole to consider. Once the questionnaire was final, we sent it to each of our panelists.

Their discussion covered many of the core issues being debated in the fire service today. It seems that when you talk about where the money comes from and where it goes, you wind up talking about the future of the fire service.

Revenue

What are your department's current funding sources? Has your department experienced a recent decline in funding? If so, why has funding declined, and how have you compensated?

Lavoie: Until recently, 100% of our department's funding originated from property and sales taxes collected by the city. These monies were then set aside in a general fund for use by all city departments with the fire department obtaining its "fair share" at budget time.

In recent years, there has been a general decrease in sales tax generation because of the weak California economy, with the accompanying decrease in the general fund and less funding available for local programs from the state. As a result the city experienced a 10% decrease in its budget income this year. We were able to streamline our department line item requests to absorb much of the deficit, but any further cuts may affect service delivery.

Grover: Current funding is through the historical property taxed citywide budget, and the department has experienced a recent decline in funding. Bridgeport is a typical New England town whose early years were spent as an industrial giant. Companies such as Jenkins Valve, General Electric, Hubbell Electric, Bryant Electric and Remington Firearms have left the city or gone out of business completely. We had middle-class flight and government leaders failing to take corrective action.

Funding has declined, and the present administration has started to reinvent government. We are using processes such as TQM, and we just embarked on a program of sharing revenues with department heads who implement innovative revenue sources and ideas.

Rielage: Our department is fairly lucky with regard to its current funding sources. We're on a continuing property levy that generates about $4 million annually. Ohio has basically three funding mechanisms. The state has an income tax, the county has a sales tax, and municipalities have an income tax. Townships must look to property taxes to provide police, fire and general maintenance.

Our budget for about 60,000 residents is based on a millage that's strictly for fire and EMS, including ALS. Therefore our budget is fairly well set, since we are expanding both in residential (in the area of 500 new home starts a year) and commercial and light industry. Nonetheless, cost containment is important, and I'll be talking about some of the things we've tried.

Bruegman: Our department is funded from the general fund, which receives its funding from taxes, both property and sales; licenses and permits; service charges; operating transfers; and other intergovernmental agreements. Our department has not experienced a decline in funding in the past several years, because of growth in the area and the increase in assessed valuation.

Simpson: Anaheim's primary source of funding is from the city's general fund, which is funded from a variety of sources. The three major sources in order of contribution are transient occupancy tax, sales tax and a distant third is property tax.

Funding has declined. Property tax has gone down, as have transient occupancy tax and sales tax. The priority in the city has been to hold the line in public safety to the extent possible. Despite that, there have been cutbacks.

Lawton: Primarily our city fire department is funded through property taxes. Funding has decreased for the fire department, both with direct budget reduction and through the effects of inflation.

In Montana there was a cap on the property tax passed by the voters in 1986, so every year the purchasing power of the dollars available loses ground at the rate of inflation. In 1989 our city faced a budget deficit and was forced to implement drastic budget cuts. A fire station was closed and 12% of our firefighters were laid off.

Stofer: We receive our funding from personal property tax through the trustee, and billing for ambulance services. We also have a county option income tax, which has a 1% cap on it. But due to the economy, the council has frozen it below the 1%.

Funding for the fire service is the topic for conversation at all fire and budget meetings. Unless other funding can be found, it will become necessary to tighten the belt and/or cut services.

Hoetmer: Fire departments have been under greater pressure over the last several years to substantiate why they need a certain level of resources, for what purpose they're using these resources, and whether they're using these resources efficiently.

They're also being asked to look more carefully as to how they can improve their service delivery to the ultimate customer, the citizen.

Both police and fire departments have been fairly insulated, for the most part, from the pressures most other departments have been under for more than a decade. If one looks at the average number of firefighters in cities across the country, that has been fairly consistent at 1.65 firefighters per thousand population since the late 1970s. What this number, of course, does not show is the increased requests for service, especially for EMS, that many fire departments now are delivering.

The question, then, is not whether the revenue picture is breaking down or the revenue decreasing, but that EMS has put increased pressure on fire departments through an ever-increasing workload. The unfortunate side effect of this has been that fire departments have continued keeping most resources in fire response, even though EMS services typically receive many more calls. The question could then be "How should we allocate the available resources differently in a more equitable manner toward areas that are in higher demand, such as EMS?"

Is your department using, or have you tried, user fees, impact fees, cost-sharing or similar methods to help meet your current or projected budget? What innovative funding ideas have you discussed, tried or heard about recently?

Rielage: While we have not used user or impact fees per se, we do have cost sharing and this has helped appreciably in our finances. We operate as part of a regional communications center that services most of Hamilton County, and we are by far their largest customer, with about 6,000 emergency runs a year and an additional 3,500 we define as service calls.

The total cost of the communications center to the township, including the police, is about $200,000. Of that, the fire department's share is somewhere around $80,000. That puts us somewhere around $15 or less per call per dispatch. Even with the police at this point we could not staff our own public safety answering point for 911 and dispatch for anywhere near the $200,000 figure.

In addition, we take advantage of county- and statewide purchasing agreements. For example, a standard Ford LTD Crown Victoria which some jurisdictions paid $22,000 for a year and a half ago, we paid $14,000 for along with the joint purchase requisition from Hamilton County.

Lavoie: As part of our marketing campaign to ensure future money allocations, our department enacted a service cost recovery fee for over 50 services being performed by the department above and beyond routine emergency service delivery. We anticipate recovering nearly $250,000 in fees the first year.

Grover: The very first thing a town should do is take a very hard look at their fire department budget. The chief should do a thorough analysis of expenses.

When we did this, we found that we were paying about $4,000 a month in phone bills for phones that were not being used at all or being used by other city agencies. For example, there was an old emergency operating center that had 18 phone lines, and the fire department was being charged $156 per month, and none of these phones were ever being used. That's just one example of where this $4,000 in taxpayer dollars was being wasted.

Besides that, we've tried to be innovative and think of ideas to gain revenues. For example, we instituted a Phase 1 hazardous materials site assessment fee. We got this idea from my previous department, from Acting Fire Marshal John Scarback. John and I were on the phone one day, and he brought to my attention that they had instituted a fee for hazardous materials site assessments.

There are companies that are in business to do environmental searches of properties. They call the local fire marshal and ask him to provide all the records of a particular site and then charge their customer anywhere from $2,000 to $3,000 for these reports that they get from the fire department for virtually no charge.

We enacted an ordinance in Bridgeport and started charging $75 per Phase 1 site assessment. It has worked rather well, although we met with some reaction from companies who cited the Freedom of Information Act. They felt that under this act these reports should be given free of charge. We got around this by having the ordinance and saying that the fee was to make up for the salary and time taken up by our fire department.

We also increased all our fire marshal fees. We were taking revenues annually of about $3,900, and through ordinances we have increased that to about $55,000.

We are also looking at offering our arson investigation expertise to smaller neighboring towns. We believe it would be less costly for them to pay for our expertise on investigations on a per-fire basis than to have a full-time fire marshal with salary and benefits. We are also exploring the possibilities of contracting out our fire department maintenance shop and mechanical services to neighboring small career departments and volunteer fire departments.

Also, we are entertaining proposing a fire education curriculum to the school board for a fee. The board of education receives state funding for such programs at a rate of $2 for every $1 of expense. These expenses are reimbursed by the State of Connecticut, and we feel this may be a source of revenue for our fire prevention bureau.

We are also looking at impact development fees for a new 100-acre theme park and marina by developer Donald Trump. Additionally, we are looking at benefit assessment charges for all new developments that may take place in Bridgeport.

Stofer: We have taken advantage of alternative methods such as the user fee on ambulance service. This method helped as a band-aid, but with collection rates so low and no way to collect from out-of-town people, who are a large part of our users, it doesn't answer the problem completely.

The county option income tax really was a large help in bringing our finances up to the cost of running the department in the '90s, but since the cap has been put on, the cost of running the department is far exceeding the monies that COIT brought us.

We have discussed billing for fire runs through homeowners insurance, but have not tried this yet.

Lawton: In 1990 I initiated a task force to discuss alternative funding sources for a projected budget deficit in the fire department's share of the general fund. User fees, along with other funding options, were explored.

As union jurisdictional disputes were interjected, talks bogged down. Talks became ideological diatribes stifling creativity. The reality of the budget deficit was ignored. It became apparent that it was management's job to be creative and responsible. We were. One-sided creativity has its limitations, and one-sided responsibility is equally limiting. The net effect was second-guessing the motives of the task force.

Some union members did not want to be implicated in the decision-making process, because the process may have affected hours, wages and working conditions, and because it's safer to be loyal to one's truck-floor colleagues. Union and personal loyalties prevailed. Exoneration from having to make unpopular decisions was attained at the cost of responsible proactive participation. Exploration of alternative funding sources died from lack of moral courage.

Simpson: The Anaheim Fire Department has a standard fire prevention fee structure for new businesses and monitoring of the established business community. The advent of hazardous materials disclosure and underground storage tank inspections has increased fee collections significantly in the prevention area, with some reimbursement to suppression. The new underground storage tank structure is a cost-versus-expense operating environment whereby revenues directly reflect cost recovery and are not to support other fire department functions.

The total revenues estimated for fire prevention activities, including arson and environmental protection (hazmat disclosure and underground tanks), are $854,000. Compared to the estimated expense of providing these services ($1.7 million), about 50% of the cost is recovered through fee and charges.

The true fee-for-service is the paramedic subscription and direct billing process. Although full cost recovery does not appear possible with a $36 annual fee, the volume of subscribers allows the department to fully fund labor premiums and operating costs associated with EMS, and still offset some additional costs that would otherwise be a draw on the general fund. This offset is about $2.3 million in the 1994/95 budget. There are labor premiums for paramedics in the suppression budget, so the actual savings to the general fund are about $500,000 less.

The total revenues estimated to offset expenses in suppression and EMS for FY 1994/95 are about $3.2 million. This includes the EMS revenues and hazmat reimbursements combined with miscellaneous fee collections. Compared to the expense budget for those services ($21.9 million), about 14.7% of the cost is funded through fees and charges.

Would the voters in your jurisdiction be in favor of a fee-for-service charge for certain fire department services? Why or why not? If so, under what conditions and for what services? Would you be in favor of creating an "assessment district" for your jurisdiction as a fire department funding mechanism?

Lawton: With the right information the public would accept fees for certain services provided by the department with the knowledge that the fees were being used to offset the cost of providing that service. It would also help to be able to offset current property tax assessments.

Eventually, this could even come from the fire insurance provider under a systems approach that recognizes the building occupant as responsible for fire protection. The homeowner would be responsible for the well-being of his domicile through available fire protection technologies. The homeowner would pay a fee in response to neglect of the prevention system. The fee would cover the cost of fire suppression.

Bruegman: With the current political climate in our area, fees for service would not be widely accepted. Having moved to the Midwest from the West Coast, where that is commonplace, I found one of the biggest changes has been the attitude of the general constituency in their expectation of what their taxes are to do for them. In the Midwest, people paying property and sales tax expect local jurisdictions to provide certain fundamental services. One of those services is fire and EMS protection.

Grover: Bridgeport, like many New England towns, has been hit harshly by the fiscal decline, so we need to be careful that we do not violate the "taxpayer is our customer" idea. Large-scale industry making a rapid exit from New England has caused the local residential homeowner, middle-income taxpayer to bear the burden for public safety in our towns. It then becomes imperative that any fee-for-service charge does not affect negatively that segment of the population.

Frankly, they are overburdened now and any more financial stress will simply add to middle-income flight. For example, recently a neighboring more affluent town enacted a $90 fee for all residential properties, single-family included, that do not have a working smoke detector. They have also implemented a similar $90 fine for false home security alarms.

That may be well and good where residents have the ability to pay, however, in Bridgeport, this would be a very sensitive issue and would not fly. You need to look at the demographics of your area and make a conscious decision, both politically and practically, before implementing any type of alternative funding.

I would favor creating an assessment district only with the prerequisite that it was acceptable to the voters. Last year, Bridgeport had to close two fire companies. One neighborhood was very incensed and averse to these closings. In a situation such as this, if we were to propose for that particular neighborhood a service charge to be included in their annual property tax bill, there is a possibility that type of assessment district could work.

Stofer: Our voters would be in favor of increases, as long as they funded fire services and kept them from losing services.

I do not agree with assessment fees. I think there should be alternatives, more of a user fee than an assessment. The taxpayers in our area would be willing to pay a user fee if money would go to fire and EMS only. There also should be some type of charge to companies that sell fire insurance in our area, because without our protection, their losses would be larger.

Lavoie: The voters in my jurisdiction recalled the entire five-member city council for enacting a 5% utility tax. Thus the introduction to the newly elected city council of a fee-for-service, or as we called it a "cost recovery" program, was proposed with great care and consideration.

The department conducted a major marketing campaign in educating the citizens and business owners of the community to the need for such a mechanism, and explaining why the program was being proposed. The proposal went before the council in open, advertised session with no opposition from the citizens or business owners being expressed and passed the council 5-to-0.

The problem with assessment districts is, most jurisdiction managers want to use the monies generated by the assessment district beyond the use intended. If the stipulation can be placed in the assessment district agreement mandating that funds can only be used for department offsets, so much the better.

Simpson: Passing taxes of any kind in California is extremely difficult. On June 7, 1994, the citizens of Fullerton, a neighboring community to Anaheim, of well in excess of 100,000 people, successfully recalled three council members, including the mayor, for imposing a 2% utility users tax in the community. Such actions make politicians very nervous.

Yet we had a utility tax in our community for a short time, and there was no real hue and cry. My instinct is if such a tax were attempted now, the result would be dramatically different. Voters, in the form of homeowner's associations and neighborhood groups, have begun to realize they have influence and are beginning to use it. We tried to pass a per parcel tax for the express purpose of funding police services, which are woefully inadequate, and it was soundly defeated.

The difficulty is the mistrust of government. People are not convinced that maximum use has been made of current tax dollars. When they become convinced of that, they are willing to be taxed. Orange County supported a 0.5% sales tax for transportation by a wide margin. The measure clearly demonstrated in quantifiable terms just what the improvements would be and how they would benefit traffic and transportation.

If the same effort were given to improvement in public safety, I believe it could be passed. Would I support it? Yes, and would work hard to ensure its passage. In the case of fire, it would need to be shown that the city enjoys a high level of not only fire protection but EMS as well. It can't be one of those "Let's put it on the ballot and let the voters decide."

Has your master plan reflected or taken advantage of alternative methods of financing your emergency or nonemergency services?

Lawton: Why does it have to be "methods of financing"? The public will pay for services it needs or desires. If the public feels it needs a fire department and the services it delivers, they will be willing to fund those services at whatever level of service delivery they desire. The rest will become a historical footnote.

Bruegman: Our five-year comprehensive plan does not address alternative methods of financing but specifically focuses on establishing service level objectives, standards of response coverage to meet those objectives and operational support issues related to providing the standards of coverage.

Lavoie: The jurisdictions that have master plans (most do not) are better prepared to address this issue, and most probably have already taken this into consideration. In my jurisdiction, cost recovery is now a very important component of the city and fire department's master plan.

Have you considered any internal consolidation of services within your municipal entity, such as combining the building department and the fire inspection bureau?

Bruegman: At present, our department has not been involved in any internal consolidation of services, although the village recently went through a reorganization whereby community development, the building department and engineering were combined into one department. This was about 12 months ago and has been working very well to date.

Lawton: We haven't really consolidated any services. The fire department began patrolling some recreation areas for the purpose of enforcing safety ordinances. Firefighters will be issuing tickets to violators and also will provide a presence to inhibit unwanted activity.

With the fire department providing this service, the police won't have to dedicate manpower for patrolling the parks. In the future there should be an emphasis on cross-training between firefighters and police.

Grover: The obstacle to this point has been basically a turf battle. The building inspection personnel are reluctant to be placed under the control of the fire department, or any other department head for that matter. This is understandable.

I have discussed this very issue with other fire chiefs, and it has been our collective opinion that initially combining the building department into the fire department is a bear of a problem to control. However, I believe the benefit to the taxpayer far exceeds the negatives.

It establishes efficient, one-stop shopping for the taxpayer. Additionally, you could charge a fee to the person who comes to the fire department for the sundry amount of work permits that he would need from the building department for development. An employee could be assigned to go through the process and obtain all the permits this customer would need and simply charge a fee of $100.

Furthermore, an advantage would be that the integrity of the inspection process would be strengthened. The fire service has a reputation for integrity and dedication to public safety. Historically, the corruption and delinquency of building departments are notorious and well documented. Placing the building department under the fire department enhances its reputation and leaves little room for the integrity of the process to be compromised.

Simpson: Anaheim recently completed a consolidation of inspection services study between the fire, code enforcement and building departments. An independent consultant recommended no changes from current practices and congratulated us for having sought to eliminate duplication of effort while encouraging cross-training of inspectors.

In many jurisdictions, the traditional system under which public fire protection was funded by real estate taxes is breaking down. Departments increasingly find themselves scrambling for new revenue sources, many of which are temporary in nature or not very lucrative. Is it safe to assume that the funding system will stabilize again at some point, say in the next decade? If so, what will that new system look like? If not, how will fire departments survive? Assuming that funding will continue to be a problem, what role will privatization play, and how can communities ensure a quality product from the private sector?

Rielage: I don't necessarily see property taxes stabilizing in the next 10 years. Rather, I think we need to use the property tax as a basis and look at other sources of funding. This would include impact fees and assessment districts as well as consolidation and merger.

We were fortunate in passing our existing levy in 1988 which at the time had not felt the adverse feelings of the taxpaying public. However, we just attempted in May a county-wide communications levy to upgrade all of the fire and police operations in Hamilton County, including the City of Cincinnati, to a combined 800MHz trunking system, thus allowing more interoperability between city and county departments.

This was to be a slightly more than 1 mill levy for five years, and it was soundly defeated by the county populace, even though there was some down-the-road efficiency that we were trying to propose, as well as the safety of the individual fire and police officers. The public, overwhelmingly, felt that they have been taxed enough.

Stofer: I don't feel that property tax will pay for the fire service in the near future, because too many property-tax payers are on fixed incomes. Possibly a sales tax will be the answer to funding public safety.

I don't see how privatization can lower the cost of providing public safety, and if it could, would we get the same quality service we get from the firefighters today? From my view of privatization, the companies that are giving this service don't provide the trained personnel to do the job. Privatization will never work in the fire service, because you will lose control of the fire service.

Grover: Labor organizations will need to take a deep look inside themselves. We can survive by working cooperatively with our labor organizations. We will need to be business-minded together and underbid any attempt at privatization. Intelligent, quality people are dispersed between the fire service management and labor equally. They need to put these collective talents together and ward off any attempt by private business to take away the camaraderie, dedication and courage we display on a daily basis all over this country.

Nobody does it better than the uniformed, municipal firefighter. Pardon my arrogance, but the private sector couldn't carry our boots. If we put our business minds together, we could do it better and cheaper than any private organization.

Simpson: It's not safe to assume that funding sources will stabilize for the fire service in the next 10 years, or maybe even the next millennium. There will continue to be taxpayer's revolts, and the public and public officials will continue to become more informed. The public has always indicated support for public safety, but not support at any cost.

Fire departments will survive because they are a vitally needed service (enhanced by the advent of EMS). The extent to which they survive will depend on whether they choose to remain parochial and how willing they are to be innovative. Single-purpose enterprises rarely ever succeed.

The threat of privatization is ever-present and will remain so. Government has finally begun to emerge from the dark ages, albeit slowly in many cases, and discover the world of public/private partnerships. They work. They work well only if they are intelligently approached, realizing that both sides may have a vital role to play.

I am not an advocate of privatizing fire departments, far from it. I gave my life to the service, and it remains my first love. There are services that are essential public services best performed by government. Fire and police may be the last bastions of those, but I consider them sacrosanct. I am, however, an advocate of exploring any and everything possible to reduce costs and maximize service.

The question of how to ensure quality service for fire protection from private enterprise is difficult. You can write tight specs, set high standards, demand quality training and do all those good things, but the real test is in delivery, and that can only be measured in actual operation. It is relative to fire loss and certainly to loss of life.

Bruegman: I believe it's safe to assume that funding mechanisms will stabilize again. If you look back at the historical ebbs and flows of different geographic areas of the country, we see that about every 10 years there's a downturn in the economic development of various regions. It usually takes three to four years to climb back out.

The issue that's looming for the fire service is not so much the funding system, but the demands from an expanding need for services. As we have seen the federal government drive down programs from the federal to the state and ultimately to the local level, fire departments all across the country find themselves having to compete for dollars to provide services that 10 years ago didn't even exist at the local level. This plays a role in the move to privatize.

As to how communities can ensure quality product from the private sector, we need to step back and ask ourselves how we can ensure quality product from the *public* sector, because that's the most critical question. If we don't ensure that we're delivering a quality level of service in the most cost-effective manner, that's what truly opens the door to privatization.

Lawton: No, it's not safe to say that the funding issue will resolve itself at any time, in fact, it will get worse. By the turn of the century, fire departments that cling to traditional roles will be able to show off their equipment and exploits in the Smithsonian Museum of History and Technology.

People are no longer willing to pay for traditional public services. Privatization, alternative revenue sources, new missions and consolidation will all have to play a larger role. Where privatization is used, quality can be controlled through effective contracting and contract monitoring.

Fire departments, like other local government services, are being asked to do more with less. In the private sector the theme has been downsizing and productivity improvement. Is the real issue not funding fire protection, but rather how does the fire service improve its productivity?

Grover: In today's fiscal environment it's a little bit of both. Municipalities need to determine what level of fire protection is required and then provide the funding for that service.

There are few municipalities that haven't taken a hard look at downsizing their fire departments. It's important that they go through this downsizing intelligently and determine a safe level of fire protection, both for the safety of the community and the safety of its firefighters. Government leaders also need to demand from their fire service leaders innovative ideas about productivity and funding.

Hoetmer: Fire departments have made great strides over the last decade. They have improved training and occupational safety and health standards, and have become more specialized to be able to respond to a variety of incidents, which in earlier years were done on a more ad hoc basis.

We now have hazmat teams, arson task forces and search/rescue parties. These are all good outcomes of a much better managed fire service. These improvements also point to how fire departments have improved their effectiveness through training.

Nevertheless, a good part of the fire service still spends a great deal of time waiting for incidents to occur. Today that mode of operation is totally unacceptable. Prefire planning, code inspections and public fire education need to be done by all members of the fire service on a continuous basis.

Transferring the cost of fire protection to the private sector via strong building codes and built-in fire protection, such as sprinklers and smoke detectors, all help reduce the cost of delivering fire services and improve the safety of communities, simply because these measures are much more effective than any fire response could possibly be.

Because public safety has always been one of the primary services that a local government promises to its citizens, police and fire services have traditionally been protected from cuts to their budgets even in hard recessionary times.

However, this should not keep a fire department from looking for efficiencies and ways to improve its effectiveness, so that other local services citizens want (such as youth programs, library services, etc.) don't face drastic cutbacks. Fire department leaders need to begin to view their service in a larger array of local government services.

Lavoie: The fire service and in particular fire suppression is a very labor-intensive operation. True, fire suppression is a small percentage of our service delivery operation today, but suppression is primarily why we are here. If we as a fire service can ever get across the point to decision-makers, the bureaucrats, that being proactive is less expensive than being reactive, then and only then, can we be less labor-intensive.

Bruegman: Depending on what part of the country you live in, the real issue can be funding for fire protection, because we've seen budgets continually cut. A good example is California.

For much of the country, however, the issue is really one of how we improve on our productivity and efficiency. There I think we can take a few pages from our fire service colleagues on the international front and from those that provide private fire protection and EMS services within the United States.

Simpson: Frankly, I find the subject of downsizing and productivity improvement for the fire service boring in the extreme.

People have tried for years to make firefighters productive without really understanding the nature of the profession.

Try thinking of productivity in terms of efficiency and innovation. What can we do better? Are we maximizing resources? The funding question is raised again here. Is the problem funding or increased productivity? It is and will remain *funding*.

Fire departments are expensive. They are labor intensive, and the station distribution system must be extensive if it is to be effective. The question fire chiefs must be able to answer is "Have we gotten the most we can out of what we have?"

Lawton: The real issue is what changes does the fire service need to make to meet the needs of the customers. Fire departments sometimes seem to be trying to find ways to be "productive" for the purposes of job justification, without really meeting the needs of the customer.

Why else would fire departments and unions spend an absurd amount of time defending suppression budgets so they can man the "ole snorkel," rather than fighting for mandatory sprinkler legislation, increasing fire prevention budgets or adopting better fire suppression technologies?

Rielage: The broader question is one of productivity in career, volunteer and combination departments. Taxpayers want to know that their dollars are being spent most efficiently. For example, will the traditional 24-hour day with 48 or 72 hours off go by the wayside, and are governmental officials finding that a 10/14 system, perhaps even without a sleeping cycle, would be more productive in the fire service?

For example, it makes sense to inspect public occupancies when they're open. If a bar is open from 7 in the evening until 2:30 in the morning, then perhaps inspection should take place at midnight. This is the kind of efficiency people are looking for, but perhaps not yet vocalizing.

As an aside, the recent change in NFPA 1500 has been heralded by some as a way for the fire service to stop the budgetary ax. I don't view it as that. Politicians will continue to try to consolidate and close fire stations or look to other methods to augment the numbers and keep stations open. By that, I mean auxiliary firefighters, combination departments or even volunteers who are qualified to a certain level, even to the same level as career personnel.

It will be interesting to see how some departments respond to such suggestions. Is the issue one really of safety, that is, four, five or six people responding on an engine or truck company, as NFPA 1500 now indicates, or is it a way of creating more jobs or less attrition in the fire service?

After reading *Reinventing Government* and hearing comments by the general public, I don't believe the average citizen will allow the genie back in the bottle. The fire service will be held to a higher standard of productivity.

If we're dealing with a true safety issue, then it should make no difference to the fire service whether the four, five or six individuals responding are career, part-paid or even volunteer, as long as they're trained to a given level. More and more states are training even volunteer personnel to the same level Firefighter I, II or even III as required by career departments. I envision all but the most stalwart departments becoming something of a combination department, whether that's with auxiliaries, part-paid individuals or volunteers of some nature.

Expenses

Even though a jurisdiction could find itself spending more than $150,000 on a fairly ordinary pumper these days, over the rig's 20-year service life, labor costs in a career department will dwarf that price. What do you envision happening to labor costs in the fire service, in both union and non-union departments? What can paid and combination departments do to keep their labor costs down?

Lavoie: Until we make the transition from being reactive (suppression) to a proactive (prevention) service, we cannot make a major impact on the very labor-intensive operation called fire suppression. Only when the decision-makers realize that every time they place an element that increases the fire loading in that community and further stress on the fire department's already limited resources, can the labor-intensive issues related to suppression, both career or volunteer, be addressed.

Cut the fire loading, we may be able to handle what we already have. Continue fire loading, I will continue to ask for more resources. My fire service delivery system is about as efficient as it can be with the resources currently available.

Rielage: If I were to look to the 21st century, I would see that career firefighters will be a cadre of the fire service. These individuals will probably be required to at least have an associate's degree in fire science prior to being hired, much the same as some of our European friends. This career nucleus will then be the linking pins keeping the department together, whatever form it may take.

Borrowing the idea from our city manager friend in Great Falls, the career department may take care of such things as initial fires, fire inspections, public education and EMS. But other departments or staffing pools such as public works may be called upon for the large surround-and-drown non-interior firefighting operations.

Hoetmer: I do see labor costs and fire services continuing to increase much faster than other capital costs and other direct costs. One of the biggest problems has been the view that static staffing requirements (personnel per unit and per shift) are required for adequate fire protection. Another is that some departments are moving toward shorter workweeks without corresponding increases in productivity, such as the willingness to do code inspections by fire companies.

Combination departments using both paid and volunteer firefighters have an advantage in keeping their costs down. This is because of their ability to attract volunteers from the community to do activities that an all-paid department may not want to do, or because labor costs have increased so much, they can't afford to gain additional personnel and keep up with population growth or demands for service. The volunteer section of a combination department can provide a check on the pressures of increased labor costs and labor demands for reduced workweeks.

Stofer: The only way to keep costs down is to cut back, but this is not the answer in the fire service. We need to get better-trained people.

With the push to have increased firefighters on the scene, there's no way to hold labor costs down. The only possible answer I see would be to have more of a volunteer reserve in the departments.

Grover: The Northeast has liberal benefits, including escalating pensions and stringent contracts that prevent management from unilaterally implementing cost-saving measures. Usually these measures are taken for granted in other areas of the country. Labor organizations need to look in the mirror and compromise or run the risk of losing more positions. It's time to give up small benefits to keep the greater good—our jobs.

Lawton: As long as there are paid fire departments, the lion's share of their budgets will go for paying those firefighters. Firefighters have maximized their pay scales in proportion to other service industry jobs as far as they are going to. In the future, smaller communities having traditional fire departments that have fought positive change will be forced to take full-time paid departments to part-paid, and part-paid to volunteer.

Simpson: The pendulum is swinging away from spiraling salary increases. Fire will be competing for raises and benefits in a much more competitive market than ever before.

There are some measures which should be explored. Apprenticeships which provide a career entrance to the service. The use of part-time help during periods of peak demand. Variable manning has been often discussed, without much result of which I am aware.

Bruegman: Labor costs will continue to rise in both union and non-union departments. As we increase our specialization and level of professionalism, we must realize that we're going to have to pay more money for a higher level of expertise.

If we're to hold our costs down, we're going to have to look at more innovative approaches to staffing, such as flex staffing based on call loads, common in the private ambulance industry. We need to look at employee costs for such things as workers' compensation and health care, which have escalated dramatically. For combination departments, continuing to use paid-on-call personnel to supplement career staff is essential if they are to minimize escalating operating costs.

Unfunded state and federal mandates have been a growing part of the fire service's financial obligations, as have consensus standards. Do you see their growth as slowing, or continuing unabated? Can the fire service do much to limit these mandates? Will it?

Bruegman: I'd like to think the unfunded mandate problem will slow down in the coming year, but I don't believe it will. I don't believe the fire service alone can do much to slow these mandates down, although collectively, major players in the fire service, the National League of Cities and other organized groups within the public sector can put enough pressure on the elected officials to at least maintain a level of awareness when they legislate these mandates and what their effect will be on our departments and local government in general.

Rielage: Unfunded state and federal mandates are a growing concern. Obviously such things as the Fair Labor Standards Act, SARA Title 3, NFPA standards and now the new pending OSHA regulations, for especially those states that are non-OSHA states, have and will have an impact on the fire service.

On the positive side, the average citizen has also about had it with federal mandates. Recently various states, including Florida and Ohio, have told the federal government that they will not adhere to federal mandates in certain areas. What I hope to see is a lessening of those federal mandates without a means of recovery such as that built into SARA Title 3 for hazmat recovery or training opportunities through local organizations such as the LEPC.

Simpson: Unfunded mandates have begun to wane. At least the legislature is aware that any such mandates will be fought on a variety of fronts. I believe the growth of such mandates in fire will continue to slow, but the best way to assure that is to be constantly on the alert and above all become a force to be reckoned with in the legislative process.

Fire is a powerful force in politics if they are banded together. They represent a great voting bloc. Sadly I still see many splintered efforts. I have also seen what can be done when we speak with one voice. Giant strides have been made in the area of safety clothing, fire protection systems and pension benefits, to name only a few.

The nation is still run by politicians through special-interest groups. Lobbying is a massive industry; there are some 80,000 registered lobbyists in Washington alone. Why shouldn't we be involved, and unashamedly so? The product we deliver is vital. Apathy is an archenemy. Maybe we should be wining and dining instead of whining.

Lawton: Local government is the only level of government that operates in a fiscally sound manner with balanced budgets. With the nearly incomprehensible federal deficit, the government is attempting to slide its responsibility off to the local level. The feds will continue to do so, and municipalities will continue to fight their attempts.

Stofer: I think the mandates are slowing, and several fire and governmental associations are pushing for no more mandates without funding. We need the support of all the fire service over the nation, both career and volunteer, to get this job done.

The fire service could be one of the most powerful lobbying groups in the nation, if we could ever get them to walk the same paths. The fire caucus group has been working on this and has alleviated some of the problems we faced several years ago, but there's still plenty of room for improvement.

Hoetmer: Unfunded state and federal mandates will continue. The mandates from consensus standard organizations will also impose more requirements on localities, probably eclipsing federal and state mandates.

The fire service can do a lot to limit these mandates by looking very carefully at what's required to do the job safely, efficiently and without passing unnecessary burdens onto local government simply because certain interest groups (such as national unions) demand them.

Whether the leadership of fire service has the gumption to do this, however, is another question. I don't believe fire chiefs can stop these forces by themselves.

In many communities the fire chief is the only one who is providing management to the fire department. His management team is essentially nonexistent, because every rank below him first serves the labor organization of which they are members, as opposed to looking at the needs of the department, the local government and the community as a whole.

If many fire departments only have their chief as their primary management, this really undercuts their ability to prevent unnecessary mandates from overwhelming the capacity to deliver quality fire services.

Lavoie: The key question is "Will it do much to limit these mandates?" We still don't have a universal reporting mechanism that can isolate our real fire problem, and because of that, we really don't know what the fire problem is. Consequently we can't make viable recommendations to our standards-makers on how we can address those problems.

Consolidation

Some people in the fire service would argue that consolidation / regionalization is the single most powerful tool for reducing public fire protection costs. Is this true? How significant are the savings? Who or what are the biggest obstacles to consolidation? Organized labor? Local politicians? Citizens? Chiefs themselves?

Bruegman: Consolidation of services can be one of the most effective tools for reducing our costs while at the same time enhancing our service levels. How significant the savings are really depends on the specific circumstances, but we have seen across this country, that the savings can be substantial, hundreds of thousands and possibly even millions of dollars yearly in operating expenditures while maintaining the same level or, in some cases, actually enhancing the level of the services provided to the local residents.

It has been my personal experience in going through two consolidations and at the present time looking at regionalizing certain support services, that overcoming the local political egos and overcoming the kingdoms that chiefs have a tendency to build up are the two greatest challenges.

Grover: Consolidation is a primary tool for providing improved services and cost savings. In New England savings can be significant. I'm not totally convinced that without careful analysis this is true in all regions of the country, or in all specific cases. Each municipality or governance needs to look at its own status.

The biggest obstacles are all of the entities listed, including chief officers. I can understand organized labor's resistance. The union mission is job security. Consolidation in most cases results in senior fire executives and middle management being displaced. There often can be power struggles between the organizations. Basically it is a turf battle. No one, including fire chiefs and local politicians, wants to lose their power.

I also believe that the residents of suburbs are resistant. Normally they want nothing to do with any of the problems of the inner city. On the other hand, they still desire and use the services provided by cities, such as hospitals. In short, they want the benefits but none of the problems of crime, fire and taxes.

On the other hand, consolidated systems are more suited to large fires and other emergency operations and can result in considerable operational cost savings and improved insurance ratings. Operational services required and a thorough cost analysis need to be projected at intervening levels of three, five, seven, and ten years. This is a long-term proposition that should be digested thoroughly.

Hoetmer: I don't think consolidation or regionalization necessarily reduces public fire protection costs. What it can do is insulate certain practices from the rigor of local review. By regionalizing, one can easily remove the service from the closer inspection of citizens and insulate it from pressure to improve or to reduce the cost of the service. So, no, I am not a believer that consolidation or regionalization necessarily reduces costs.

Simpson: Consolidation or regionalization provides the greatest potential for cost savings and, further, providing a far better level of service.

You need only drive throughout the nation to see the proliferation of small cities and fire protection districts to realize the potential of regionalization. Each city or district may not need its own autonomous department.

There are classic examples of regionalized fire protection. In California there are the contract counties of Contra Costa, San Diego, Santa Barbara, Kern and Los Angeles. All provide an excellent level of service with a vast depth of resources for handling large or even campaign fires.

It's not an overnight process, and part of the planning must be extensive meetings with the public and chambers of commerce and other civic groups. Some years ago we put together a plan for fire protection for eight cities in northern Orange County.

The project was an outgrowth of a class assignment by a couple of guys on the Anaheim Fire Department. I found out about the project and suggested they expand their horizons, make some arbitrary decisions on boundary lines and build a complete fire protection system. They did so with help from a number of others. It was a comprehensive look at fire protection for that area.

It was completely self-supporting within existing budgets. It realigned stations, did some combinations of stations, and totally ignored boundary lines. It even contained a complete mechanical service facility. All stations were manned with four men. The overall EMS system was enhanced, and the fire protection system met all accepted guidelines. All this, and it still produced a savings of $8–$10 million.

The word got out that the planning was being done and the factions became polarized. It was killed before it had even a fair chance of evaluation by the various agencies. The biggest barrier? The chiefs. City councils tend to be parochial and as a result are easily swayed. Labor was not the chief obstacle. By the way, salaries were brought to the level of the highest-paid department.

It was my feeling that if something were not done, eventually economics would drive an even more drastic change. That is currently happening.

Stofer: I don't feel that consolidation is the answer to cost problems. It doesn't lower the cost and leads to longer response time, and the taxpaying public does not feel that consolidation is the way to go. Just because you make the service big doesn't make it less expensive.

Consolidation by itself sometimes creates more problems than it solves. Before consolidating any type of service, there should be many months of study, because consolidation of anything from cities to businesses has not improved the services.

Lavoie: Because of the control it can exercise, a community should maintain its own fire department if it can afford to do so. If the jurisdiction cannot provide the resources to adequately and efficiently address the fire loading of the community and provide the service on its own, alternatives must be looked at, and consolidation and/or regionalization is a viable alternative.

Even if a jurisdiction were to maintain its own service delivery system, partial consolidation of like services such as dispatch, training, inspections, computers, maintenance and even administration could provide savings to the jurisdiction while maintaining local autonomy.

What potential is there for separate fire departments to save money by sharing stations, communications, training centers and programs, computer facilities, apparatus maintenance, or purchasing? How can this be accomplished, and what are the obstacles?

Rielage: Our department is considering adding a fifth station in the northeastern area of our township, and it is already being discussed that this may be a station shared with one of three other jurisdictions in that area. We already have automatic joint response with several of our neighboring communities, and the shared-station concept is only an extension of that kind of thinking.

Bruegman: There's a great potential for separate entities to save money through the sharing of resources; from dispatch, to training, other support services, such as finance, personnel, all can provide a more cost-effective, higher-performing program under a consolidated system.

The obstacles are the same as you'll find if you're talking about a full merger or consolidation of two separate entities. You still have the territories to overcome, the political land mines, and it's clear that for consolidation, whether it be of two organizations or of service, there needs to be a champion for the cause, and that is usually the fire chiefs involved.

Stofer: We have discussed consolidation and are not sure it would work for us. We have combined communications under what is called MECA, Marion County Emergency Communications Authority, and this has helped alleviate communications costs. We have looked into county-wide purchasing, but have not come to any conclusion as to whether this will alleviate costs.

Grover: It could be accomplished by doing a thorough analysis of services required, which I consider being part of the marketing that would need to be done to sell this product of consolidation. The time is ripe.

Some small surrounding towns in New England have already begun to work on consolidated or combined dispatch centers. The obstacles are turf battles and egos of politicians, fire chiefs and your local citizenry. These can be overcome by proper research and marketing, advertising and selling techniques that simply amount to clear and objective facts to support the argument of savings.

Simpson: There are economies to be realized by combining stations near boundaries in some cases. Such an opportunity exists in Anaheim now. Two cities have stations near a common boundary. It could be done by contract. There are no doubt other examples.

We have for many years operated a joint training and communications facility at a tremendous savings. There were originally four cities involved, and the facility was built with federal funds as a demonstration project. Communications are currently being moved into a new and larger facility with much more sophisticated computer and communications capability. It is easily expandable to accommodate other cities.

Would joint purchasing make sense? I think so even if only in economies of scale. If we could break with tradition and have uniforms alike and all the various peripheral equipment the same, even more economies could be realized. (Careful now! We can't have these guys looking alike.) Joint training makes sense and doubly so if we are willing to standardize.

Would we ever dare to think about standard specs for fire trucks? Innovations and advances in design need not be lost because of a common spec. As a matter of fact, the opposite would be true. Certainly the cost of development of specs and the bidding process would go down.

How could it be accomplished? Simple! Buy on a regular and standard basis. Stop having the signature of fire chiefs on fire trucks and equipment. Let the experts in the field design equipment based on performance standards. Sit down in a solution-oriented manner and set aside parochialism.

Services

Does your organization intend to add or delete emergency or non-emergency services as a way of mitigating financial constraints? Is the fire service providing services that could or should be provided by another entity?

Lawton: That depends. You see, we've got this fire department with some excellent people, and some who need to achieve greater levels of excellence. As their employer, I feel a responsibility to try to help them achieve the tools required to survive. The tools needed for our department's survival include the means to generate revenue to offset the costs of providing the service.

Some of the fire department staff don't fully understand this concept. They believe that if revenue is produced, it should result in the hiring of more firefighters. They fail to recognize that those additional funds are needed just to maintain the current costs and keep up with inflation.

Grover: We need to look at the internal process and job tasks we're doing that are not needed to support our mission of fire prevention and fire protection. I found that there is much redundancy in the process of running our fire department. We've looked at this with the thought of eliminating, not necessarily jobs, but the duplication of processes, for example, the processing of fire reports. There are too many people doing the same thing, completing the same process or the appropriate people not handling that process. We are looking for productivity rather than eliminating services.

Simpson: During periods of economic instability, the deletion of services often becomes a focus as a cost-saving measure. Perhaps a more rational approach is to seek more efficient ways of delivering the service.

For example, two years ago, we had two full-time 40 hour/week arson investigators. Call-outs for nighttime and weekend fires, which occurred often, required a minimum call-out period at time-and-a-half. We saved $135,000 by reassigning the arson investigators to suppression duty (24-hour schedule), and increasing the number from two to three so we had one on each shift.

We then hired a retired investigator part-time to provide continuity between shifts and coordinate issues with the staff. The work is getting done, perhaps not at the same level of quality as when they were full-time, but for substantially less money.

Lavoie: Our recently enacted cost-recovery fees will certainly help in addressing this issue. I see in some jurisdictions "environmental services" departments being established to monitor hazardous materials concerns of the jurisdiction, complete with fee-collection mechanisms to completely pay for hazmat mitigation and response programs, while the local fire department doesn't want to become involved, but sooner or later does anyway.

Rielage: I don't believe our department will be necessarily looking for new emergency or non-emergency services in the immediate future. However, I do envision the fire service as a whole adding environmental protection as one of its next steps. We've seen the progression from EMS to hazmat to specialized rescue, and that's the beginning of seeing the fire service have additional responsibilities in public safety, probably up to but not including law enforcement.

EMS, for example, is the greatest public relations tool the fire service has. In our department there is better than a three-to-one ratio in the number of EMS runs to fire runs. We could not survive or have the support that we have without having Advanced Life Support and all that goes along with it, including patient transport.

In pursuit of additional funding, many departments have gotten into EMS, and many departments have also become more aggressive about taking on patient-transport duties. Where do these elements fit into a fire department's total funding picture? Does EMS, with or without patient transport, truly have the potential to subsidize fire protection? Should a fire department bill private ambulance companies that operate in its town for the department's first-responder services?

Bruegman: It's a myth that EMS and patient transport have the potential to subsidize fire protection. It's been my experience that you're lucky to break even with the transport service. The benefits far outweigh the costs as you gain additional people for response to other emergency incidents, and the goodwill created by an effective EMS program is tremendous.

The question of fire departments billing private ambulance companies who operate in this town is really one of local preference and of competition. I personally don't favor fire departments billing private ambulance companies as a revenue source, although I do think it's appropriate that the services we provide as first responders from our ALS engine companies be included as part of the bill from the private EMS provider, as we are truly subsidizing their response.

Simpson: It is almost tragic to me that the fire service as an entity nationwide has not embraced EMS. Every expert in the field readily admits that paramedics provide the most dramatic advance in emergency medicine in this century. The number of lives saved by this system is probably incalculable, but one thing is sure: It's a service for which people are willing to pay.

The fire service has a delivery system already in place and a high caliber of people easily capable of assimilating the training to deliver a high level of service. The pilot study done for paramedic service was to determine if firefighters were capable of performing the service. They were and are.

EMS with or without patient transport is certainly capable of subsidizing fire service costs. We have a *voluntary* subscription fee in Anaheim which raises about $2.3 million per year, which more than pays for an EMS system that, by the way, far exceeds normal standards. It also helps maintain manning at four firefighters per unit, all of which helps Anaheim maintain its Class I rating. EMS is delivered from engine companies as opposed to squad units. It is a proven concept from both a fiscal and service standpoint.

Stofer: Our department does furnish EMS and ambulance transportation and has for many years. We find that we either break even or lose money on this, because there is a problem with collection from individuals who use our service and live all over the country, or who have no insurance, or who simply don't want to pay. There would have to be an improved way of collecting for the service we have today before this service could provide an increased savings for running the department.

Lavoie: Those departments that have become involved with EMS have a better case for helping to justify their existence. Seventy percent of our jurisdiction's responses are EMS-related. The department does not transport, but does provide ALS services.

Our local ambulance company transports and provides back-up ALS services. We have established a good working relationship with that private entity that is cost effective and benefits our citizens. Our citizens appreciate this working relationship and would, in my opinion, be against any change.

Lawton: The ability of EMS to help with the funding of the fire department probably depends largely on each individual community. If EMS is going to help with funding, it needs to be delivered without a proportionate increase in manpower. If EMS is delivered with completely separate manpower, it does nothing to solve the funding issue, it just funds the delivery of EMS.

One thing though. If fire departments are going to deliver EMS, they need to make a commitment to the level of service and quality. If they don't, eventually fire department EMS programs that aren't setting a standard of excellence will be ripe for slaughter.

The last part of your question hits home. We've been in the process of negotiation with several private providers looking into the possibility of a joint venture for the delivery of EMS. The city would be compensated for first-responder services, and I think most fire departments should be. Fire department response allows private providers to rely on their services.

For example, recently we had a problem of private providers calling for lift assistance when their employees should have been able to handle the situation. As one firefighter put it, "I love it when Brand X calls us for lift help and my guys do all the work, and the EMTs stand and watch" and then collect the payment. We implemented a $50 charge for lift help.

Hoetmer: The question talks about subsidizing fire protection via another service, specifically EMS. This is a poor way to look at whether or not to take on a particular service. Each service delivery, whether it's EMS or some other service, should be able to stand on its own with the resources it needs. One should not have EMS unless one is willing to fund EMS. One shouldn't have paramedic service unless one is prepared to pay for that level of service.

You shouldn't have one service subsidizing another. A fire department really does need to look very carefully as to the level and types of services it offers. If a fire department feels that an EMS service will complement its other services, and it is willing to provide the necessary resources to adequately deliver those services, then by all means it should recommend that to its city council or its county commission.

The question as to whether or not a fire department should bill private ambulance companies that operate in town for the department's first-responder services is also a policy question that should be addressed by the city council or the county commission.

The question should be, "Does the community want first-responder services?" If it does, that becomes a service the community should be willing to pay for. The existence of private ambulance companies has little to do with whether a department offers a first-responder service. Now, if a community decides they can only afford first-responder service, but can't afford transport to the hospital without charging the person who is being transported, a fee for that service or contracting with a private firm for transporting are perfectly legitimate ways to fund that portion of the service delivery.

Grover: I absolutely believe that we should take on patient transport duties. This is where the monies are made. Without patient transport, it has been my experience that EMS does not have the potential to enhance fire department revenue.

It's time for fire department leaders to look at billing private ambulance companies who operate in their municipalities for the fire department's first-responder services. Often, the private provider cannot meet the time frames required of four minutes for Basic Life Support to begin. They depend on us, and we should be charging for that service.

I discovered that our city was paying the local private ambulance company $100,000 per year to provide services. I suggested to the city leaders that the opposite should be true, that they should be paying us for the benefit to come in and make a profit in our city.

I read of an interesting case, I believe on the West Coast, where a private provider was put to the test by city fathers. When all the negotiating was done, the company went from zero to the hefty sum of $500,000 that they were now willing to pay.

Whether in search of additional funding, constant staffing levels or simply a stronger reason to exist, some departments are moving into broader missions than just fire, EMS and hazmat response. Will assuming more diverse missions help departments broaden their funding bases, or will many find themselves expected to carry out extra responsibilities without the training or other resources to perform them properly?

Hoetmer: The question presumes that you should consider adding additional services in order to pay for other services you perhaps like better. This is obviously a bad reason to add additional services. One should not add services simply to help pay for other services that are not as high a priority or aren't needed as much according to the priorities of the citizens of that community.

Adding services on a premeditated basis is not the way to look at service delivery. Each service delivery should be able to stand on its own, based on the assessment of the community need as well as the cost of that particular service.

Lawton: To maintain the vitality of any organization, it must be constantly seeking to redefine itself, its mission and to engage the community it serves. Diversifying missions at a time when taxpayers demand change is a survival tactic that opens up options for future task assignment.

The problem is that firefighters sometimes apply old versions of success to new realities. The tried-and-true expectation of fighting fires courageously after the fire has started is archaic thinking. In the current climate it would be more heroic to insist that prevention and detection systems be installed and then, only after failure of those systems, would physical courage be applied to suppression efforts.

Stofer: Expanding the fire service any further than fire suppression, EMS, hazmat and prevention will not provide additional income to us. We added hazmat to our department several years ago, as many other departments did also, and with training and equipment, it will take many years to recoup this cost.

Fire prevention, if handled in the right manner, could increase income and cut down on fire runs and lessen the cost of running fire departments. We need to improve our fire prevention programs and offset fire suppression, possibly by starting fire prevention in lower grades than we are doing today. Our brothers in law enforcement agencies are now starting programs in kindergarten classes. When we find that children from 8 to 10 years old are in the fire-setting business, we need to start training fire prevention at earlier years.

Grover: Assuming more diverse missions will help departments broaden their funding bases and will result in revenues for the fire service. As the federal and state governments put out mandates, the fire service is currently expected to carry out the responsibilities—such as confined-space rescue and infectious-disease control—and are mandated by government to be trained to carry these out. Since we need to be trained to do them anyway, it would behoove fire service leaders to pursue any revenues that may be garnered for providing such services. As I said, confined-space rescue is a clear example.

Lavoie: First, how many fire departments have a written mission statement, approved by the decision-makers of that jurisdiction, that clearly defines, to the citizens of the community and the department itself, why it exists? Defining that mission would be the first step in providing meaningful services to the community.

Second, if the mission statement has been prepared and your budget is based on accomplishing specific goals and objectives, also approved by the jurisdiction to achieve the department's mission, the mission, goals and objectives will have to be changed, or adequate resources will have to be provided to achieve the results agreed upon. The departments that do not have a specific mission and accompanying goals and objectives will have the most problems with "servicing beyond their means."

Fire prevention has always been an underfunded activity within fire departments. Is there a potential for increasing revenues by allocating fire code inspection fees back into the code enforcement and fire education areas of the fire department?

Hoetmer: Fire prevention has always been an underfunded activity within fire departments, yet it has the greatest potential for making a difference as to property and life loss. If a community does charge a fee for code and building inspections, these fees should be a part of the revenue base of those programs and be allocated back to enhance those program areas.

Grover: There is a great potential for this, and code inspection fees are an acceptable way of garnering revenue, particularly the issue of reinspections. In the future of the fire service I see fire prevention divisions increasing in size and number. They are truly a division that can produce revenue for local government.

In countries other than the United States, their fire prevention and education divisions are sometimes three-quarters of the total strength of the department. This is mind-boggling to the fire chief in the United States. However, I believe that with the advent of residential sprinklers and the movement to better education and thorough code enforcement, the size of the fire prevention bureaus in our country will increase.

Bruegman: I don't agree that fire prevention has always been an underfunded activity, as it's been funded as a part of our mission, protection of life and property. There does exist a potential for increasing our revenues through fire inspection fees and charging for public education, fire education, but I think it gets back to the central core of the discussion we've had, and that's that the people are paying the freight in our communities. What is their level of expectation for service for the taxes they are paying?

There is no one correct answer. One community may feel that the taxes they pay should provide a full range of services from fire suppression to paramedic services to public education to inspections, while another community may feel the taxes they pay are solely for fire prevention or fire suppression. It truly is a local issue.

Rielage: There is no question that fire prevention and public education are probably the most underfunded areas in the fire service today. A rule of thumb I have is that fire prevention and public education should invest at least a dollar a year per citizen out of the department budget. If we're to include salaries in that $1 per year per citizen, then those individuals should be assigned strictly to fire prevention/public education duties, not someone who has a shared responsibility for fire or EMS as well.

Lavoie: Until the jurisdiction's decision-makers, including some fire chiefs, are really educated about proactive vs. reactive fire service delivery and shown the actual costs related to the delivery of both, underfunding of fire prevention bureaus will continue to exist.

Mini-max codes adopted by some states have assured that building departments will continue to receive additional resources, possibly at the cost of fire department appropriations.

Given that the United States spends less per capita on fire protection than any industrialized nation, and has one of the highest rates of fire deaths and property loss, how can a city manager tell the fire chief that the fire department is not essential to the city operation?

Hoetmer: This is a loaded question that makes certain presumptions, which I must obviously challenge first. Working at ICMA for the past 16 years and in local government prior to that, I have never known a city manager to say to a fire chief or anyone else in the fire service that the fire department is not an essential city operation. Police and fire operations are absolutely vital services and one of the most fundamental services any community delivers.

As to whether the United States spends less per capita on fire protection than any other industrialized nation, this is a patently false statement. The World Fire Statistics Center shows that the U.S. is not the lowest nor the highest as far as expenditures.

Now, these statistics are somewhat fuzzy, because of the difficulty in measuring what fire protection is. Suffice it to say, however, most countries in the world operate with much smaller fire departments on a per capita basis than the U.S. does. However, they tend to spend much more in prevention and built-in fire protection than the U.S. does.

Response forces are smaller in many other countries, but prevention, education and built-in protection expenditures are higher. Nevertheless, even with those expenditures included, the U.S. still does not spend less per capita on fire protection. It's about in the middle.

The part of the question that clearly is correct, is that the U.S. does have one of the highest fire deaths and property losses in the world. Again, this is due to the U.S. putting more of its dollars into response as opposed to where it would do a lot more good: prevention, education and built-in fire protection.

Grover: The fire service is really up against it on this issue. The problem seems to be the frequency of occurrences: Most times government leaders will say, "That never happens here." Clearly, if you look back in history it has happened here and probably will again; it simply doesn't happen on a regular basis.

Certainly if a fire chief were to document the tragedies and emergencies that occur around the country on a daily basis, he could provide a strong argument to city managers and mayors for the essentiality of a fire department. We need to do collective research and have fire service leaders who are willing to take the time to present a well-documented and -researched, educated presentation to the city fathers.

Unfortunately, particularly in New England, I doubt that this is done regularly or with the intensity it deserves. It's the best way for senior fire officers to protect and support the firefighter on the back step.

Rielage: One of the key problems in the fire service today is illustrated by this last question. I don't know of any progressive department that is resting on its own laurels, maintaining the status quo. Even the most successful departments have to sell themselves daily to the citizens, the administration and the politicians. Those departments with direction, vision and planning will be better at surviving potential budget problems than those who passively sit back and await the ax.

It's very easy for a city manager to tell a fire chief that the fire department is not essential to city operations, if all he or she sees is firefighters waiting at the fire house for an alarm, whether it be fire or EMS.

A fire department has to get out in the community, meet with the movers and shakers, and become the focal point of the community. The closer the community can identify with the fire department, the less likely it will be that the politicians will take a major ax to the budget. However, the citizens need to know that they're getting the most efficient use of their tax dollar, whether in fire, EMS or related services.

The fire service will be changing. As progressive fire service leaders, we have the responsibility to lead that change in our own community, or else suffer the consequences when the system is changed for us. I really do not envision when the fire service will not be in transition. Financing is just one element of this very dynamic situation.

Bruegman: Very simply, we as a fire service have not proved that there is a direct correlation between the money we spend on fire protection and the rates of fire death, property loss and injury between the United States and the industrialized world. There are many other factors that go into such an international comparison, such as cultural attitudes, density, building construction, prevalence of fixed fire protection. These all play a critical part in how we analyze the fire experience within a given country and try to compare it to that of the United States.

However, the fire chief can state to the city manager that we are an essential part of any local operation, because we are a quality-of-life issue. The expectation of most people in the United States is that when they dial 911, a fire truck will be there immediately if their house is on fire. If their husband or wife is having a heart attack, they expect competent medical help to arrive quickly. The fire service must begin to look at ourselves as a quality-of-life issue, and when we begin to think of ourselves in that light, so will our managers and elected officials.

Lawton: Obviously this is a loaded question and maybe the whole reason for this exercise. The city manager can tell the fire chief that his department isn't essential. He can do it like this: He'll say, "Your department is not essential."

Or he can ask questions such as "How many actual fires has the department fought this year? How many EMS calls did you go to this year? How many other duties did the department perform last year? . . . This surely must be a life safety or emergency services department, and not a fire department."

He can ask even more questions: "Have you been asking our customers what services they want from you? Have you been actively participating with a customer committee to define areas of interest and concern? What have you done to train your people about the need for change?"

He can say fighting fire may be essential to the city, but a stagnating, anemic department held back by people unwilling to redefine service isn't. He may conclude that some other organization can do it better.

Lavoie: A fire chief and his staff should be spending a large percentage of their time marketing their department to anyone and everyone who will listen. In our jurisdiction, the fire department costs our citizens 25 cents per day per capita for all the services (also listed) we provide. Doesn't that sound better than "The fire department has a $4 million-plus budget"? We were also 99.958% effective in saving our assessed valuation.

That's what our citizens want to hear. It's about time we told them.

EMS: An Overview

Mary Jane Dittmar

Over the past two decades, the public has come to expect many more services from fire departments. In addition to fire suppression, departments are engaged in fire prevention and protection, public education, heavy rescue, haz-mat management and response, and emergency medical services (EMS). Of these functions, EMS has made the greatest demand on fire department personnel and time; some would argue, however, that the fire service has not allotted to EMS the same management and training priorities given to other functions.[1] As an example, Don H. Hiett, Jr., treasurer of the International Association of Fire Chiefs (IAFC) EMS Section and chief of the Atlanta (GA) Fire Department, cites the following typical fire department budget breakdown: 96 percent, firefighting operations/training; 3 percent, fire inspection/prevention; and 1 percent, EMS and other programs—despite the fact that "better than 64 percent of the calls are emergency medical calls."[2]

The issue of EMS as a fire service responsibility has been controversial, and the inability of the firefighting and EMS systems to intertwine and function as one complete system in some departments has caused EMS to be less "consistent" than other fire department functions.[3] The relationship of the fire service to EMS varies drastically on a state-by-state basis. "Each town or city, each county, each region or state seems to reflect the attitudes of fire officials who were influential at various turning points during the past 50 or so years," observes James O. Page,

Adapted from Mary Jane Dittmar, "Fire Service EMS: The Challenge and the Promise. Part 1—An Overview," *Fire Engineering* (July 1993). Reprinted with permission of *Fire Engineering*.

publisher/editor-in-chief of *JEMS* and executive director of the Advanced Coronary Treatment (ACT) Foundation. Many fire departments, in fact, have completely avoided any significant involvement in EMS over the years.[4]

Despite this lack of centrality, however, most of the EMS services have developed in the fire service.[5] Many departments have become involved in EMS, and their operations are professional and efficient. A 1981 study, in fact, showed that 73 percent of all American fire departments, career and volunteer, are involved at some level in EMS service.[6]

The EMS vs. firefighting debate

The explanations offered for the disparity in reception given EMS by fire departments range from a philosophical difference stemming from the dichotomy between the old and the new, and the traditionalist vs. the innovator,[7] to misunderstandings of workers' job descriptions to career issues such as compensation and promotion policies. Yet, the consensus inside and outside the fire service is that since the common goal of the firefighting and EMS functions is to save lives, the two services should work as a team to successfully fulfill the public's needs.[3,2]

Basic to the EMS-vs.-firefighting mentality that has existed within pockets of the fire service have been the following factors.

Tradition   The mission of the fire service "has been the same since the burning of Rome by Emperor Nero: to prevent and suppress fire." Relatively speaking, EMS is a newcomer to the fire service and is not bound by the same traditions.[7,2]

The fire service, especially in large urban areas, "has always done things in a certain way," notes Gordon Sachs, EMS program manager for the U.S. Fire Administration. "Just as change is inevitable, it is inevitable that the old dogs will resist the new ideas of the young pups. When a new program is forced, rather than eased into, it can cause problems in delivery."[8]

In some departments, EMS has been looked on as "a stepchild—a responsibility that the fire service faces reluctantly."[8,30] Whenever the topic of incorporating EMS into these departments has arisen, fire officers have retorted with "Firefighters should fight fires."[9] Some of these departments have tolerated EMS as a "necessary evil," since both EMS and firefighting provide lifesaving functions to the public.[10] Proponents of this "old-guard" theory have looked on anything other than fire suppression as an intruder into the department.[8,30]

Accountability to "outsiders"   Fire departments, traditionally closed organizations used to operating independently and without much scrutiny, sometimes have found it difficult to have to account to the "outside" agencies responsible for EMS, explains Page. EMTs and paramedics, for example, are licensed or certified by "outsiders." Fire departments that provide EMS services, consequently, find themselves accountable to "outsiders" ranging from private ambulance personnel to doctors and nurses to hospital administrators to local and state health agencies.[11]

Included in the areas subject to the scrutiny of the medical community are education/training, advancement, and discipline. As Page points out, some fire officers, in resisting the incorporation of EMS into their departments, have "appeared uncooperative at best, and obstructive at worst in their contacts and relationships with the health-care community." Some of them have even tried to override medical protocols established for EMS personnel. In addition, some volunteer fire departments and organizations have lobbied to have training, continuing education, and certification standards for EMS personnel relaxed; in several cases, fire service organizations have fought for the right to evaluate their members' qualifications to provide emergency medical care instead of having the state health agency make the determination.[4,16]

Stepchild mentality   With regard to ambulance service, some departments—especially those departments that had inherited the responsibility for it—began exhibiting a "stepchild" mentality toward it during the 1940s. No established mandated criteria for training ambulance personnel or courses beyond basic first aid existed at that time. "The job required minimal knowledge, few skills, a tolerance for blood, and a strong back," recalls Page. "In many fire departments, assignment to ambulance duty became an unofficial form of punishment."[4,14]

Morale problems have existed in some departments because old-line chief officers and firefighters in those departments took on EMS without accepting it as an integral component of their organizations. They view EMS "as a temporary assignment taken on by an organization whose job it is to fight fires" and, consequently, see firefighter/paramedics as temporary personnel. As a result, these departments do not have promotional policies that incorporate the two services or provide additional compensation for cross-trained employees.[3,2-3]

Issues of contention

Major EMS-related issues of contention among firefighters have been the following:

- Some firefighters just want to be firefighters; they do not want to be EMTs. In some cases, firefighters have had to accept new EMS responsibilities or lose their jobs. The prospect of performing EMS can make some firefighters anxious, as was the case when the San Diego (CA) Fire Department first placed defibrillators on its engines.[8,30]

- The workload vastly increases when EMS functions are brought into a department. During 1982, for example, one major fire department responded to 2,621 structure calls and 81,210 EMS calls, with at least one engine company and one paramedic rescue unit per call.[11,31]

- EMS work increases personnel exposure to many communicable diseases and often brings personnel in contact with human blood, vomit, feces, and body fluids.[11,31]

Firefighter/EMTs or firefighter/paramedics also have grievances, such as the following, that increase stress and lower morale:

- Inaccurate perceptions of EMS personnel's functions and responsibilities have led to misconceptions that affect the image of the EMS worker, who has not always enjoyed the same positive image as the firefighter. One of these misconceptions is that being a member of EMS is relatively safe when compared with firefighting. This viewpoint, point out observers, is "ironic," since many statistics citing firefighting injuries and illnesses include EMS workers who are part of the fire service.

  This view of EMS as a "safer" career has been changing, however, for various reasons. EMS professionals face many of the same hazards as firefighters, including the occupational dangers related to lifting and bending and exposure to contagious diseases, including those that are incurable, such as AIDS. These personnel often find themselves at dangerous scenes involving violent crimes or domestic disputes. The high volume of run activity makes EMT personnel more vulnerable to vehicular accidents, which account for a large percentage of emergency service worker deaths and injuries each year.[3,4]

  In addition, EMS workers serving in a dual role also perform suppression functions, which subjects them to all the risks associated with firefighting. EMS personnel and firefighters are reaching parity in occupational risk levels, and the difference between what is perceived and what is occurring may cause strife or division between EMS workers and fire suppression forces.[3,5]

- Many EMS workers do not want to be firefighters. "Many of them don't want to drag hoselines, search buildings, and participate on the fireground, except for caring for victim(s) retrieved from a burning building." This attitude, although not prevalent throughout the combined services, could lead to morale and political problems within various jurisdictions. In the combined services, many EMTs do not feel they should assist "smoke-eaters" in cleaning and restoring equipment so that it is ready for the next alarm. This attitude creates friction.[10,38]

- Some paramedics or EMTs think of themselves as health-care professionals and do not care to fit into the quasimilitary fire structure. Others feel that firefighters are not qualified or motivated to give quality medical care.[8,30] Not all firefighter/paramedics agree, of course.

  "I have seen just the opposite," asserts Firefighter/Paramedic Paul Harvey, president of the Seattle (WA) Fire Fighters Union, International Association of Fire Fighters (IAFF) Local 27. "Its underlying military discipline means the fire service is inherently able to give quality control." In Seattle, EMS functions are completely within the fire department. Some firefighters cross-train as paramedics who ride advanced life support (ALS) units. Paramedics maintain firefighting certification and occasionally ride fire apparatus.[8,30]

  Chief Hiett of Atlanta agrees. "There is no group in the United States capable of enforcing EMS," he says. And, he adds, there is no enforcement group overseeing on a moment-to-moment basis emergency services given outside of a hospital. "The fire department," he stresses, "is capable of such enforcement."[2]

- Ambulance runs generally take longer than an hour per call. In the volunteer service, this time usually is time the worker would spend with family or pursuing personal activities. In addition, ambulance calls are much more numerous than fire calls in most fire departments.[10,38]

Outside opposition

In many areas of the United States, the firefighting/EMS controversy within the fire service has become public and has created the impression that the fire service is "a house divided." Since the ultimate product of EMS is patient care, the dissension has caused some influential physicians to become concerned about the negative impact the stress of the ongoing conflict can have on the EMTs and paramedics—and patient care, which, of course, is the bottom line.[11,37] Some observers have even been led to ask whether the fire service has any "paternal" obligations toward EMS at all.[8,28]

For the most part, the fire/ambulance personnel seem to work out their differences before and after the emergency call so that the political ramifications behind the delivery of the service are not evident to the recipient of the services. As M. "Mick" Mastrino, a 35-year veteran of United Fire Company #3 in Frederick, Maryland, observes: "The political climate in most fire/ambulance stations can be in turmoil; however, when the alarm sounds, most leave the problems behind."[10,39]

Another argument critics have used against locating EMS in fire departments is that fire protection and EMS services are too diverse to combine. One of these critics, a "very respected" fire department physician, in 1974 charged that the fire service looks on fire department EMS services as a "bastard offspring" of rescue and medical care. He also cited "significant differences" in the training, education, and experience required for fire and EMS duties."[12]

The negative attitudes of the fire service toward EMS led to government actions in 1980 that could have taken EMS out of the fire departments. The fire service, however, rallied as a unified force to maintain EMS. At that time, a study group was commissioned by the U.S. Department of Transportation (DOT) to evaluate the concept of "third-service" prehospital emergency medical services: local government public agencies other than fire or police departments that would have prehospital EMS as their sole function. Third-service EMS agencies already were operating in Austin, Texas; Pittsburgh, Pennsylvania; Wichita, Kansas; Cleveland, Ohio; San Francisco, California; and other locales. The DOT's actions had no significant effect other than to bind the fire service together,[9,38] and its suggestion to establish EMS as a separate or third service was made to eliminate some of the conflicts.[12,49]

Other members of the EMS community welcome the fire service's involvement in EMS. Among them is Jerome M. Hauer, executive director of the Indiana State Emergency Management Agency. "You cannot separate EMS and the fire service. . . . Some of my colleagues are myopic when they say they don't want the fire service (particularly the National Fire Academy) involved. It's about time someone in Washington got interested."[13]

Adding to the debate has been the question of whether EMS is a public health-care or public safety issue, adds Hauer. "I would argue it's both. It's the first step before entering the health-care system. If you're not successful in defibrillating, the patient won't enter the health-care system." Addressing this recurring issue, Sachs (USFA) says that after consulting with a number of experts, the USFA has taken the position that "EMS is a public safety entity charged with delivering a public health service."[14]

EMS and the fire department: a natural duo

Despite the reluctance of some fire departments to embrace EMS and the opinions of some critics to the contrary, the fire service and EMS seem to be natural partners from several perspectives. Among them are the following:

- *Image.* The firefighter has always been perceived as a brave public servant who can help when there is danger. Traditionally, the one source of help that comes to mind when a situation appears helpless has been the fire department.[9,38]
- *Cost effectiveness.* As an already existing and functioning service, the fire department provides a more cost-effective means of providing paramedic service, points out Tim Butler, a fire captain/paramedic with the City of Anaheim (CA) Fire Department. The public gets two services for the price of one.[15] Staffing and equipment are already available. Most fire stations already have in place the components—such as communications, dispatch, vehicle maintenance, training, rapid response, and personnel—needed for EMS; modifications can make them suitable for medical purposes.
- *Decreased workload.* The decrease in the fire workload has left firefighters with more time between alarms for EMS activities.[5,1]
- *Improved response time.* Fire stations are situated so that response time often is improved; the time difference between the arrival time of the fire engine and the ambulance in outlying areas can be dramatic.[8,30]
- *Noninterference with fire suppression duties.* Most fire stations find that assuming EMS duties does not interfere with fire suppression, points out Chief Ricky Davidson, chief of EMS for the Shreveport (LA) Fire Department and the past chairperson of the IAFC EMS Section. In many areas, the ever-increasing number of medical calls being handled by the fire departments already has caused them to assimilate EMS duties into their daily routines.[8,30]
- *Incident command system.* The fire department has another advantage in that it uses the standardized incident command system (ICS) to manage large-scale emergencies. The ICS provides a framework for coordinating on-scene and available resources so that actions at a chaotic scene are controlled, explains Butler.[15,15]

Some steps toward improvements

The fire service began to move gradually to reorganize its EMS programs during the 1980s. Some departments entered directly into EMS and instituted separate job standards and career ladders, as well as different pay scales for these personnel.[12,49] They devised solutions to the problems that had been fostering discontent within the fire service EMS. In some locales, for example, the job description for fire chiefs has been revised to require that future applicants have a significant EMS background. In jurisdictions such as Beverly Hills, California; Idaho Falls, Idaho; and Abilene, Texas, fire chiefs have served on the streets as EMTs or paramedics.[11,36-37]

Such changes, of course, are not likely to occur everywhere. Some fire departments have been "captives of their own history and hiring policies; many of them do a bad job of fighting fires and a bad job of [rendering] emergency medical care," observes Page. These are the departments, he predicts, that the emergency physicians, who will become more involved in prehospital care on behalf of the patient, most likely will pressure into dropping EMS so that it can be provided by a private or hospital-operated ambulance service.[11,37]

Changes are in the air

If the fire service is to be at the forefront of EMS in the future, indications are that it must be able to adapt to the many changes underway in our society. Some of these changes were begun in the early 1980s when some communities began to see their possession of EMS programs challenged. Potential competitors began assembling data to show the economic and service advantages of a hospital-based, public utility, or private ambulance program. Hospitals throughout the country with a surplus of hospital beds, for example, are looking to the control (or ownership) of the ambulance service as a means of bringing a flow of patients to their hospitals. Some private ambulance companies are offering these hospitals "turnkey" contract arrangements that will provide the hospital with ambulance service overnight.[4,16-17]

Changes in Medicare reimbursement policies and new hospital financing approaches have produced potential competition for the local volunteer ambulance service. The changes being proposed in the national health-care delivery system and the fire service's EMS-oriented initiatives now underway nationally and in Washington, D.C. also will affect the overall EMS system. "It will be very interesting to see what's going to happen when a new national health-care delivery system is proposed and implemented," notes Bill Madison, former deputy executive director of the IAFC and a registered EMT/P. "If everyone becomes covered under the plan, will our business go up? How will the new health-care plan affect EMS, and will we be involved in it?"[16]

A reorganization of Medicare, Medicaid, and private insurance could help ambulance companies, which have trouble collecting their fees. Many American Ambulance Association (AAA) members are concerned that health-care reform might include rationing and price fixing, which if incorrectly administered could put many ambulance companies out of business.[17]

In Congress, Steve Gunderson (R-WI) introduced H.R. 4256, which would create a federal EMS office under the Department of Health and Human Services and would provide grant money for state EMS offices and for improving rural EMS services.[17]

According to Toffler and other esteemed futurists, major societal and economic changes are occurring every two to five years. Unless those segments of the fire service still saddled with the "traditions of constancy" respond to the accelerated change timetable, they may find themselves "vulnerable" with regard to EMS, warns Page. A warning sounded in 1983 still appears appropriate: "While the current parents of EMS are treating it as an old shoe, others—just around the corner—are perceiving it as a glass slipper."[4,17]

EMS, the "savior" of some fire departments

Many observers, in fact, credit the move into EMS with helping many fire departments to keep their fire suppression service viable. "We can only speculate on what the fire service would be like today without the public and budgetary support it has reaped from its EMS role," noted a 1984 *JEMS* report, which posed the following question: "Could a single-function fire service have endured the economic pressures of two oil shortages, double-digit inflation, taxpayer rebellions, and the longest of postwar recessions?"[9,40]

In many areas, EMS is the function that has been winning public and political support for the fire department and providing the productivity needed to keep the engine and truck companies adequately staffed.[11,34]

In departments where personnel are cross-trained in firefighting and EMS, there seems to be less of a tendency to eliminate positions; two-thirds of all calls to these departments commonly are for emergency medical assistance. In addition, the departments also enjoy strong public support. Where sampled, public sentiment has shown that the public ranks EMS as the most valued public service, Page notes. The tax-concerned public, on the other hand, showed little concern over whether a three-firefighter pumper is as effective as a five-firefighter pumper, he points out.[4,15-16]

"How can one justify a multi-million-dollar budget if the system doesn't get used?" asks Madison. ". . . It's a matter of time before cost-efficiency comparisons will be made." These analyses, he adds, will reveal fewer calls for fire suppression, more expensive fire suppression equipment, and escalating firefighting personnel costs. The progressive fire departments, he says, understand that EMS runs are one way to resolve the budget problem. Fifty percent of the ambulances sold in this country are sold to fire departments, something every fire chief has to look at closely, Madison notes. His department, in Norfolk, Virginia, took over EMS from a third service.[16]

Providing EMS services seems to be a natural way for fire departments to build rapport with community residents. In one study based on an estimated total of 30,000 fire departments, 21,900 of them were shown to provide EMS in one or more of 26 distinct profiles of service. If each of those departments provides EMS to only two patients per 24 hours year round, in a year's time nearly 16 million people would have received fire service EMS. Theoretically, that means that fire department EMS personnel will have contact with every man, woman, and child in the country once every 12.5 years. No other public agency has such an opportunity to provide valuable service while establishing a relationship with taxpayers, stresses Page.[4,16]

These factors have led some advocates to encourage the incorporation of EMS into the fire service. Harvey, of the Seattle Fire Fighters Union, says the question should not be "Should EMS be in the fire service?" but rather "How can a fire department meet the demand of EMS?"[8,28]

The truth, say others, is that many fire departments believe they have no other choice but to take on EMS,[8,29] since it no longer may be realistic to continue to support two departments with duplicate expenses for leadership, administration, and training staffs, as well as individual training facilities for similar responses.[18]

Looking on EMS as "the emergency treatment for ailing fire service budgets" seems to be a logical position for many departments. Keep in mind, however, that many other critical factors in addition to the economic benefits must be evaluated when considering whether to add the EMS function to a department. Also, keep in mind that not all fire departments are ready to provide a full scope of services. Moreover, departments in cities and counties that have private or third-service EMS providers might not welcome the suggestion of a budget-saving fire-EMS merger.[8,29]

Whether local fire departments should provide EMS depends on factors such as the community's needs and wishes, the resource capability of the locality, the political impact of the decision, and the attitude of the fire department that is to undertake the additional responsibility.[19] As Lieutenant Harold C. Cohen, EMS director of the Baltimore County (MD) Fire Department and head of the Fire Rescue Academy, points out, a department in which management "vehemently resists" EMS is not conducive to quality EMS.[8,30]

Jim Thornton, a firefighter with the Department of Fire and Paramedical Services in Norfolk, Virginia, agrees: "Cross-training of firefighters for any level of EMS certification should never be forced." Norfolk's third-service EMS provider was merged with its fire department in May 1991; it is operated by cross-trained firefighters who want medic certification. "Some firefighters are not good at the EMS angle, and not everyone in EMS can do fire suppression," Thornton explains.[8,30]

While it appears that most fire officials accept that there is a legitimate role for the fire service in EMS, some are wrestling with decisions such as what the nature and extent of the role should be.[12,48]

Fire and EMS in the future

Despite the problems, challenges, and competitors, the future of fire service EMS appears to be bright. Even those who believe that creating combination fire/EMS services throughout the country was "a mistake that will forever be a problem" also believe that "the political process will prevent their dissolution and that good management can prevent or minimize the friction that will be persistent between the services."[10,39]

Even in the 1980s, when many of the problems associated with fire service EMS came to prominence, statements such as the following appeared in various fire service publications.

It "seems safe to say that fire departments, the public, and perhaps a large segment of the medical community have come to accept the fire service as a major EMS provider. . . . There certainly is no suggestion that the fire service should not continue to play a leading role."[12,49]

"I feel no community can run a truly effective EMS system without the involvement of the fire departments on some level. . . . Some of the best EMS services in the country are provided by fire departments. . . . The reason they perform so well is that they understand that EMS is different and demands a different type of thinking. Fire departments bold enough to look beyond themselves and their traditional approaches to fighting the 'enemy' will achieve their full potential of excellence."[20]

There have been warnings in these publications as well. One is that the fire service will have to work harder to keep EMS services in the future than many departments have had to work to acquire them. In a nation flirting with bankruptcy, other sources point out, decisions affecting the fire service and health-care arenas will be based on "cold-eyed analyses of quality and cost."

These factors keep in the forefront the question, Can the fire service maintain its role in EMS in such an environment?[9,40]

Fire service EMS will encounter various challenges and obstacles in the future, observes Kevin Brame, battalion chief in charge of strategic planning and legislation with the Orange County (CA) Fire Department. Among those he cites are the following: the medical establishment's mandating of local standards of care without giving any consideration to how they will be financed; overregulation; changing social environments that will place the fire service on the front lines of providing the first, if not the only, access to cumbersome and bureaucratic systems of health care; labor concerns relative to the increasing dangers within the work environment; political processes that tell the fire service how to do its job, based on the need for votes or political contributions; and a continuing medical community belief that members of the fire service are still "just firefighters."[21]

National EMS initiatives

Indications within the fire service are that EMS is and will continue to be an integral component of fire departments, as evidenced by the IAFC and IAFF Joint Resolution on Emergency Medical Services, issued on January 9, 1991. The document recognizes prehospital emergency medical care as a major service provided by fire departments and maintains that the "fire service must continue to provide emergency medical care." The document also urges "all elected officials, professional associations, and health care providers to recognize and support the provision of emergency medical care by the fire service." In addition, the IAFC established an EMS section; the Congressional Fire Services Institute (CFSI) formed an EMS advisory committee;[21,32] and the CFSI hired Michael Smith as its EMS coordinator, as of November 1, 1992, with the aid of a $25,000 grant from the AAA—his duties will include facilitating the flow of information from the CFSI to Capitol Hill staff members and members of the Federal Interagency Committee on EMS.

The USFA has committed itself to increasing the efficiency and effectiveness of the management of the overall prehospital emergency medical system. "Patient care is the top priority in EMS," stresses Sachs. He points out that 80 percent of the fire service provides EMS and that, therefore, EMS management is a critical part of fire service management. The goal of the USFA, Sachs says, is to promote unity throughout the EMS community.[14]

A significant portion of the agenda for accomplishing this objective was developed at the National Forum on EMS Management, held in February 1992 in Arlington, Virginia. Leaders of all major national EMS organizations and federal agencies involved in EMS met to discuss various issues related to EMS, including the scope of the role the federal government should play. A report on the forum was being prepared at press time.[22]

To increase coordination and cooperation between the federal agencies and the EMS community, the Federal Emergency Management Agency (FEMA) reassigned the chair of the Federal Interagency Committee on EMS to the USFA and expanded its role. The chair's functions now include maintaining a liaison with national EMS trade and professional organizations and associations.[22]

At the NFA, Jeff Dyar, director of prehospital education at Creighton University in Omaha, Nebraska, was hired to supervise the development of the NFA's proposed comprehensive EMS management program. EMS leaders at an EMS forum and participants in a National Highway Traffic Administration's Public Information, Education and Relations conference recommended that the NFA expand its curricula to include EMS. Among revisions the NFA has made is the replacement of its two-week EMS management course with a new Advanced EMS Leadership course.[22]

Prospects for EMS

The fire department's role in EMS in the 1990s will vary with each department. No single model will fit the needs of every community. In rural areas, for example, the fire department may be the only provider of EMS. In cities, on the other hand, the fire department may provide basic life support with another city agency or an outside (third-service) agency providing advanced life support and/or transportation to the hospital.

Fire service EMS is a complex, vital, and controversial issue whose future prospects invoke both "euphoria" and cautiousness in fire service members such as Brame of the Orange County (CA) Fire Department, who on the one hand is celebrating that "the fire station light has come on, waking everyone up to the realization that fire service EMS is here to stay," and, on the other hand, is warning that without proper attention, EMS will become a "nightmare." Brame emphasizes: "EMS management is a must, for if we do not manage our EMS operations, they will be managed by others."[21,32-33]

1. McKeen, D.K., N. Rynning, B.J. Weaver, K.M. Smith. "The Illusion of Gorgeous Uniqueness of the Fire Service Toward EMS." Research Project, National Fire Academy, Jan. 7-18, 1991, 1.
2. D.H. Hiett, Jr., treasurer of the International Association of Fire Chiefs EMS Section and chief of the Atlanta (GA) Fire Department, telephone interview, May 10, 1993.
3. Harley, G., D. Johnson, G. Kantak, et al. "Fire/EMS—A Marriage in Trouble." Research Project, National Fire Academy, Aug. 6-17, 1990, 1.
4. Page, J.O. "Trends in Fire Service EMS." *Fire Service TODAY,* 50:2, Feb. 1983, 14.
5. Hunter, K., J. Holt, D. Saunders, et al. *Improving Attitudes of Firefighters Towards E.M.S.* Management of Emergency Medical Services Course, National Fire Academy, Feb. 1-12, 1988, 1.
6. Nemwan, M. "Born of Necessity and Thriving: A Survey of Fire Service Involvement in Emergency Medical Services." *JEMS,* 1982 Almanac, Jan. 1982, in "Trends in the Fire Service," as cited in No. 4 above, 16.
7. Alguire, W.J., J.C. Cosby, D.B. Jackson, et al. *Patching up the marriage between fire service and EMS.* Research Project, National Fire Academy, Apr. 11-22, 1988, 3.
8. Benson, K., "EMS in the Fire Service." *Emergency,* Nov. 1992, 30.
9. "Fireman, Save My Child!" Staff Report, *JEMS,* June 1984, 38.
10. Mastrino, M. "EMS & the Fire Service: Has It Hurt Delivery?" *Firefighter's News,* Oct./Nov. 1992, 38.
11. Page, J.O. "Understanding the Fire Service." *JEMS,* June 1984, 34.
12. Gratz, D.B. "EMS in the fire service TIME OUT! *Fire Chief,* Nov. 1983, 48.
13. Hauder, J.M. executive director, Indiana State Emergency Management Agency, phone interview, Feb. 1993.
14. Sachs, Gordon, EMS program manager, USFA, telephone interview, April 1, 1993.
15. Butler, T. "Call the Fire Department." *Emergency,* Dec. 1989, 45.
16. Madison, Bill, deputy executive director, IAFC, and nationally registered EMT/P. Telephone interview, Jan. 27, 1993.
17. *Washington Watchdog.* Congressional Fire Services Institute, Nov./ Dec. 1992, 7.
18. Land, D.W. "Integration of Fire and EMS Delivery System, NFA executive development program, Nov. 1989, 9.
19. Peterson, W. "Improving Public Support for the Fire Service Through EMS." *Fire Engineering,* Nov. 1983, 55.
20. Dernocoeur, J. "A Bold Approach to Fire Service EMS. *JEMS,* June 1987, 8.
21. Brame, K. "EMS Perspectives": Fire service EMS comes of age." *Fire Chief,* May 1991, 33.
22. *NASEMSD SCANNER,* National Association of State Emergency Medical Services Directors, Fall 1992, 7.

Fire Investigation: Change and Evolution

James H. Shanley, Jr.

Fire investigation is changing at a rapid pace. These changes are the result of a number of developments in the understanding of fire behavior as well as direct efforts to transfer new knowledge into fire investigation technology. Years of basic research in fire behavior by the National Institute of Standards and Technology's (NIST's) Building and Fire Research Laboratory (BFRL, formerly the National Bureau of Standards, Center for Fire Research), Factory Mutual Research Corporation, and numerous universities and private companies have led to greater understanding of how fires start and grow.

For instance, the phenomenon of flashover and its importance to a developing fire only now are being understood and have just started to make their way to fire investigators. Another milestone of progress for fire investigation was reached when the National Fire Protection Association (NFPA) published the first edition of NFPA 921, *Guide for Fire and Explosion Investigation,* in February 1992. This manual was the first of its kind in the field of fire investigation written by a committee of people who each contributed special knowledge of and experience in fire investigation.

Unlike many previously published materials in the field, its facts were carefully checked to ensure they agreed with the laws of science, and it will undergo periodic updates. The committee has reviewed NFPA 921 numerous times, and the Guide was open to comment by the general public twice before being adopted.

Adapted from James H. Shanley, Jr., "Fire Investigation Change and Evolution, Part 1: An Overview," *Fire Engineering* (January 1994). Reprinted with permission of *Fire Engineering.*

Even today, fire investigation seminars are being conducted that are seriously flawed in their science, have not been updated to reflect the latest technology and research, and make no mention of NFPA 921. These seminars serve only to reinforce the "old wives' tales" and fire investigation myths that hurt investigators' credibility. It is hoped that this and future articles bring these deficiencies to the attention of the fire investigation community as well as to those who employ them in the interest of advancing the science.

Fire research

Modern fire research really began during World War II. The vulnerability to and resulting damage from incendiary attacks in Europe and Japan led many countries to develop methods for evaluating the ability of structures to withstand fire. This research continued and expanded in the postwar years to become what it is today. One problem, however, has continued to characterize the fields of fire research and fire protection: Often it takes a major fire with multiple casualties before codemaking groups, legislators, and the fire research community act on a particular fire problem. (Such was the case with the problems of combustible ceiling finish, inadequate exits, and open stairs.) And even after the magnitude of certain problems are recognized, fires still occur where the lessons learned are the same as they were 50 years ago. Examples are the fires at the Happy Land Social Club in New York City and the DuPont Plaza Hotel in Puerto Rico.

Early on, it was recognized that the size and complexity of buildings and their contents made full-scale tests to evaluate fire behavior in them expensive and difficult. Today, environmental regulations prevent or restrict much fire research. For these reasons, fire researchers have sought to understand the fundamental rules of fire behavior and then apply that understanding to predict fire behavior. One of the results of this approach is fire modeling. With a fire model, it is possible to predict how a particular fire will affect a room or rooms within a building under specific conditions. Fire models typically run on a computer, which uses the data collected from fire tests and the results of fire analysis to predict outcomes. Some models specialize in predicting the toxicity of smoke or determining the likelihood of occupant escape from a building. Fire models have become a new and powerful tool for the fire investigator as well. Now it is possible to look at a fire scene after the fact and, with the help of a model, gain insight into aspects of the fire, such as the following:

- How long did it take for the fire to reach flashover?
- What was the carbon monoxide concentration in the room next to the room of origin?

- When should the first smoke detector and automatic sprinkler have activated?

These and numerous other examples show what these new tools can do for fire investigation, things that, until recently, were impossible to determine or could only be estimated unless a reliable eyewitness was available.

Fire research also has provided fire investigators with scientifically sound explanations for phenomena fire investigators have observed for years at fire scenes. Conversely, it has opened to question things considered to be undisputable evidence for a particular fire effect. An example is burn patterns on the floor, which long have been held as evidence that an ignitable liquid had been burned on the floor. However, research into the flashover phenomenon and other fire effects has shown that floor burn patterns may have other causes.

For many reasons, integrating new technology and fire research data into the fire service and fire investigation field has been slow. Many fire investigators have their roots in the fire service, where the inertia of tradition sometimes has been difficult to overcome. Research findings often are published in language incomprehensible to anyone without a Ph.D—making them useless for most fire investigators; and, until recently, this research was not geared specifically to fire investigation problems.

Training for fire investigators typically has involved classes or seminars produced by local, state, or federal agencies; insurance companies; and investigator associations. The system has been successful, educating many competent fire investigators; but when changes started to occur and new technology became available, some trainers did not update their programs.

For example, one seminar included a presentation on the uses of a computer in fire investigation. The presentation centered on how fire investigators could use word processors to keep notes. No mention was made of fire models, computer-aided drawing (CAD), or other uses of real value to fire investigators. Curriculum changes have been met with resistance for many reasons, most of which probably fit into the category of "because we've always done it this way." For this and other reasons, the NFPA formed the Technical Committee on Fire Investigation in 1984, which was charged with developing a manual on how fire investigation should really be done.

NFPA fire investigation committee

Once the NFPA decided to form a fire investigation technical committee, it solicited membership applications from its members and the general public. NFPA rules mandate that its committees be "balanced," that is, they must represent all the groups to which their documents would apply. Members of the fire investigation committee represent the fire service, insurance companies, the federal government, state fire marshal offices, researchers, the legal profession, private investigators, and special experts. This group was charged with writing a new manual and also became responsible for NFPA 907M, *Determination of Electrical Fire Causes* (1988 edition), which had been written by an electrical fire investigation committee that first met in 1977.

In November 1991, at the NFPA Fall Meeting in Montreal, Canada, members voted to accept the first edition of NFPA 921, *Guide for Fire and Explosion Investigation*. It was published in the spring of 1992. Since that time, the members of the Fire Investigation Committee have been preparing new material for inclusion in the second edition.

The first edition of NFPA 921 has 14 chapters: Administration, Basic Methodology, Basic Fire Science, Fire Patterns, Legal Considerations, Planning the Investigation, Sources of Information, Recording the Scene, Physical Evidence Examination and Testing, Safety, Origin Determination, Cause Determination, Explosions, and Referenced Publications.

NFPA 921 now is being used in whole or part as a textbook by such agencies as the Connecticut State Fire Marshals Office, the National Association of Fire Investigators, and the National Fire Academy. It has been and will continue to be used in the courtroom as an authoritative reference on fire and explosion investigation. The next edition of NFPA 921 will include chapters on incendiary fires, automobile fires, major fires, appliances, and investigating electrical fires. It is anticipated that the current NFPA guide for electrical fires, NFPA 907M, will be absorbed into NFPA 921 as a new chapter with much updating.

NFPA 921 was written for beginning and experienced fire investigators. This broad audience made writing the manual difficult, since it had to be technical enough to present the science accurately but not so technical that a beginner could not use it as a textbook. NFPA 921 presents the science behind the "tools" of fire investigation, such as fire patterns, so that the investigator understands their origin and meaning. It was hoped that this would dispel the fire investigation myths still prevalent and prevent new myths from forming. The survival of myths threatens the credibility of individuals and the fire investigation community at large.

Fire investigation myths

It was the persistence of repeatedly repudiated myths that in part prompted the formation of the NFPA Fire Investigation

Committee. These myths originated in the days before fire models, gas chromatograms, and fire research. They were based on rules of thumb and general observations made at fire scenes. In their day, they had some merit, but they were not scientifically based and did not change to reflect changes in the science of fire investigation. Like the flat-earth concept, many of the myths appear rational under narrow scrutiny—they seem valid as long as you do not look too far or expect the myth to conform to basic physical laws. These myths, however, have retained credibility because of the number of fire investigators and fire experts using them.

Certain elements of fire investigator training have been based on these myths and other unscientific principles. For example, many investigators have been taught that there are four modes of heat transfer: convection, conduction, radiation, and direct flame contact. The engineering and scientific communities recognize only convection, conduction, and radiation; direct flame contact is a combination of convection and radiation heat transfer. Other popular fire investigation myths include those regarding V-patterns, low burning, depth of char, origin based on greatest fire damage, floor burn patterns, spalling of concrete, fire seeking oxygen, and arson indicated by "fast" fires. Each of these myths and others are discussed in a later article.

Fire investigation fundamentals

Before exploring these myths, it is important to review and reinforce the fundamentals of fire investigation, which should be second nature to all fire investigators. Objective and valid investigations into the origin and cause of fires depend on knowledge of these fundamentals. An investigation must start as an objective collection of data and facts from which theories will be formulated. This requires the investigator to have an open mind and not be prejudiced toward any particular fire cause. Information is collected by visiting and documenting the fire scene. No conclusions are made at this point, but data, in the form of diagrams, photographs, interviews, and other observations, are collected. Data also may be collected remote from the fire scene. As the quantity of data increases, the investigator analyzes it and begins to formulate theories and a hypothesis with regard to the fire's origin and cause. Before this hypothesis can be put forth as a conclusion, it must be tested by considering and eliminating all other reasonable origins and causes.

If the hypothesis cannot withstand this test, it must be discarded or modified and retested. If no hypothesis can withstand this type of scrutiny, then the cause must be listed as "unknown." Listing a fire as "suspicious" based on inconclusive data is not valid and contributes nothing to the field of investigation. This term should not be used in reports or incident forms unless conclusive evidence of an incendiary fire exists, in which case the fire should be listed as incendiary or arson. The collection, preservation, and presentation of investigation data without conclusions are valuable because at a later date additional data may be developed or the original data may become useful to someone with specialized expertise.

The Impact of ADA

Karin L. Foster and
Michael T. Reynvaan

After the Americans with Disabilities Act (ADA), what kinds of questions can public safety employers such as fire departments still ask job applicants? Should employers still rely on approved hiring standards for physical and mental fitness? Does an employer need to make a job offer before requiring a medical examination? Are there any additional restrictions on drug tests? Are "wellness incentives" still lawful? Can light duty jobs still be filled based on seniority?

Public safety employers across the nation have grappled with these and other questions as they have prepared for the impact of the ADA on their employment practices. This Congressional Act has received more attention since it was signed into law than any other civil rights legislation in recent memory.

Focus on individual abilities

The cardinal rule of the ADA is for employers to focus on the individual abilities of job applicants and employees with disabilities, rather than on their disabilities. The ADA seeks to provide equal access to jobs by knocking down barriers that historically have stood in the way of individuals with disabilities. Those barriers include myths, stereotypes and assumptions about the jobs they can and should hold in our society.

The first ADA case was decided in March 1993 and illus-

Adapted from Karin L. Foster and Michael T. Reynvaan, "The Impact of the Americans with Disabilities Act on Public Safety Employers," *Firehouse* (July 1993) and "The Americans with Disabilities Act, Part 2: Specific Issues: A Closer Look," *Firehouse* (August 1993). Reprinted with permission of *Firehouse* magazine.

trates the importance of focusing on an employee's current abilities to perform. A federal jury in Chicago is reported to have awarded $572,000 in damages to the former director of a security firm who was discharged after his employer learned he had terminal brain cancer. The jury apparently found that, although doctors had told the employee he had less than a year to live, his present ability to perform the job was unimpaired.

This article will provide an overview of the ADA's employment provisions and illustrate how to analyze ADA problems, then take a closer look at specific issues related to hiring standards, interviews, pre-employment testing, substance abuse and contractual arrangements.

Overview

What does Title I prohibit?   Title I of the ADA, which covers public safety employers, prohibits disability discrimination in all aspects of employment. It covers recruitment, hiring, promotion, award of tenure, transfer, termination, compensation, job assignments, job descriptions, seniority lists, fringe benefits, training, conferences, social and recreational programs and any other term or condition of employment.

Title 1 covers public safety employers with 15 or more employees. It specifically prohibits:

- Using qualification standards that tend to screen out individuals with disabilities.
- Administering a test so that the results reflect sensory, manual or speaking disabilities, rather than the ability to perform the job, unless the purpose of the test is to measure sensory, manual or speaking abilities.
- Except as specifically permitted, asking questions of a job applicant as to the existence or nature of a disability or requiring a medical examination before making a job offer.
- Except as specifically permitted, asking questions of a current employee as to the existence or nature of a disability or requiring a medical examination that is not job-related and consistent with business necessity.
- Entering into a contract or other arrangement—such as with an employment agency, a union or a training academy—that has the effect of subjecting a job applicant or an employee to discrimination on the basis of disability.
- Discriminating against a job applicant or current employee because someone with whom he or she has a relationship or association has a disability.
- Coercing, intimidating or retaliating against a person based on the exercise of rights protected by the ADA.

What does Title I require?   An employer must reasonably accommodate the known physical or mental limitations of a qualified individual with a disability, unless the employer can show that the accommodation would cause an undue hardship.

Who is protected by Title I?   Title I protects a "qualified individual with a disability." That term is defined as "an individual with a disability who satisfies the requisite skill, experience, education and other job-related requirements of the employment position such individual holds or desires, and who, with or without reasonable accommodation, can perform the essential functions of such position."

Applying the ADA to a decision whether to hire or retain a worker is a two-step process. Assuming the worker has a disability, the first question an employer must ask is whether the worker is qualified, i.e., whether he or she satisfies the skill, experience, education and other job-related requirements for the position. If the worker does not satisfy those requirements, the employer may reject that individual without considering whether he or she needs a reasonable accommodation.

It is critical, however, that before rejecting an individual on the basis of lack of qualifications, the employer consider whether the qualification standards are job-related. Qualification standards that are not job-related and consistent with business necessity, and which tend to screen out individuals with disabilities, will violate the ADA.

If the individual is qualified, the next question is whether he or she can perform the functions of the job with or without accommodations. Some individuals with disabilities will be able to perform all functions of the job without any special accommodations. Others may need workplace modifications, changes to the way the job is performed, assistive devices or other reasonable accommodations.

Once it becomes apparent that an accommodation may be needed, an employer needs to find answers to the following questions: Does the individual have a covered disability? Is the individual able to perform all functions of the job? If not, are the functions the individual is unable to perform essential job functions? If so, is there a reasonable accommodation that will enable the worker to perform the job without presenting an undue hardship on the employer?

What is a "disability"?   A disability is "a physical or mental impairment that substantially limits one or more of an individual's major life activities." An individual who does not presently have a disability may be covered by the ADA if he or she has a record of such an impairment, or is regarded by the employer as having such an impairment.

To illustrate how an individual who does not presently have a disability may be covered, consider an individual with a record of mental illness which is presently controlled, or someone with a record of having been hospitalized for cocaine addiction who is now successfully rehabilitated. Basing an employment decision on a record containing such information may be a discriminatory practice. Likewise, an individual who is regarded by the employer as having an impairment, such as someone with a prominent facial scar, would be covered.

What is a "physical or mental impairment"?   Nearly any physical or mental disorder will qualify as an impairment. The definition of physical impairment covers all body systems. It also covers cosmetic disfigurement or anatomical loss. A mental impairment is defined to include mental retardation, organic brain syndrome, emotional or mental illness and learning disabilities.

Some disorders are specifically excluded from coverage. For example, sexual behavior disorders—such as transsexualism, pedophilia, exhibitionism and voyeurism—are excluded. Compulsive gambling, kleptomania or pyromania are also not covered. Likewise, psychoactive substance use disorders resulting from current illegal use of drugs are excluded.

Employers must bear in mind that state law may cover these conditions, even though the ADA does not. For example, transsexualism has been recognized by some state courts and agencies as a covered disability. In what has been described as the first case reinstating a public employee with transsexualism, the city council of Jacksonville, Florida, returned a corrections officer to work and approved a $149,500 settlement of her claims that she was discharged in violation of Florida's law against discrimination based on handicap.

Other conditions are excluded from ADA coverage on the basis that they do not result from disorders. These include homosexuality, pregnancy, characteristic predisposition to disease and common personality traits such as poor judgment or a quick temper, so long as they are not symptoms of an underlying disorder.

Stress and depression may or may not be considered impairments, depending upon whether these conditions result from an underlying disorder. Thus, if an employee requests that he or she be reassigned to a less stressful job as a reasonable accommodation, the employer should proceed to consider the request. Reasonable accommodation is discussed later in this article.

When does an impairment "substantially limit" a "major life activity"?   Just having a physical or mental impairment is not enough to constitute a disability; the impairment also must substantially limit a major life activity. Major life activities include functions such as caring for oneself, performing manual tasks, walking, seeing, hearing, speaking, breathing, learning and working.

The impairment substantially limits a major life activity if it causes the individual to be unable to perform a major life activity that the average person in the general population can perform, or significantly restricts the way he or she can perform it. An impairment is more likely to be a disability if it is severe, expected to endure for a length of time or expected to have a permanent or long term impact.

An individual with an impairment that does not limit any other major life activity may still have a disability if the impairment substantially limits his or her ability to work. The inability to perform a single, particular job does not qualify, however, if the impairment causes the person to be unable to perform a class of jobs or a broad range of jobs that utilize similar knowledge, skills or abilities in a particular locale, the impairment may be a disability.

If an individual has a disability covered by the ADA, i.e., a covered impairment that substantially limits a major life activity—the next question is whether the individual can perform the essential functions of the job with or without a reasonable accommodation.

What are the "essential functions" of a job?   The essential functions of a job are the "fundamental job duties of the employment position the individual with a disability holds or desires." Employers must focus on essential functions, rather than marginal functions, in determining whether an individual with disabilities can perform the job. Therefore, it is important for employers to identify, in advance, which functions are essential.

An employer should first ask whether employees who already hold the job perform the function. If not, it may not be essential; if so, the next question is whether removing that function or changing the way it is performed would change the job fundamentally. The focus should be on the purpose of the function and the result to be accomplished.

While this list is not exclusive, a job function may be essential to a particular job if:

- The reason the position exists is to perform that job function.
- There are a limited number of employees available among whom that job function can be distributed.

- The function is highly specialized and the individual is hired for his or her expertise or ability to perform that function.
- The employee spends a significant amount of his or her time on the job performing the function.
- The consequences of not requiring the employee to perform the function are significant.

An employer who wants to establish that a job function is essential should analyze the job under the foregoing criteria and then prepare a written job description which lists the function as essential before advertising or interviewing applicants for the job. It is important that job descriptions be current and accurate, for they can be used at trial by both sides as evidence of what the job actually requires.

Public safety employers should be alert to the danger of identifying a function as essential to a position when some of the employees in that position do not perform the function. For example, a job description for a firefighter defining the ability to carry a person from a burning building as an essential function could be a problem if there are firefighters within the department who will never be required to make such a rescue.

On the other hand, the consequences of not requiring a firefighter employee to be able to perform these types of functions could be life-threatening. Such functions may be considered essential if, in fact, all personnel may be required to respond in emergency situations. Employers with smaller workforces may have an even greater need to require that each employee be able to perform all functions of the job.

If a public safety employer determines—ideally, based upon an accurate and up-to-date job description—that a job applicant or employee with a disability is unable to perform an essential job function, the next question is whether a reasonable accommodation can be made.

What is a " reasonable accommodation"? A reasonable accommodation is essentially a change to the employer's practices, procedures or facilities that does not cause an undue hardship. Employers may need to make a change to enable an individual to apply for a job, to perform the essential functions of a job or to enjoy equal benefits and privileges of employment.

Generally, an individual who needs an accommodation must inform the employer. However, once put on notice that an accommodation may be needed, the employer must seek to identify the precise limitations caused by the disability and what modifications are possible. An employer may need to consider:

- Modifying existing structures, facilities, and transportation, including offices, job sites, cafeterias and vehicles.
- Restructuring a job to assign marginal functions to other employees.
- Permitting flexibility as to when work is performed or when breaks may be taken, including a part-time or modified work schedule.
- Modifying existing equipment used on the job or acquiring special equipment specifically to assist in job performance.
- Modifying tests, training materials or policies.
- Providing a qualified reader, a job coach or other professional assistance.
- Reassigning a current employee to a vacant position for which he or she is qualified.

An employer is not required to lower its standards for quality or attendance in order to make an accommodation. Nor need an employer provide personal use items, such as glasses or wheelchairs, unless those items are specifically required to meet job-related—rather than personal—needs.

A designated employee who is familiar with the ADA should participate in discussions with a job applicant or employee about what accommodation is needed. If the employer doubts that the individual actually needs a particular accommodation, the individual may be asked to provide medical documentation. An employer who cannot readily identify a reasonable accommodation may need to consult a community resource agency before deciding that an accommodation cannot be made.

A reasonable accommodation need not be the best accommodation available, as long as it is effective for the purpose. An employer has the right to choose among effective accommodations. An individual with a disability has the right to refuse an accommodation; however, if the individual cannot perform the essential functions of the job without the accommodation, he or she may be disqualified.

In summary, the ADA is a comprehensive statute which covers nearly all aspects of employment. It protects an individual with a disability who has the qualifications for the job. If an individual is the best qualified and able to perform the essential functions of the job, with or without accommodations, the employer may not reject that individual based on a disability. If a reasonable accommodation is needed, the employer must provide it.

Specific issues
Hiring standards   Over time, public safety employers have developed rigorous physical and mental criteria for police and

firefighter jobs. Job applicants have had to pass medical examinations and fitness tests to show that they are in good health and fit to perform without presenting a safety risk. In some states, certain medical standards for hiring have been approved by professional associations and are widely used.

Some of these criteria will violate the Americans with Disabilities Act (ADA) unless an employer can show that they are job-related and consistent with business necessity. For example, a requirement of 20/20 uncorrected visual acuity might violate the ADA, unless the employer can show that corrective lenses would interfere with proper job performance. Likewise, a requirement to read at a stated level might unfairly exclude persons with learning disabilities, unless the employer can show that the requirement is job-related.

A professional association's stamp of approval on a set of standards will not necessarily make them lawful under the ADA. In a case in Washington state, a fire district disqualified a firefighter with Crohn's disease from employment because the absence of Crohn's disease was among the minimum medical standards approved as guidelines for firefighters. The firefighter claimed handicap discrimination under state law and the fire district moved to dismiss on the basis of the approved guidelines. The court found for the firefighter and held that the guidelines did not show that the absence of Crohn's disease was sufficiently job-related.

Public employers must review their hiring standards to make sure that those standards are actually related to proper job performance and that they do not unfairly exclude individuals with disabilities from jobs.

Interviews   A job applicant may need a reasonable accommodation in order to complete an application or be interviewed. Public safety employers may require persons who need accommodations to request them in advance of applying or interviewing for a job.

On applications or in interviews, a public safety employer may not ask questions to elicit information about a job applicant's medical condition or history prior to making a job offer. For example, an employer may not:

- Present a laundry list of medical conditions and ask job applicants to indicate whether they have had them.
- Ask if there is any health-related reason the job applicant may not be able to perform the job.
- Ask if the applicant has ever been treated for drug addiction or alcoholism.
- Ask if the job applicant has ever applied for disability benefits.

An employer may tell a job applicant what the attendance rules are and ask whether he or she can comply with those rules. However, even if an applicant has an obvious disability, the employer may not ask how severe the disability is, how it happened or how much time off the applicant might require to receive care.

An employer may inquire into a job applicant's ability to perform job functions or ask him or her to describe or demonstrate how he or she will be able to perform those functions. If an employer requires an applicant with a disability to demonstrate how he or she will perform a job function, the employer must provide the accommodation the applicant needs, if any, and the demonstrations must be required of all applicants.

Public safety employers must review their job applications to make sure that they contain no impermissible questions. It is also a good idea to make sure that interviewers understand what types of questions will violate the ADA. This can be done by conducting short training sessions for interviewers and distributing a list of what should and should not be asked in an interview.

Medical examinations   The ADA prohibits requiring a medical examination before making a job offer. Between having made an offer and when work begins, the employer may require medical examinations of all new hires entering the same job category. If one person's initial examination indicates a problem, more tests may be required of that person without testing the others.

Unlike a current employee, a new hire may be required to undergo a medical examination that is not job-related. An employer may also condition the offer on the results of the examination.

However, in order to withdraw a job offer based on those results, the employer must be able to show that the offer was withdrawn for reasons that were job-related and consistent with business necessity, and that no reasonable accommodations could be made.

For current employees, a medical examination must be job related and consistent with business necessity. A current employee may be required to undergo a medical examination if necessary to determine whether the employee is still able to perform the job or whether a reasonable accommodation can be made. An employer may also administer periodic medical examinations to evaluate fitness for duty, if all employees in the same job category are examined.

Any information obtained about the medical condition or history of a job applicant or current employee must be maintained on separate forms and in separate medical files and must be treated as a confidential medical record. The release of such information is limited to informing supervisors and safety personnel about accommodations, and providing relevant information to worker's compensation offices, second injury funds and insurance companies.

Fitness tests   In contrast to medical examinations, fitness tests may be administered at any time. They should be administered to all job applicants for similar jobs, without regard to disability. If a test screens out an individual on the basis of a disability, the employer must be able to show that the standard the applicant failed is job-related and consistent with business necessity.

The ADA limits an employer's ability to ask about a job applicant's medical condition before the fitness test. For public safety employers who want to guard against injuries from the fitness test, the Equal Employment Opportunity Commission (EEOC) suggests giving each applicant a description of the test and asking for a doctor's note stating whether he or she can safely be tested. A potential disadvantage is that the job applicant will know what test to expect, unless the description covers many test options.

One area of particular interest to public safety employers is whether a psychological examination is a medical examination, with its attendant restrictions, or a fitness test that may be required at any time. If the test measures emotional or psychological instability, it may be considered a medical examination; however, if it tests only for personality characteristics, it may be a fitness test. The conservative approach would be to postpone any psychological testing until after making an offer of employment and to make sure any psychological testing of current employees is job-related.

Substance abuse   Employers may make and enforce rules prohibiting the use of illegal drugs in the workplace, and may hold employees who currently use drugs to the same performance standards as other employees. Employers also may require compliance with the Drug-Free Workplace Act of 1988. Tests of illegal drug use are not considered medical examinations, so the ADA does not affect an employer's ability to administer such tests during the hiring process or to current employees.

The ADA does not clearly define "current use." The House-Senate Conference Committee Report vaguely states that it means the "illegal use of drugs occurred recently enough to justify a reasonable belief that a person's drug use is current." The distinction between current and former drug use is important, because a former drug user who has been successfully rehabilitated or is in the process of completing a rehabilitation program may be a covered individual with a disability under the ADA.

An employer ordinarily is prohibited from rejecting an applicant or taking disciplinary action against an employee on the basis of former drug use. However, the EEOC has stated that certain employers, such as law enforcement agencies, may be able to exclude individuals with a history of illegal drug use upon a showing that the standard is job-related and consistent with business necessity. The ADA prohibits rejecting an individual with a disability because the public may have a negative reaction; however, police departments could take the position that former drug users are more likely to associate with criminals, making them unfit to be police officers.

Contracts and union agreements   The ADA prohibits entering into a contract that has the effect of discriminating on the basis of disability. Public safety employers that require job applicants or employees to go to a training academy should consider whether the training academy complies with the ADA. If the training academy violates the ADA, then the public safety employer could share liability. One way to address this would be to insist upon an indemnification clause in any training academy agreement.

An employer who relies on a union agreement to refuse to provide a requested accommodation risks sharing liability with the union for a failure to accommodate. For example, assume a union agreement restricts light duty positions by seniority and a junior employee requests light duty as a reasonable accommodation. The employer may have to choose between breaching the union agreement or violating the ADA. The employer could argue that it would be an undue hardship to violate the agreement. One way to avoid this would be to negotiate a clause in the union agreement authorizing the employer to comply with the ADA.

Many union agreements contain "wellness incentive" provisions that give employees extra vacation time as a reward for not having taken sick leave. An individual who has had to take sick leave because of a disability may not qualify for a wellness incentive; however, as long as a wellness incentive is not adopted for a discriminatory reason, it should not violate the ADA.

Employer defenses
A legitimate, nondiscriminatory reason   The traditional defense to a charge of intentional discrimination is that the challenged action was justified by a legitimate, nondiscriminatory reason. One example of this type of defense might be that a dis-

charge was justified for the reason that the employee was not performing the job satisfactorily. Documentation that the employee was evaluated and counseled before discharge can be valuable evidence.

It is critical for the determination that an employee cannot properly perform the job to be based on evidence of present abilities, and not upon assumptions or predictions that the employee will be unable to perform in the future.

Job-related standards and no reasonable accommodation   If the charge is that the employer's qualification standards were discriminatory, the employer may defend with evidence that the qualification standards were job-related and consistent with business necessity, and that the job applicant or employee could not meet those standards even with a reasonable accommodation.

It should be noted that the ADA preempts state and federal laws that are less protective than the ADA; thus, it is a weak defense to claim that the physical, medical or safety standards were imposed by state or local law, if those standards violate the ADA.

A direct threat to health or safety   Another defense to a charge of discriminatory standards is that the individual posed a direct threat to the health or safety of the individual or others in the workplace. A "direct threat" means "a significant risk of substantial harm to the health or safety of the individual or others that cannot be eliminated or reduced by reasonable accommodation." This particular defense should be relied upon with caution, because the burden of proving a direct threat rests squarely with the employer.

To sustain this defense, an employer must have made an individualized assessment of objective and specific medical or other factual evidence. The evidence should show that the particular individual is currently unable to perform essential job functions without presenting a direct threat, rather than on general assumptions or speculations. An employer must consider whether a reasonable accommodation would reduce the risk of harm, and may not consider the possibility of future harm.

Relevant factors are (1) the duration of the risk, (2) the nature and severity of the potential harm, (3) the likelihood that the potential harm will occur and (4) the imminence of the potential harm. If the risk is expected to be long term, the potential for harm is severe and imminent and the likelihood that harm will occur is significant, then a direct threat defense may be appropriate.

A case under Section 504 illustrates the importance of objective medical evidence. A District of Columbia fire department refused to hire a job applicant who had disclosed that he was HIV-positive, relying on negative public perception and general safety concerns. Medical witnesses testified at trial that the applicant was asymptomatic and would present "no measurable risk." The court likened the fire department's approach to racial prejudice and awarded damages for disability discrimination.

Undue hardship   The defense to a charge of failure to accommodate is that the accommodation would impose an undue hardship, which is defined as a "significant difficulty or expense." Among the factors to be considered are the net cost of the accommodation (after outside funding), the financial resources of the facility and the covered entity, the type of operations, the number of other employees at the facility and the covered entity and the impact of the accommodation upon the ability of other employees to perform their duties.

It will be difficult for many employers to establish an undue hardship based solely on expense. It is unclear under the ADA whether the evaluation of undue hardship will be based on the resources of a city's fire department or on the resources of the city as a whole. Notably, Congress specifically rejected an amendment proposing that an accommodation costing more than 10% of an employee's salary be treated as an undue hardship.

Remedies   Before bringing a lawsuit under Title I of the ADA, an individual must first file an administrative charge with the EEOC. After the EEOC has made its determination, there is a 90-day private suit filing period. The remedies available to a successful plaintiff include hiring, reinstatement, promotion, back pay, front pay, reasonable accommodation, attorneys' fees, expert witness fees and court costs. Punitive damages are not available against state and local governments.

Conclusion

The ADA presents nearly as many questions as it does answers about what is required of the employers it covers. Until the courts have had an opportunity to interpret some of its provisions, the actual force of the ADA's impact has yet to be felt.

Public safety employers need to review their practices—hiring, interviewing, medical examinations, training academies and any others—related to employment. Employers who base employment decisions on the *abilities* of individuals with disabilities will be well prepared for the ADA.

The Experience with Smoke Detectors

John R. Hall, Jr.

From 1975 to 1984, the United States experienced remarkable growth in the use of home smoke detectors, principally single-station, battery-operated, ionization-type smoke detectors (see Figure 1). This rapid growth in use, coupled with clear evidence of the life-saving effectiveness of detectors, made the home smoke detector the fire safety success story of the decade.

Since 1984, the growth in use has been much less rapid, but it remains fairly steady. As of 1993, only 1 home in 12 remained unprotected.

However, the percentage of *fires* occurring in homes with smoke detectors has lagged far behind the overall percentage of *homes* with smoke detectors. There are two principal factors that could explain why there are, proportionally, so many more smoke detectors in homes in general than in homes in which fires have been reported. One is that households that have fires tend, for a variety of reasons, to be the kind that would be less likely to buy or own smoke detectors. The other is that smoke detectors discover some fires so early that they can be controlled by the occupants without involving the fire department. There is no way to develop a conclusive analysis of the relative importance of these two factors, but some exploratory analysis suggests that the more significant factor is the impact of smoke detectors in detecting fires early so that people are able to control them without involving the fire department.

Adapted from John R. Hall, Jr., "The U. S. Experience with Smoke Detectors." Reprinted with permission from *NFPA Journal* (September/October 1994, vol. 88, no. 5) © 1994, National Fire Protection Association, Quincy, MA 02269.

Figure 1. Growth in home smoke detector use, 1970–1993.

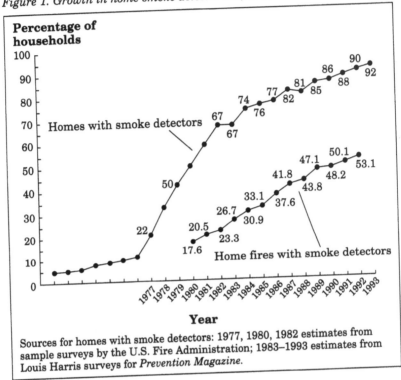

Sources for homes with smoke detectors: 1977, 1980, 1982 estimates from sample surveys by the U.S. Fire Administration; 1983–1993 estimates from Louis Harris surveys for *Prevention Magazine.*

The major population groups that are at risk from fire have all been included in the country's strong move to smoke detector use. All national surveys that have examined smoke detector use by major population group have found that detector use for all population groups is far higher than it is in homes that have fires (see Table 1).

To some degree, households that are poor or have other risk-related characteristics still lag behind the others in smoke detector use. But the gap is not large enough to explain the high concentration of fires in homes without smoke detectors. Apparently, the households that still do not have smoke detectors are more risk-prone, but in ways that do not correlate strongly or neatly with the socioeconomic characteristics of poverty, race, age, and so on that usually correlate with the risk of having a fire.

How effective are home smoke detectors?

Homes with smoke detectors have slightly more than half the risk of incurring a death should a fire occur than homes without

Table 1. Detector usage by major population group in 1982, 1989, and 1991.

	Percentage of group having home smoke detectors		
	1982	1989	1991
Total population	67	85	88
Apartments	63		
Rural households	62		83[a]
Households headed by person over 65 years of age	62		83
Households headed by person who did not complete high school	61	72	83
Households in the South	60	80	85
Households not headed by married couple	56		
Households with incomes below $7,500 per year	55	79	84
Non-white households	53		86[b]
Smokers			87
Heavy drinkers			83
People who ever use drugs			83
Homes with fires	23	47	

Source: 1982 figures from Figure 1 (homes with fires) and John R. Hall, Jr. and Sid Groeneman, "Two Homes in Three Have Detectors," *Fire Service Today,* February 1983, pp. 18–20; 1989 and 1991 figures from "The Prevention Index '90 and '92," *Prevention Magazine,* 33 East Minor Street, Emmaus, Pennsylvania 19098, 1990 and 1992. Some figures available for 1982 were not available for 1989. Some additional material on these demographics for 1991 was provided to the NFPA by *Prevention Magazine.*

[a]Outside SMSA but not necessarily rural.

[b]African-American households, specifically.

smoke detectors. To put it another way, smoke detectors cut the risk of dying in a home fire by roughly 40 percent. Table 2, which shows this pattern, also reveals that the estimated impact of smoke detectors on death rates fluctuates somewhat from year to year. In the last 12 years, there has been a slight downward trend in the estimated impact of smoke detectors, which may be attributable to increased problems in keeping them operational.

Table 2 probably understates the power and value of home smoke detectors. First, the death rates for homes that have smoke detectors include those deaths that occurred in homes with nonoperational smoke detectors or incomplete smoke detector coverage. Households should do even better if they follow the

Table 2. Life-saving effectiveness of home smoke detectors.

| Year | Deaths per 100 fires | | How much lower is death rate with detector present? (%) |
	Detectors present	No detector present	
1980	0.54	1.00	46
1981	0.53	0.92	42
1982	0.43	0.90	52
1983	0.55	0.90	39
1984	0.43	0.84	49
1985	0.62	1.02	39
1986	0.55	1.07	49
1987	0.59	0.99	40
1988	0.66	1.16	43
1989	0.65	1.06	39
1990	0.61	1.14	46
1991	0.53	0.84	37
1992	0.57	1.03	45
Last 10 years averaged (1983–92)	0.58	0.99	42

Source: 1980–92 NFIRS, NFPA Survey.

NFPA's recommendations for installing and maintaining smoke detectors and practice the closely related rules for developing and practicing an escape plan.

Second, the figures in Table 2 are based on reported fires only; as noted, smoke detectors are able to discover some fires so quickly that they can be extinguished by occupants before they have to notify the fire department. Indeed, smoke detectors may cut the number of fires reported to fire departments by 75 to 80 percent, relative to the number that would have been reported if there had been no smoke detectors. Still, analysis of this issue is very uncertain because the limitations of available data require an indirect analysis, and some estimates of the likely range for values cannot be directly measured.

A 10-year analysis that separates single-family dwellings, duplexes, and manufactured homes from apartments, townhouses, and condominiums produces a surprisingly large difference in the statistical estimate of the life-saving effectiveness of home smoke detectors. In single-family homes, duplexes, and manufactured homes, smoke detectors are estimated to reduce the risk of dying in a fire by 50 percent. In apartments, townhouses, and condominiums, the estimated reduction is only 14 percent, based on fires that occurred between 1983 and 1992.

According to our best estimates, the problem of nonoperational detectors is of equal size in both types of homes, so apparently that is not the reason for the discrepancy. Apartments might have fewer or longer escape routes, less complete coverage, or more success in preventing fires from growing large enough to report. However, none of these hypotheses can be analyzed with the available data.

It is also possible that apartment fires are more dangerous, that more apartment dwellers are unable to act on an early warning, or that more apartment dwellers ignore detector warnings. This last situation might occur, for example, if the occupants are more likely to assume that any detector alarm from outside their unit is a nuisance alarm.

Table 3 presents an overview of the characteristics of victims and the fires that killed them in apartments and in single-family dwellings, duplexes, and manufactured homes, with and without smoke detectors. Many of the differences found in Table 3 are small. In addition, some groups of characteristics seem to be measuring the same or similar phenomena, but show inconsistent patterns in doing so.

The most striking difference has to do with the victim's proximity to the fire. Roughly one-third of the victims of fatal fires in single-family dwellings, duplexes, and manufactured homes are in the room of fire origin at the time of ignition. Roughly half the apartment victims are that close to the fire. This suggests that there are proportionally more people in apartments who are so close to the fire that they may not have time to escape, even if they have an operational detector.

Other NFPA analyses have shown that one-third of fatal apartment fires begin in bedrooms, compared to one-fourth of fatal fires in single-family dwellings, duplexes, or manufactured homes.[1] This may help to explain why fire victims in apartments are closer to the fire in so many cases.

How many home smoke detectors are operational?

Published studies of the operational status of detectors focus almost exclusively on home smoke detectors. Within this population, there are two different kinds of studies: those that look at smoke detector performance in fires and those that look at the operational status of smoke detectors in homes in general (see Table 4). The latest study—and one of the best—was done for the National Smoke Detector Project and shows that one-fifth, or 20 percent, of homes with smoke detectors have detectors that do not work.

Another way to estimate the fraction of smoke detectors that are working is to estimate what percentage of homes that experi-

Table 3. Characteristics of fatalities in home fires, with and without smoke detectors present.

Characteristic	Dwellings and mobile homes		Apartments	
	Detector present (%)	No detectors (%)	Detector present (%)	No detectors (%)
Victim in room of fire origin at ignition	36.7	39.2	52.2	44.1
Fire spread flames beyond room of origin	74.5	83.8	67.6	75.3
Fire spread smoke beyond room of origin	94.0	92.1	93.2	91.1
Victim impaired physically or mentally, including by age or by drugs or alcohol	26.5	29.5	31.5	29.9
Victim age 65 or older	24.6	26.5	27.3	15.9
Victim age 5 or younger	22.5	20.6	16.9	22.5
Victim unable to act or irrational	19.6	17.3	19.1	18.8
Victim attempting fire control or rescue	6.2	5.2	5.4	5.1
Victim incapacitated before fire	14.3	11.8	14.8	11.1
Fire between victim and exit	18.5	18.4	19.5	25.9
Victim's clothing on fire	6.1	4.9	8.3	4.9
Victim blocked by locked door or illegal gates or locks	3.5	3.4	1.5	2.9

Source: 1983–92 NFIRS, NFPA survey.

Note: Victims with characteristics unknown have been proportionally allocated.

enced fires are reported to have had an operational smoke detector (see Table 5).

Since we already know that homes that have fires are much less likely to have smoke detectors than homes in general, we might also suspect that smoke-detector-equipped homes that have fires are more likely than smoke-detector-equipped homes that do not have fires to have allowed their smoke detectors to become nonoperational. The argument would be that having a

Table 4. Percentage of operational home smoke detectors.

Results of several studies	
1. Twelve communities[a] (principally Montgomery County, Maryland), 1978–1979	92
2. Santa Barbara, California, 1983[b]	64
3. Oregon, 1984[b]	75
4. DeKalb County, Georgia, 1985[c]	70
5. Inference from two national studies[d]	83
6. Unreported fires study (fires with smoke spread beyond room of origin)[e]	68
7. National Smoke Detector Project Survey[f]	80

[a]Raymond E. Hawkins, *An Evaluation of Residential Smoke Detectors Under Field Conditions: Final Phase,* Washington, D.C.: International Association of Fire Chiefs Foundation, March 1983, p. xiii.

[b]Leon Cooper, "Why We Need to Test Smoke Detectors," *Fire Journal,* November 1986, pp. 43-45.

[c]Centers for Disease Control, U.S. Department of Health and Human Services, *Morbidity and Mortality Weekly Report,* July 18, 1986.

[d]"The Prevention Index '87," *Prevention Magazine,* 33 East Minor Street, Emmaus, Pennsylvania 18098, 1987, and R.E. Hoffman, "Tracking 1990 Objectives for Injury Prevention With 1985 NHIS Findings," *Public Health Report* #101, November-December 1986, pp. 581-586. The former estimated 76% of homes had at least one detector in 1985, and the latter estimated 63.3% of homes had at least one functioning detector in 1985, which would mean an 83% rate of operationality.

[e]Audits & Surveys, Inc. *1984 National Simple Survey of Unreported Residential Fires,* Final Technical Report, Contract C-83-1239, for the U.S. Consumer Product Safety Commission, June 13, 1985.

[f]Charles L. Smith, *Smoke Detector Operability Survey–Report on Findings,* Bethesda, Md.: U.S. Consumer Product Safety Commission, November 1993, p. ii.

fire correlates with a lower concern for fire safety, which might be expected to produce a lower rate of smoke detector use and a higher rate of nonoperational smoke detectors where smoke detectors are present. In fact, the figure for homes equipped with smoke detectors that experienced fires in 1992, taken from the National Smoke Detector Project, is substantially lower than the figure for such homes found in Table 4.

Note that Table 5 also indicates that the percentage of operational smoke detectors is roughly the same for apartments as it is for single-family dwellings, duplexes, and manufactured homes. Where they differ, the percentages for apartments are usually better, although not significantly so, except in 1985.

Table 5. Estimated percentage of fire-involved homes[a] with operational smoke detectors.

Year	Single-family dwellings, duplexes, and manufactured homes (%)[b]	Apartments (%)[b]
1980	75.7	76.0
1981	72.5	73.9
1982	71.5	71.1
1983	68.3	70.5
1984	67.4	67.9
1985	62.5	69.7
1986	68.0	69.4
1987	68.0	70.4
1988	67.1	68.9
1989	68.1	69.3
1990	68.2	68.0
1991	67.5	69.4
1992	67.5	69.6

Source: 1980–92 NFIRS, NFPA Survey.

[a]Homes are all structures that households may occupy, other than properties such as hotels, boarding homes, dormitories, or barracks, where households share some building services. The dwelling category encompasses one- and two-family units, including manufactured homes, while apartments include all other homes—that is, buildings containing three or more housing units.

[b]Estimated as percentage of fires where detectors activated within set of fires deemed large enough to activate an operational smoke detector. Set excludes fires coded as too small to activate smoke detector, fires in which the extent of smoke was unknown or unclassified or confined to object or area of origin, and fires originating in a room without a smoke detector and having extent of smoke confined to room of origin.

This may seem surprising to urban fire experts accustomed to seeing a disproportionate level of smoke detector problems in poor, multifamily housing. However, we should remember that, in the United States as a whole, poverty and other household characteristics that one might expect would correlate with poor smoke detector maintenance are found in rural dwellings and manufactured homes as often as they are in urban, multifamily housing. Of course, we do not know whether the operational status of smoke detectors is correlated to poverty, although most measures of fire frequency and use of fire protection equipment are.

Figures 2 and 3 show how problems with nonoperational home smoke detectors have produced a widening gap between the percentage of fires in homes with smoke detectors and the percentage of fires in homes with *operational* smoke detectors. In

Figure 2. Smoke detectors in dwelling fires, 1980–1992.

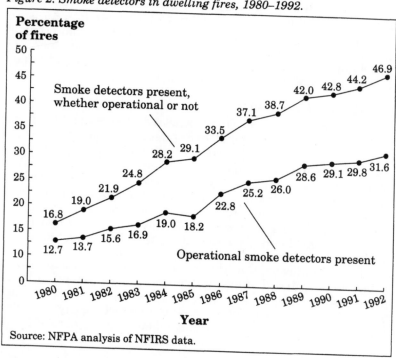

Source: NFPA analysis of NFIRS data.

Figure 3. Smoke detectors in apartment fires, 1980–1992.

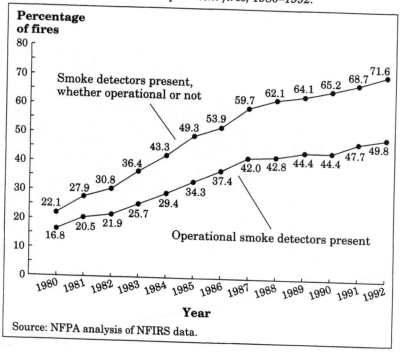

Source: NFPA analysis of NFIRS data.

1985, the decline in operationality actually overtook the rise in smoke detector presence in dwellings that experienced fires, resulting in a net decrease in the percentage of fires that occurred in dwellings with operational smoke detectors. Since then, the trend has reversed again, and each year has seen a higher percentage of homes with operational smoke detectors.

What does this mean?

If 92 percent of homes now have smoke detectors and 20 percent of those have nonoperational smoke detectors, then 8 percent of homes have no smoke detectors at all and another 18 percent have smoke detectors that do not work. Thus, 74 percent of homes—or three out of every four—have at least one working smoke detector. Even though the homes without detectors still have nearly half of the fires, restoring operational status to the nonworking smoke detectors could have a major impact and should be considered a priority, along with installing smoke detectors in the remaining homes that have none.

Table 5 indicates that the problem of nonoperational smoke detectors in homes that experience fires has leveled off. It is encouraging to see that the erosion of smoke detector protection appears to have stopped, but a situation in which nearly one-third of smoke detectors are not working when they are needed is not acceptable for the long run. More must be done.

Why are so many smoke detectors nonoperational?

The National Smoke Detector Project has provided current information on nonoperational smoke detectors 10 years after the last large-scale study of smoke detector performance produced statistics that helped explain the reasons for detector nonperformance. Both studies showed the principal problem to be dead or missing batteries.

In the 1983 study, dead batteries, missing batteries, and other power source problems accounted for 69 percent of the 314 cases in which smoke detectors failed to activate for known reasons in fires that produced enough smoke to cause activation.[2] The other principal problems the study identified were incorrect installation, which accounted for 12 percent of the cases, and incorrect location, which accounted for 11 percent. The installation errors included placement in a dead air space, too low on a wall, too close to an air return, and without a cover. In other words, the principal problem is the human factor: lack of knowledge, neglect, or misapplication.

The National Smoke Detector Project found that the 20 percent of households that have nonoperational smoke detectors could be further subdivided into households in which the detector's battery was missing, dead, or disconnected, or in which the ac power source was disconnected. Batteries were missing in 11 percent of households without operational smoke detectors, dead in 5 percent, and disconnected in 3 percent, while the power source was disconnected in 1 percent.[3] The more-than-10-to-1 ratio of battery problems to ac power problems contrasts with a 3-to-1 ratio of battery-powered to ac-powered detectors.[4] Clearly, dead, missing, or disconnected batteries account for nearly all the nonoperational detectors, and battery-powered detectors are much more susceptible to power source problems that leave them inoperable. Note that the National Smoke Detector Project focused on nonoperational detectors, which constitutes a narrower group than that with detector-related problems in general and excludes such factors as improper location.

The use of battery-powered versus ac-powered detectors follows some patterns that would be expected in light of recent codes and regulations. Overall, 72 percent of the detectors involved battery power only, compared with 23 percent hard-wired ac detectors, 2 percent plug-in ac, and 2 percent ac with battery backup. Seventy-six percent of the smoke detectors in single-family dwellings, excluding manufactured homes, were battery-only detectors. In apartments, 62 percent were battery-only detectors.[5] And in manufactured homes, which have been required to have hard-wired, ac-powered detectors since 1976, 38 percent were battery-only detectors. In addition, homes built in 1980 or later, including apartments and manufactured homes, had 31 percent battery-only detectors, while homes built before 1980 had 83 percent battery-only detectors.[6] This parallels the requirement for hard-wired smoke detectors in new construction that has been in place for several years in such codes as NFPA 101, the *Life Safety Code®*.

The leading reason that batteries were missing or disconnected was that they had been deliberately removed as a reaction to nuisance alarms. Removal for this reason was eight times as likely as removal to permit use of batteries in other places.[7] The leading nuisance alarm problems cited—responding to cooking fumes and responding continuously when powered—were cited with roughly equal frequency.[8] Alarming too often for unspecified reasons was the next most frequently cited nuisance alarm problem. And reacting to steam or humidity was cited about one-third as often as either of the two leading problems.

Nuisance alarms can often be reduced by adjusting the detector's location or by switching from ionization-type detectors to photoelectric-type detectors. One-third of the detectors studied for nuisance alarms in the National Smoke Detector Project were located less than 5 feet from a potential source of smoke, steam, or moisture that was sufficient to produce a nuisance alarm.[9] In addition, 97 percent of the detectors were ionization-type detectors, which accounted for 87 percent of all detectors in the study.[10] More important is the fact that the particles associated with cooking smoke are generally small enough—less than one micron—to activate ionization-type detectors. Photoelectric-type detectors are generally activated by larger particles.

The likelihood of nuisance alarms can also be reduced by decreasing the sensitivity of the detector. The National Smoke Detector Project found that the detectors involved in nuisance alarms were more sensitive, on average, than those that were not involved in such alarms.[11] However, the project report cautioned that reduced sensitivity could adversely affect a detector's ability to provide timely warning of a real fire.

Roughly half the inoperable detectors studied in the National Smoke Detector Project were more than 10 years old—older than the currently recommended replacement age.[12] Among the problems of aging detectors are "sensitivity drift," which refers to a shift in the range of visibility obscuration or particulate density that will activate the smoke detector. Such a shift can mean either an increase in nuisance alarms, if sensitivity increases, or a decreased ability to react promptly to real fires, should sensitivity decrease.[13]

The few studies of field experience with nuisance alarms have shown consistently that detectors produce far more nuisance alarms than real alarms. A 1989 study of Veterans Administration hospitals found 15.8 nuisance alarms for every real alarm, or 1 nuisance alarm for every 6 detectors per year.[14] An earlier study of home smoke detectors as units in an automatic remote residential alarm system in The Woodlands, Texas, found 27 nuisance alarms for every real alarm, or nuisance alarms in 6 of every 7 homes each year.[15]

While both studies identified a number of steps that could be taken to sharply reduce the rate of nuisance alarms, the current rate is so high that neither study expects that nuisance alarms can be made to occur less frequently than real alarms. Thus, nuisance alarms may continue to induce smoke detector owners to deactivate their smoke detectors.

What other issues have to be addressed?

Most smoke detector owners do not test or maintain their smoke detectors as often as they should. As of 1982, 60 percent said that they did not test them as often as once a month, and 16 percent said that they never tested them.[16] Somewhat more encouraging was the information found by the National Smoke Detector Project: The majority of the respondents who stated their testing frequency had tested their detectors within the past month.

The value of testing was borne out in other parts of the study. Of those surveyed, 78 percent believed that all their detectors worked, in the majority of cases because they had tested them. Of that 78 percent, 88 percent proved to have working smoke detectors when testing was done. Another 11 percent of those surveyed did not know whether their detectors were working, and of those, only 61 percent proved to have working smoke detectors when testing was done. The final 11 percent of those surveyed believed that at least one detector was not working, usually because they knew that the battery was dead or missing or that the power source had been disconnected. Of this 11 percent, only 40 percent proved to have working smoke detectors when testing was done— and it is surprising that the percentage was that high.[17]

Even among households that have tested their detectors, many have not developed escape plans that would allow them to use to best advantage the extra warning time the detectors provide. One 1985 study found that 59 percent of the population had developed an escape plan.[18] But a 1980 survey found that the majority—56 percent—of households with escape plans had never practiced them.[19] If these two figures can be used together, then only one-fourth of U.S. households have both developed escape plans and practiced them. Obviously, there is still considerable room for improvement.

Most homes need more than one smoke detector to comply with code requirements for complete protection, so even if a home has one working smoke detector, there may be room for improvement here, as well. The National Smoke Detector Project found that 26 percent of the households surveyed had fewer than one detector per floor, which indicates too few detectors for code compliance. Other households may have had too few detectors to protect widely separated sleeping areas on the same floor. The National Smoke Detector Project also estimated that 43 percent of the households had fewer than one *working* smoke detector per floor.[20]

There is a similar concern about the extra protection provided by integrated, wired-in smoke detector systems. The *Life Safety Code* requires that smoke detectors be powered by the house electrical service in all new housing. The *Code* also requires indirectly—by performance requirements—that smoke detectors be interconnected within the dwelling unit. Since single station, battery-operated units still predominate in most existing homes, the possibility of wider use of wired-in smoke detectors is another opportunity for further improvement in the home smoke detector problem.

The National Smoke Detector Project also found that 6 percent of households with smoke detectors had them connected to a central alarm system.[21] This provides even more protection than interconnected detectors alone.

Recapping what we found

Home smoke detector use in the United States rose in 1993 to 11 homes in 12, or 92 percent of homes in the country. Most of the groups that have the highest fire rates, such as poor households, are lagging slightly behind in smoke detector use, but a large majority of households in all such groups does have smoke detectors.

How operational are detectors outside the home?

Tables 6 and 7 (pp. 98–99) use NFIRS data to develop, for most major classes of property, percentages of fires in which detectors were present and percentages of fires in which the detectors were operational. These figures are much less dependable than the figures for homes for several reasons. For some property classes, the sample sizes are low enough that statistical uncertainty becomes a concern. Unusually large 1-year jumps or drops in estimated operationality are one effect of this.

Further, nonresidential properties are more likely to use heat detectors than smoke detectors or to have very limited partial coverage. The analysis procedures used here will tend to underestimate the percentage of properties with operational detectors in those cases because smoke spread beyond the room of origin will no longer be a good proxy for a fire that is large enough to activate an operational detector.

Note, too, that some properties use automatic suppression systems such as sprinklers to detect and control fires, and these systems are probably not coded as detection systems at all. Nevertheless, the results are useful as exploratory analysis and to give a sense of the relative performance of different property classes.

In Table 8, (p. 100) the major property classes are separated into low, medium, and high levels of usage and operationality, based solely on 1992 figures.

Using Tables 6 through 8, we can draw several interesting conclusions. First, as we might expect, the percentage of detectors in the home that are operational is lower than the percentage of operational detectors in most other property classes. The only occupancies that had a comparably low level of operational detectors

---

These slight differences in smoke detector use are not enough to explain why the 8 percent of homes without smoke detectors account for nearly half of all reported home fires. The principal reason for this seems to be that households with smoke detectors are able to control far more of their fires without involving the fire department.

One-fifth of homes with smoke detectors and one-third of homes with smoke detectors that have reported fires have no smoke detectors that work. The latter percentage has held fairly steady since 1983. Since 92 percent of homes have smoke detectors, this means that 18 percent of all homes have nonoperational smoke detectors. This is more than twice as many homes

---

in 1992 were public assembly occupancies, stores and offices, and storage facilities other than dwelling garages.

Second, one would expect that properties that care for persons who are sick, very young, or very old would have both high usage of detectors and high operationality. However, this has not always been true—for instance, educational properties did not qualify as high operationality in 1988 or 1990—and this is a cause for concern.

Third, nearly all property classes, except storage facilities, showed dramatic increases over the 1980s in the percentage of fires in properties in which detectors were present.

Another difference between detectors used outside the home and those used in the home is the reason given for nonoperationality. Some of the reasons recorded in the NFPA's Fire Incident Data Organization (FIDO) for the failure of detectors used outside the home illustrate this difference. Human actions, such as shutting down the detector system as part of a renovation or maintenance activity or in response to an earlier alarm, were cited in several instances. These are the nonresidential counterparts to missing batteries in home detectors. Mechanical problems, such as sprinkler waterflow switches sticking, were also cited, although a waterflow alarm should not be relied on for detection. Also given as reasons for nonoperability were the weather, including lightning strikes and high winds that disabled the detection system or the telephone or electrical systems that support it, and the effects of fire, including burnthrough of the telephone lines that relayed detector alarms to a central station.

These human and mechanical problems can be addressed through appropriate testing, maintenance, and inspection provisions, and some of the weather and fire effects can be addressed through the provision of appropriate backup.

as have no smoke detectors at all, although the latter group still accounts for nearly half of home fires. Homes with smoke detectors experience just over half the rate of deaths, given fire, as homes without smoke detectors.

Power source problems are the leading reason nonoperational home smoke detectors do not work. Dead, disconnected, and missing batteries are by far the most common problems and can be traced back to a pattern of not testing often enough.

What we recommend

Strategies for dealing with this growing problem have not been evaluated in the field, but two observations seem consistent with the evidence. First, wired-in detection systems do not require periodic power source replacement, do not permit occupants to remove their power sources for use elsewhere, and are statistically much less susceptible to power source interruption.

Second, the reduction of the nuisance alarm problem, which is closely linked with the problem of disconnected or missing batteries, would also reduce the possibility that people will come to assume that all smoke detector alarms are nuisance alarms because of the very high percentage that are. Nuisance alarms can be addressed by relocating detectors, substituting photoelectric-type detectors for ionization-type detectors, reducing detector sensitivity, and cleaning detectors more frequently or effectively.

Of course, reduced sensitivity may affect detector performance in real fires. The National Smoke Detector Project also raised concerns about consumers' abilities to clean detectors effectively.[22]

On the other hand, there are a number of new technologies that may help address the nuisance alarm problem. Some detectors now on the market have a silencer button, which can be pressed to silence the alarm for up to 3 minutes. If the smoke around the detector is too dense, however, the unit will stay in alarm until the smoke is no longer heavy enough to suggest a serious situation.

In 1989 and 1991, the NFPA's Learn Not to Burn® Foundation's Technical Advisory Council issued several recommendations for testing and maintaining smoke detectors. These include installing new batteries in all smoke detectors on the day you change your clock from daylight to standard time or when the detector chirps, warning that the battery is dying. You should also replace all batteries as soon as you move into a new home. Detectors should be tested monthly, in accordance with NFPA 72, *National Fire Alarm Code*, using the test button or an approved smoke substitute, and cleaned in accordance with the manufacturer's instructions. An open-flame device should not be used because of the danger the flame could pose. Finally, the batteries should always be left in smoke detectors, never borrowed for some other purpose.

Certain design problems with the detector unit itself must also be considered. The National Smoke Detector Project identified some cases of horn deterioration or corrosion leading to detector failure. However, the project was unable to determine whether regular testing produces a "self-wiping" effect that eliminates this problem, as manufacturers maintain, because most, though not all, of the problem detectors had not been tested as often as recommended.[23]

Home smoke detector use also needs attention. Most homes that need more than one smoke detector have at least one smoke detector, but most do not have as many as they need to comply with the code requirements for every-level protection. And, though most households say they have an escape plan, they have never rehearsed it.

The U.S. fire service, fire protection professionals, and the media all played a large role in placing detectors in most U.S. homes. Indeed, many fire departments continue to promote home smoke detectors, installing and maintaining them in high-risk households. Perhaps it is time for these agencies to take on the equally important role of teaching the public how to maintain and test their smoke detectors, letting them know how many smoke detectors are needed for full protection, and telling them where the detectors should be placed.

Table 6. Trends in detector presence by major property use from 1983 to 1992.

Property use	Percentage of structure fires where detector was present[a]									
	1983	1984	1985	1986	1987	1988	1989	1990	1991	1992
Dwellings and mobile homes	24.8	28.2	29.1	33.5	37.1	38.7	42.0	42.8	44.2	46.9
Apartments	36.4	43.3	49.3	53.9	59.7	62.1	64.1	65.2	68.7	71.6
Public assembly	16.0	18.6	20.7	23.9	26.7	29.9	31.9	33.2	34.0	36.3
Educational	40.0	40.6	46.1	46.2	51.3	54.6	56.1	59.3	59.4	63.9
Care of aged	80.4	79.1	82.4	86.0	88.1	90.2	90.8	90.9	91.8	92.7
Care of young	60.0	61.4	67.7	70.7	75.6	79.4	81.6	84.7	84.1	86.8
Hospitals and clinics	70.4	74.4	80.3	85.5	86.0	86.4	87.0	87.3	87.2	89.1
Prisons and jails	46.6	48.2	52.0	41.6	63.7	74.2	86.4	79.7	86.7	91.3
Care of mentally handicapped	63.7	67.5	71.4	73.9	82.8	85.4	89.8	92.1	90.0	93.0
Hotels and motels	47.3	52.2	56.4	63.8	66.7	69.6	72.4	71.9	74.3	75.4
Dormitories	66.6	73.8	77.0	81.1	80.5	82.6	87.3	88.4	90.6	90.8
Stores and offices	13.3	14.8	17.2	18.8	23.4	26.3	28.7	28.1	30.6	32.1
Industry and manufacturing	17.1	18.0	19.9	20.6	22.5	23.9	24.7	26.8	27.4	28.8
Storage (excluding dwelling garages)[b]	3.2	3.3	3.9	4.2	5.1	5.3	5.5	6.3	6.2	6.0

Source: 1983–92 NFIRS.

[a] Estimated as the number of structure fires with detectors present divided by number of structure fires with detector status known. Does not distinguish type of detector or completeness of coverage.

[b] Storage facilities include tool sheds, barns, silos, and other storage buildings that are not the warehouses one might think of in connection with this category.

Table 7. *Trends in detector operationality in fires by major property use from 1983 to 1992.*

Property use	Percentage of structure fires where operational detector was present[a]									
	1983	1984	1985	1986	1987	1988	1989	1990	1991	1992
Dwellings and mobile homes	68.3	67.4	62.5	68.0	68.0	67.1	68.1	68.2	67.5	67.5
Apartments	70.5	67.9	69.7	69.4	70.4	68.9	69.3	68.0	69.4	69.6
Public assembly	67.1	70.7	62.2	65.2	68.6	69.0	68.4	67.0	72.0	68.4
Educational	75.7	75.7	69.0	72.9	80.9	76.5	77.2	79.6	80.7	80.4
Care of aged	84.7	86.4	80.0	84.0	82.1	86.7	86.6	85.8	86.1	87.0
Care of young	82.2	79.2	79.0	88.2	82.1	84.0	87.5	87.4	85.0	85.0
Hospitals and clinics	80.0	84.0	78.0	80.9	82.1	85.2	84.2	87.2	85.4	86.0
Prisons and jails	84.2	85.3	81.2	81.0	81.9	84.0	89.1	84.7	85.2	85.5
Care of mentally handicapped	82.1	91.3	81.0	88.5	89.5	84.9	88.3	88.9	87.3	93.5
Hotels and motels	78.4	74.1	77.1	82.2	77.5	78.4	77.9	78.5	77.8	76.4
Dormitories	86.8	88.9	82.8	83.5	88.6	87.8	82.0	84.2	89.0	89.6
Stores and offices	70.0	72.5	66.2	73.3	71.0	71.4	72.8	75.7	71.1	73.1
Industry and manufacturing	83.2	81.0	78.3	80.5	81.0	78.1	80.4	79.1	79.9	80.5
Storage (excluding dwelling garages)[b]	65.0	70.8	67.6	67.9	71.6	62.9	68.6	69.9	68.9	68.3

Source: 1983–92 NFIRS.

[a]Estimated as percentage of structure fires where detectors activated within set of structure fires deemed large enough to activate operational detector. Set excludes fires coded as too small to activate detector, fires with extent of smoke unknown or other or confined to object or area of origin, and fires originating in room without detector and having extent of smoke confined to room of origin. CAUTION: This procedure may be less dependable as a proxy for true reliability in properties that use primarily heat detectors or that tend to have very limited partial systems.

[b]Storage facilities include tool sheds, barns, silos, and other storage buildings that are not the warehouses one might think of in connection with this category.

Table 8. Overview of detector operationality by major property use in 1992.

Usage	Operationality		
	Low (under 75%)	Medium (75 to 80%)	High (over 80%)
Low (under 40%)	Public assembly Stores and offices Storage[a]		Industry and manufacturing
Medium (40 to 65%)	Dwellings and manufactured homes		Educational
High (over 65%)	Apartments	Hotels and motels	Care of aged Care of young Hospitals and clinics Prisons and jails Care of mentally handicapped Dormitories

Based on 1992 NFIRS statistics. Usage measured as percent of fires, not percent of properties in general. For example, usage levels for dwellings (46.9%) and apartments (71.6%) were taken from the fire-based statistics in Table 6, not the general population usage level for all homes (90%) in Figure 1. Reliability estimated as percent activations in fires deemed large enough to activate operational detector, for fires where detector was present.

[a]Excludes dwelling garages.

1. J. R. Hall, Jr., *The U.S. Fire Problem Overview Report*, Quincy, Mass.: NFPA, December 1993.
2. R. E. Hawkins, *An Evaluation of Residential Smoke Detectors under Actual Field Conditions—Final Phase*, Washington, D.C.: International Association of Fire Chiefs Foundation, March 1983, p. 17.
3. Charles L. Smith, *Smoke Detector Operability Survey—Report on Findings*, Bethesda, Md.: U.S. Consumer Product Safety Commission, November 1993, p. 18.
4. Charles L. Smith, *Smoke Detector Operability Survey*, p. 6.
5. Charles L. Smith, *Smoke Detector Operability Survey*, p. 7.
6. Charles L. Smith, *Smoke Detector Operability Survey*, p. 9.
7. Charles L. Smith, *Smoke Detector Operability Survey*, p. 12.
8. Charles L. Smith, *Smoke Detector Operability Survey*, p. 22.
9. Charles L. Smith, *Smoke Detector Operability Survey*, p. 23.
10. Charles L. Smith, *Smoke Detector Operability Survey*, pp. 20-21.
11. Charles L. Smith, *Smoke Detector Operability Survey*, pp. 20-21.
12. Charles L. Smith, *Smoke Detector Operability Survey*, p. 23.
13. Joan L. Gancarski and Tom Timoney, *Research Report on Home Smoke Detector Effectiveness*, Quincy, Mass.: NFPA, 1984.
14. P M. Dubivsky and R. W. Bukowski, *False Alarm Study of Smoke Detectors in Department of Veterans Affairs Medical Centers (VAMCS)*, NIS-TIR 89-4077, Gaithersburg, Md.: National Institute of Standards and Technology, May 1989, p. 45.
15. *Remote Detection and Alarm for Residences—The Woodlands System*, Washington: U.S. Fire Administration, May 1980.
16. John R. Hall, Jr. and Sid Groeneman, "Two Homes in Three Have Detectors," *Fire Service Today*, February 1983, pp. 18-20.
17. Charles L. Smith, *Smoke Detector Operability Survey*, p. 15.
18. The Prevention Index '85, *Prevention Magazine*, 33 East Minor Street, Pa. 18098, 1987.
19. Elrick and Lavidge, Inc., *A Detector in Every Other Home: Full Report*, Washington, D.C.: U.S. Fire Administration, November 1980.
20. Charles L. Smith, *Smoke Detector Operability Survey*, p. 24.
21. Charles L. Smith, *Smoke Detector Operability Survey*, p. 3.
22. Charles L. Smith, *Smoke Detector Operability Survey*, p. 22.
23. Charles L. Smith, *Smoke Detector Operability Survey*, pp. 18-19.

Residential Fire Sprinklers

Greg Gorden

Residential fire sprinklers are starting to have a significant impact on fire service management. Cities and counties that have enacted ordinances requiring new homes to have sprinkler systems have reported reduced property loss because sprinklers extinguish or prevent the spread of fires; reduced growth of fire department costs; increased flexibility in assigning fire suppression personnel to other department services; and savings on projected infrastructure costs. Today, fewer than 1 percent of homes in the United States have sprinklers, but as local fire departments continue to expand their service area and stretch their personnel, local government leaders are looking more and more to residential fire sprinkler (RFS) ordinances as a means of curbing costs.

Case studies

Each community has its own reasons for adopting an RFS ordinance, but the experiences of Port Angeles, Washington; Napa, California; Scottsdale, Arizona; and San Luis Obispo, California, demonstrate the positive role residential fire sprinklers can play in fire service management.

Because few communities have enacted RFS ordinances as comprehensive as those enacted by these cities, their experiences may appear anomalous. However, the achievements of fire departments that use residential fire sprinklers as a fire prevention tool may serve to encourage others to consider the applicability of RFS ordinances in their community.

Port Angeles, Washington Port Angeles, Washington, is a small city located in the northwest corner of the state, nestled between the Olympic Mountains and the Strait of Juan de Fuca. The city, which has a population of 18,000 but serves a fire district of 35,000, has been using residential fire sprinklers as a proactive method of fire protection.

As part of its comprehensive fire prevention plan, Port Angeles has adopted a four-minute response time and required any new residential development outside the four-minute response area to be equipped with sprinklers. Fire Chief Larry Glenn believes the ordinance has postponed the need for new substations and saved his department $500,000 a year in personnel costs alone. Because residential fire sprinklers act as a fire fighting and containment device—reducing the number of personnel needed to fight a blaze—the department has been able to cut the number of personnel posted at a station. Chief Glenn has reassigned some staff to form a top-notch EMS service at no extra cost to the community and has reassigned others to areas such as hazardous waste disposal, public education, and permit and code compliance.

In March 1994, the Port Angeles fire department completed its first test of a combination sprinkler/domestic plumbing system, which convinced fire officials that affordable fire protection from residential sprinklers can be provided in all new residential construction. According to Bruce Becker, the Port Angeles fire marshal, "The city likes the idea of saving thousands of dollars annually by not having to build new fire stations, while at the same time providing greater fire protection to the homeowner. We are at the point in our city's growth that additional fire stations had been planned for, but the requirement for residential sprinkler installations has allowed us to delay construction. Each year the city saves thousands of dollars because of the built-in protection provided by sprinklers."

Port Angeles has also granted additional savings to developers of several residential areas because they have installed residential sprinkler systems. For example, less fire flow is required and fewer fire hydrants are needed because of the reduced fire flows and increased spacing of hydrants. Street widths have been reduced, leaving more land available to develop. Probably the most common remark made by developers is that residential fire sprinklers give them more flexibility in designing their projects.

For Fire Marshal Becker, widespread acceptance is the key to effective use of residential fire sprinklers. "Accepting the concept of residential sprinklers as part of community development is catching on quickly in some sectors of the fire service community because of the greater flexibility in response time permitted by new single-family residential developments equipped with sprinklers. Saving money for government entities while providing greater life safety can continue only if we in the fire service realize the direct benefits of the technology at our disposal."

Napa, California   Since 1982, Napa, California (population 62,000), has adopted a series of ordinances requiring automatic sprinkler protection in more and more residences. Today automatic sprinklers are required in new homes that are (1) located more than 1.5 miles from one of the city's three fire stations; (2) inaccessible to fire department equipment because of narrow driveways or roads; or (3) built on hillsides or in hazardous fire areas near wildlands.

There are two primary reasons for Napa's RFS ordinance; one is response load. Napa's fire service has operated under a thirteen-person minimum staffing level since 1979 and currently assigns sixteen fire personnel per shift. Responses increased from 2,941 in 1979 to approximately 4,600 in 1990. The increase was particularly notable in EMS calls, which totaled 3,000 in 1990. Essentially the same number of firefighters were responding to almost twice as many emergency service calls as in 1979, and the department needed a cost-effective way to provide fire protection when firefighters were tending to increased EMS demands.

The second reason for Napa's RFS ordinance is terrain. The city is located in a valley surrounded by steep mountains. More and more homes are being built in the hills, where fire department access may be difficult, and average response times for those areas may be five minutes longer than the departmental average of three minutes. One fire in particular captured the public's attention and dramatized the need to find a way to provide rapid service to homes in remote areas.

In late 1987 a fire occurred in a home located approximately three miles (or nearly six minutes) from the nearest fire station. The home was one of many in Napa located on a steep incline with a circular driveway, two factors that affected fire department access. The home was a total loss. The fire vividly demonstrated to Napa residents how one fire in an isolated area can put the entire community at risk. In responding to this fire, Napa's entire fire suppression force was moved as much as 7.5 miles from some response areas, and almost twenty minutes passed before off-duty personnel were able to staff reserve apparatus.

The ensuing ordinance mandated installation of residential fire sprinklers in homes where a fire could recreate the same scenario. By the end of 1990, the 2,591 sprinkler activations recorded by the city's fire department protected not only city residents and their property, according to Fire Marshal Tom Johnson, but also the resources of the department. For example, the department once spent twenty-six personnel hours and used personnel from five fire companies to fight a fire that started in the kitchen of an apartment without sprinklers. Johnson estimates that if sprinklers had been installed, one engine company would have logged half an hour, tops, fighting the fire.

Scottsdale, Arizona In Scottsdale, Arizona, the Rural/Metro fire department was faced not only with the problem of providing effective fire protection, but also with substantial growth: the city's population increased from 107,900 in 1985 to 137,000 in 1991, and annexation of outlying areas was occurring at record levels. In 1992 Scottsdale covered approximately 190 square miles, more than twice its size ten years before. Some fire departments see rapid growth as a drawback, but Rural/Metro saw it as an opportunity to save lives and money by building a fire prevention program—with a strong residential fire sprinkler ordinance at its center—directly into the growing community's plans for development.

The majority of the areas to be annexed by the city had yet to be developed, which gave the department the opportunity to set strict fire code guidelines for over 70 percent of the city's new construction and protect it with the most modern fire systems available. In 1985 the city council passed what was at the time the nation's most comprehensive RFS ordinance, which required an automatic sprinkler in every room of every commercial, industrial, and residential building in Scottsdale.

A study conducted by an independent consulting firm showed that when Scottsdale's development is complete, the sprinkler ordinance will have saved the city more than $7.2 million in water transmission costs alone (water reservoirs, underground water mains, pumping stations, etc.). The ordinance has also generated other infrastructure savings: hydrants can be placed farther apart with no decrease in safety or the quality of service delivery, and fewer fire stations are required for sprinkler-protected areas. In addition, fewer personnel are needed to fight fires because the sprinklers decrease the incidence of out-of-control blazes, and the ordinance has provided Scottsdale residents with fire service that costs 30- to 50-percent less than comparable service in surrounding communities.

At the same time, according to Rural/Metro officials, the fire service is able to employ 50-percent more fire prevention personnel than the regional average. These individuals spend their time in public education, building inspection, plan review, arson investigation, and fire prevention administration, allowing reallocation of available resources to meet growing EMS demands or to provide other basic public services.

Rural/Metro's experience with residential fire sprinklers has been positive, to say the least. From implementation of the ordinance in 1985 to 1991, Scottsdale's fire losses dropped by 84 percent. Sprinklers have proven 96.8 percent effective in either completely extinguishing fire or, at a minimum, keeping flames from spreading. And the widespread use of residential fire sprinklers has allowed Chief Robert T. Edwards to begin building a program in which fire education and prevention are at the forefront of the department's assault on fire.

San Luis Obispo, California   San Luis Obispo, California (population 42,000), is another community whose fire services have been positively affected by use of residential fire sprinklers. Fire Chief Bob Neumann and fire protection personnel have documented the impact that the RFS ordinance has had on city fire services:

- The department was able to reduce the fleet by one engine, saving the city a few hundred thousand dollars.
- The city incorporated a major new subdivision outside the four-minute response time area because the response time gap was mitigated by the ordinance, which required the residences to have sprinklers. The ordinance also eliminated the need to build a new station house, which would have been staffed by fifteen new personnel at a cost of $250,000.
- The zero-foot ordinance implemented by San Luis Obispo has allowed the department to increase hose drag from 150 to 300 feet, allowing builders to develop housing in marginal lots at no extra cost.
- The city has been able to increase other services by cutting down to two-person engine companies from the usual three, with the third person switching to EMS and/or fire prevention and education duty.
- The city has been able to maintain current personnel levels while extending the city limits.

Although systematic, nationwide studies of the comparative costs of fire service operations in communities with and without RFS ordinances have not yet been completed, experience in individual communities suggests that increases in costs are reduced, especially where rapid growth has occurred that would otherwise have required significant expansion of fire services. Several high-growth California communities—Fresno, San Clemente, Palm Springs, and Mountain View—reported reduced growth of fire department costs, with no reduction in the level of service. The California state fire marshal has noted how his service "used sprinklers as a means of controlling the fire problem without enormous increases in fire stations, equipment, and staff, as the communities were being built up."

The *Barriers* project

One major obstacle to the widespread installation of residential fire sprinklers is the perception of high cost and low value among the public and in the building industry. However, a project undertaken by the National Association of Home Builders Research Center (Research Center) and the International City/County Management Association (ICMA) under contract with the United States Fire Administration found that, in some circumstances, a combination cold water plumbing and sprinkler system can be installed at considerably less cost than a traditional, separate RFS system.

Project description   The project, called *Barriers to the Installation of Residential Fire Sprinklers*, developed sixteen demonstration sites across the nation. Both project staff and demonstration site participants employed nonpartisan, objective research methods. Participants installed a combination domestic water and sprinkler system based on the *Express Residential Fire Sprinkler Design Guide* developed by the Prince George's County, Maryland, fire department and the Research Center. The *Design Guide* provides a simplified method for determining sprinkler spacing, performing hydraulic calculations, and determining the layout of sprinkler heads. This rules-based method is a safe, simplified alternative to the more traditional, costly process used in residential and commercial sprinkler installations.

The project staff focused on the following objectives:

- The feasibility of systems that combine sprinklers with domestic water systems
- Alternative sprinkler designs and associated inspection and approval procedures
- Ways to increase the number of qualified sprinkler installers
- Identification of protective barriers in state and local codes, traditions, and practices that retard innovation in residential sprinkler technology and mandate non-value-added requirements.

Fire officials and building inspectors who used the *Design Guide* at a number of the demonstration sites had favorable reactions. In many instances the express methods, procedures, approvals, and inspections contained in the guide lowered overall costs by as much as 20 percent, and the demonstrations seem to confirm that combined cold water plumbing and sprinkler systems can produce these savings with no reduction in performance.

The methods outlined in the *Design Guide* are rules-based, not plans-based, and are applicable to about 90 percent of home designs today. The rules-based approach can make it unnecessary to submit separate design plans for local approval, a widely required procedure that now adds delay and expense for both builders and local governments. With the rules-based approach, existing house plans can be used and sprinkler head locations determined in twenty to thirty minutes without a computer.

In sum, express procedures eliminate the need for special residential sprinkler plans. Instead, "target zones" are drawn on house plans using a convenient template. An express hydraulic calculation worksheet is prepared, by hand, using specific data on the house and the pre-engineered information in the *Design Guide*. The resulting design and layout are NFPA 13-D compliant. Design review is eliminated, since the system is pre-engineered. As-built drawings are also eliminated. A thorough, precise field inspection is required, but it is structured and simplified.

Participants in the *Barriers* project demonstrated a willingness to experiment and make significant departures from business as usual in order to explore the benefits of change and innovation. The team of builders, contractors, suppliers, fire officials, and local government authorities set aside traditional practices to take advantage of what they see as an opportunity for progress. Cooperation and common goals were the driving force behind the activities at the demonstration sites. For example,

- In DuPont, Washington, city officials, builders, and RFS installers created a partnership committed to high-quality, economical installation—using the *Design Guide*'s simplified process—of RFS systems that complied with NFPA 13-D standards. Their cooperation led to DuPont's implementation of a pilot program—with approval from the Washington State Fire Protection Policy Board—to grant temporary certificates of competency (Level I, 13D) for licensed plumbers working in the city to install combined domestic/fire plumbing systems generated by the *Design Guide* process. Under this program, the city verifies to the state the competency of the applicants. Upon verification, the state issues a certificate. This cooperative working environment enabled DuPont to fully explore the potential for increasing the number of qualified sprinkler installers and the widespread feasibility of combined domestic/fire plumbing systems.
- In Cedar Rapids, Iowa, the demonstration involved the voluntary installation by a local builder of automatic sprinkler systems in three four-plex buildings in one subdivision. The plumber-completed installation resulted in a 75 percent de-

crease in installation costs, when compared to the costs of installing a separate system. The city expressed its interest in the concept by considering an initiative to provide a tax credit to further offset costs for any builder who elects to install RFS systems in the jurisdiction.

- The Prince George's County, Maryland, demonstration site proved that cooperation could produce innovative, cost-saving installations. As stated, the Prince George's County fire department co-authored and developed, with the Research Center, the pre-engineered *Express Residential Fire Sprinkler Design Guide* in order to make domestic installation of sprinkler systems more feasible. The *Design Guide* was originally developed at the Prince George's County demonstration site, but quickly became a project centerpiece, providing an invaluable tool for reducing cost and red tape while opening the door to RFS installations completed by licensed plumbers.

Barriers to implementation

The installation of residential fire sprinklers still faces formidable barriers, the major ones being high installation costs coupled with public perception of low value. The examples described above highlighted cooperation and open-minded interest in the use of sprinklers to provide increased fire safety and to make maximum use of resources. However, the project demonstration sites ran headlong into numerous barriers that stymied attempts to install RFS systems generated by a simplified process. These barriers, in general, included

- Widespread lack of understanding of and misinformation regarding the technology and its costs, applications, and benefits
- Lack of agreement on life safety aspects of sprinkler use
- Codes that impose redundant safety requirements
- Long and complex design reviews
- Regulations requiring residential sprinklers to conform to engineering standards for industrial and commercial installations
- Limitations on competition that are created by controlling the number of qualified installers.

Outlook

Any combination of the barriers mentioned above will impede widespread installation of any type of residential fire sprinkler system, even though these systems have had a significant impact on fire suppression and fire service management in cities and counties across the nation. In the *Barriers* project, demonstration site participants overcame installation barriers in order to provide increased fire safety through innovative means that reduce the costs traditionally associated with the installations. The future success of RFS installations depends on the willingness of local fire and building officials, builders, municipal officials, and local home builder associations to work together and put aside preconceived notions, special interests, and historical animosities. The examples of project "breakthroughs" described above show how cooperative working relationships can contribute to safer, resource-efficient communities.

The approach of the *Barriers* project may not work for every community, but in many cases it can make a major contribution in those communities interested in increasing the installation of residential fire sprinklers in order to maximize limited resources. It is up to each community to explore the potential for success in its own environment.

PART 2

New Insights into Critical Operations

EMS: Issues, Alternatives, and Case Studies

Mary Jane Dittmar

Proactivity is as vital to an EMS system as it is to a fire-suppression department. Being proactive in the EMS service area entails taking the time to select and develop the EMS profile or configuration best suited to the characteristics, needs, and resources of your jurisdiction and continually monitoring that system so it can be modified to meet changing community needs. It also means identifying any "troublesome" areas that initially may interfere with establishing the EMS-delivery system and, ultimately, with its performance. Some of these areas identified by our sources and their suggestions for addressing them are presented below. The issues are presented in alphabetical order.

Issues

Accountability An integral part of EMS systems since their inception, accountability can pose challenges for some fire managers. "In general," says Gary Morris, deputy chief of the Phoenix (AZ) Fire Department, "EMS is subject to more standards than the fire service. . . . It is interesting to note when looking at the fire service," he continues, "that it is the last public agency whose manner of delivering services has not been held up to intense public scrutiny." He cites as an example police departments. "So many outside bodies review how police work is performed today, and issues raised relative to their performance can go all the way up to the Supreme Court to be resolved." Fire service delivery

Adapted from Mary Jane Dittmar, "Fire Service EMS: The Challenge and the Promise, Part 2—Planning Vital to Success," *Fire Engineering* (October 1993) and "Fire Service EMS: The Challenge and the Promise, Part 3—EMS Case Studies," *Fire Engineering* (July 1994). Reprinted with permission of *Fire Engineering*.

has not been evaluated to that degree, Morris says, but he predicts that it will be. Probably the most significant evaluation, he adds, will be by the public (the customer). Referring particularly to EMS, he suggests that community residents who have been observing the standard performances of EMS personnel on television programs such as *Rescue 911* one day will go to their local governing officials demanding comparable standards of service with regard to response times, personnel skills, and other components vital to their well-being.[1]

"The monitoring and management of patient care and system performance has become an issue during the past few years and will be critical to the future success of EMS programs," according to the *JEMS* survey of the 200 most populous cities. For the first time, therefore, the 1992 survey included the area of quality management with reference to programs, system performance requirements, and the management tools used to monitor system performance. (Questionnaires were sent to the responding agencies in each of the 200 most populous cities in the United States, based on the 1990 U.S. Census Bureau statistics. Survey responses were received from 278 agencies representing 200 cities.) Of the 172 respondents who reported having such programs, 40 percent indicated they have a quality assurance program; 16 percent, a quality improvement program; 25 percent, both programs; 12 percent, a quality management program; and 7 percent, no monitoring programs.

More than half (55 percent) of the systems with quality management programs use in-house and outside monitoring and analyses, 40 percent use in-house monitoring exclusively, and 5 percent use outside agencies only.

Sixty-five percent of the systems have full-time quality program managers, 34 percent have full-time medical directors, and 66 percent have part-time medical directors.

Fifty-six percent are required to meet a response-time performance requirement. Eighty percent use the percentile assessment method (e.g., 10 minutes or less 90 percent of the time.) The remaining 20 percent monitor average response times.[2]

Suggested approaches

- Poll "customers" to assess their satisfaction with the kinds and quality of services they are receiving.
- Develop standards, policies, and procedures that will improve efficiency, professionalism, and continuity. Include guidelines that EMS personnel, the line officer, or the shift commander can follow when making necessary emergency medical decisions. EMS training, certification, medical con-

trol, and management of service delivery are some of the areas that should be addressed. Consider also that if the line officer is not trained in EMS, his/her decisions may be based on fire-related experience only and may not be appropriate for the emergency medical situation.

- Review long-standing mutual-aid agreements to see if they must be updated with respect to the department's mission and the community's needs. Such documents also will offer some protection should liability issues concerning patient care arise.

- Become actively involved in standard-development organizations. Failing to do so increases the possibility that your department/the fire service may be forced to comply with impractical directives.[3]

- "'Voluntary' standards can have a great impact on the fire service," points out Deputy Chief Morris. They will remain "voluntary," he explains, only until they have been adopted as standards, regulations, or statutes by various states, increasing the possibility that the courts will look at them closely in liability actions involving the quality of patient care to see how they were applied (3).

- Financial accountability also must be part of the EMS organization. "Few of us in public service have a hold on what it costs to run EMS," observes Mary Beth Michos, chief of EMS and specialties teams coordinator for the Montgomery County (MD) Department of Fire EMS and Rescue Services. "The fire service is not doing the planning it needs to do. Maybe it's time to look back to see if there's anything in the system that should be changed. Research is needed to validate the expenditures for these systems."[4]

Burnout/stress   Firefighting and EMS are both stressful, and real or perceived problems between firefighters and EMS personnel can add to EMS personnel "burnout" and firefighter "rustout." The former is caused by too heavy a workload (caused predominantly by misuse and abuse of the system by citizens for nonemergency calls), and the latter is triggered by too few fire calls, which creates boredom and a feeling of uselessness.[5]

Suggested approaches

- The dual-role profile incorporating firefighter/paramedics or firefighter/EMTs offers one solution for the phenomena of burnout and rustout. Such a system makes it possible to transfer EMS personnel approaching burnout to another company where responses to medical calls are fewer; they later can return to their original responsibilities or be reassigned. Similarly, firefighters experiencing rustout can be recruited to serve on the paramedic/EMT companies.

- Institute priority emergency/medical dispatching programs.
- Implement programs aimed at reducing the volume of EMS nonemergency calls by educating the public with regard to which kinds of emergencies actually fall under the EMS category.

EMS personnel/fire officer interaction in the field   In life-threatening situations, EMS personnel are directed by the medical director and often cannot wait for orders to filter down through the fire command system. In some instances, nonofficer EMTs might have to direct fire officers, a situation that could cause dissension if fire officers do not fully understand the reasons for this behavior and were to interpret these occurrences as threats to their authority and power.[6]

Suggested approach

- Institute protocols/policies that provide for such situations so that the patient and operations are not adversely affected.

Promotions   The promotion policy can drastically affect morale in a department providing fire suppression services and EMS.

Suggested approach

- Institute policies that make it possible for EMS personnel to serve as chief officers and command officers, allowing them to advance and remain within the system.

Such promotability usually is built into a dual-role profile. The promotional opportunities, in conjunction with the option to remain within the "mainstream" of fire suppression, improves morale.[7] The costs of recruiting and training will decrease; and efficiency, based on the extended experience of these employees, will increase.

Recruiting/training   The fire department's emphasis on training makes it especially suitable to EMS. Firefighters' training in all facets of rescue work, including firefighting, search and rescue, vehicle extrication, rope and above-ground rescue, water rescue, and confined space entry, make them extremely versatile as firefighter/EMS personnel (7). Fire departments' policies and standards, therefore, should reflect this commitment to EMS training.

Suggested approaches

- Bring recruiting, hiring, and training practices into conformance with the department's expanded mission of providing EMS. Look to colleges and universities offering courses in fire and health sciences for recruits.[8]
- Give EMS training the same priority as firefighting training. Establish regular programs and continuing education sessions. Stagger the class schedule so that all personnel will be able to attend on a regular basis.
- Appoint an officer experienced in EMS to supervise the training program. Ensure that the EMS supervisor/coordinator has adequate time to do the job efficiently. In some departments, it has been customary to assign the EMS supervisor all EMS responsibilities—from supply procurement to representing and speaking for the department at meetings, seminars, and conferences—or to delegate EMS continuing education responsibilities to paramedics (if the department provides an ALS level of care) assigned to a regular shift.[9]
- To maintain EMS skills and knowledge in small, all-volunteer departments with a low demand for medical services, institute continuing-education programs that provide constant practice (6).

Staffing   Maintaining adequate staffing levels in these days of government/fire department downsizing is no easy task.

Suggested approaches

- Dual-role, cross-trained EMS personnel "correct the perception of the underutilization of firefighters" and lend significant support to the justification for increased staffing levels on fire apparatus. Studies made by some fire departments, including the Anaheim (CA) Fire Department and Dallas (TX) Fire Department, have found that just as a minimum of four firefighters is needed for successful fireground operations, so too is a minimum of four personnel needed to effectively administer medical treatment in a typical EMS scenario (5). This is the level of staffing advocated also by the American Medical Association (AMA), which says in its issue on cardiopulmonary resuscitation (CPR) and emergency cardiac care (ECC) guidelines, "Most experts agree that four responders [at least two trained in Advanced Cardiac Life Support (ACLS) and two in BLS] are the minimum required to provide ACLS to cardiac arrest victims."[10]

Wages   Before EMS, most firefighters' salaries were based on longevity and position, and promotions were from the ranks and based on testing or longevity or a combination of the two. The structure has been changing, especially in departments providing EMS as well as fire suppression services. In some departments, firefighter-paramedics or -EMTs are given a salary differential that, in most cases, places their wages a few percentage points above firefighters in the department. This differential can be an area of contention. Some of these EMS personnel feel that the extra pay does not adequately compensate for the additional work, education/training, and responsibilities associated with EMS. Firefighters, on the other hand, feel that EMS personnel are overpaid. They believe the duties of EMS personnel most of the time are less physically and emotionally taxing than theirs.[11]

While the first-responder training program generally is not significantly different from the first-aid instruction traditionally given to firefighters—usually 40 hours of instruction—training to the BLS level through an EMT program usually takes 84 hours, which may be followed by an additional 20 hours or so each year for continuing education and recertification.

The additional training demands may be especially difficult for volunteers to meet. (Nevertheless, a large number of fire departments have been able to implement the EMT level of training.)[12]

Training requirements for paramedics are significantly greater. The number of training hours required for Firefighter I, II, and III averages about 300 hours. On the other hand, training and continuing education requirements for firefighter/paramedics include complying with firefighter training standards and continuing education requirements as set by individual jurisdictions and, in addition, with initial paramedic course training that ranges from 1,000 to 2,500 hours. In Phoenix, Arizona, for example, paramedics must be trained for 2,500 hours, which are evenly split between classroom and field work (1). Continuing education requirements can range from 15 to 60 hours a year, depending on the state. Continuing education courses are mandatory for maintaining certification and, in some cases, employment (11,9).

Suggested approaches

- To offset any friction that may develop over the wage differential, promote communications among all levels of department employees and educate them with respect to co-workers' concerns, perceptions, and grievances.
- Create an environment that encourages and supports all department members so they believe that their roles are vital to department operations and community/customer service.

- Managers should know and understand all of the jobs, give support when needed, and instill confidence in employees.
- Initiate a study with the objective of establishing equitable salary scales for all positions within fire departments; provide all employees the opportunity to evaluate the study.
- Using engines or truck companies for first-response EMS provides the EMS and firefighting staffs with opportunities to become familiar with each other's role.

Some common configurations

EMS planning includes determining the level of services to be provided and the structure of the system that will deliver them. Following are a few of the EMS system profiles commonly found in the fire service. Even within these configurations, however, system components and characteristics can vary from department to department. Some departments, for example, transport, while others do not or do so only under extreme, predetermined emergency conditions. Some departments respond with engines or pumpers, others with squads or rescue vehicles. Some departments train firefighters to the BLS level, others to the ALS level, and still others to both levels. Some profiles include hospital, private, third services, or combinations thereof. Some departments provide defibrillator services, while others do not. The possibilities are endless and are based on the many factors that define a community's needs and wants.

Fire department first responder (BLS); private ambulance (ALS)   A dual-role, career, nontransporting BLS engine (first responder) used in conjunction with a privately owned civilian, ALS ambulance. Personnel are trained as firefighter/EMTs. For this system to be efficient, there must be a quality ambulance service, and fire department and ambulance personnel must interact positively.[13]

Fire department rescue unit (ALS); private ambulance (BLS) (13)   A nontransporting ALS unit and a transporting BLS unit (as seen on the television show *Emergency*). Generally, the closest ALS rescue unit, staffed by two paramedics, responds. Simultaneously, the private company handling BLS transport responds with an ambulance. Response time should be between four to six minutes, or preferably less. This system generally makes it possible to provide rapid response because the rescue units are responding from strategically located fire stations.

Implementing this profile necessitates that a sufficient number of and appropriate vehicles be acquired and that additional personnel be hired to maintain the prevailing level of staffing on firefighting apparatus. A contingency plan also must be devised for the times all of the BLS transport units may be unavailable. Some departments resolve this situation by maintaining a transport-capable unit that is housed with a generally low-response piece of apparatus so that personnel from the other apparatus can respond in this transport vehicle. Another option is to have in the system ALS units with transporting capability that are used to transport only in special situations, which are stipulated in written guidelines.

Fire department engine ALS; private ambulance BLS (13)
The ALS engine and a BLS ambulance are used together. The dispatch center assigns the closest ALS engine on receipt of an emergency medical call. (In some jurisdictions, the closest BLS engine or ladder simultaneously responds if the response time of the ALS engine is expected to exceed four to six minutes or if the location is in a BLS engine's first-response area.) Also, a transport unit, usually with BLS capabilities, is dispatched simultaneously or at the request of the ALS engine officer. The ambulance units, fewer in number than the ALS units, can be expected to arrive within 10 to 15 minutes.

Among benefits reported by departments using this profile are the following:

- The ALS engine establishes a link between EMS and the fire department for the public.
- Firefighters retain EMT skills (or the department-required skill level of all personnel) much longer; in fact, skills usually improve dramatically by observing the paramedics.

Among the situations that must be anticipated with this profile are the following:

- It is possible that a fire call may come in for an ALS engine's first response area while the engine is out on an EMS call. Therefore, analyze the frequency and locations of second-due companies and the call load in the district when researching the feasibility of a type of system.
- Fire apparatus generally take longer to accelerate than traditional rescue-type vehicles or ambulances. Evaluate the impact of this delay on your community. The Fresno (CA) Fire Department, for example, reported only a .5 minute increase in response time after switching from traditional nontransporting rescue vehicles to ladder trucks.
- Obviously, ALS engines are not suited for transport. This could be a problem when transport units tend to have excessive response times (more than 10 to 15 minutes) or when no transport units are available for service calls. In this case, a trans-

port unit(s) could be retained and a firefighter from a relatively low-response company be assigned to respond with it.

Regardless of the level of care a department provides, stresses Ricky G. Davidson, chief of EMS for the Shreveport (LA) Fire Department, "You need a big commitment. Departments that go into EMS only to justify their fire stations are not going to make it." The trend, he observes, is going to favor the provider of a quality service at a reasonable cost. It appears, he adds, that some private ambulance companies "are causing fire departments to clean their own houses. . . . They are pretty much defining what quality is."[14]

Additional components
Other components that often arise in discussions related to fire service EMS systems are the following:

Dual-role, cross-trained firefighter/paramedics   Departments in which personnel are trained to this level report benefits of improved response times and increased efficiency of the emergency medical team as a result of members' training and working closely together. In addition, in situations requiring paramedic transport, one or two of the paramedics off the engine can ride in the ambulance, upgrading its status from a BLS ambulance to an ALS unit (5).

Ensuring efficiency and satisfaction within a department employing cross-trained personnel depends on how adept management is at anticipating and resolving issues, such as field supervision, that may arise during the transition period. In departments that provide ambulance service, for example, assigning a field supervisor in addition to the fire command officer to an emergency incident can facilitate the quality of prehospital care that may be needed and decrease the burden on a nonparamedic company officer.

Another issue to be resolved is, How involved will the paramedics become in fire suppression operations? One determining factor is the rate of EMS and fire calls in the jurisdiction. If EMS and fire calls frequently occur simultaneously, it would be most logical to assign cross-trained EMS personnel a limited role in the fire operation. In this case, these personnel would function primarily as EMS personnel and would be available to respond immediately to medical emergencies. Under this arrangement, the department would not have to rely on EMS response from adjacent districts.

Limited-suppression duties vary widely from department to department. When EMS personnel are restricted to a few firefighting functions, departments must act to prevent them from losing their firefighting skills by rotating them in suppression roles or providing in-service training on a regular basis (6). (Likewise, when firefighting personnel are only limitedly involved in EMS functions, ongoing training programs to maintain their EMS skills should be provided.)

EMS firefighters usually become involved in total suppression duties in departments where EMS duties have been assumed by existing personnel instead of by newly hired additional personnel. In some cases, EMT firefighters are needed to maintain suppression staffing at acceptable levels. EMS crews in nearby districts must be available to cover for these personnel when they are engaged in fire suppression duties. In departments in which truck companies are not staffed or have extended response times, firefighter/paramedics sometimes can be assigned traditional truck company functions such as forcible entry, utilities control, and rescue (6).

Transporting   The locality's volume of calls is a major consideration when deciding whether to transport. The demand for EMS must be high enough to support a private transporting ambulance without the department's having to charge high service fees.

Among the advantages cited for departments that find transporting appropriate are that it permits continuity of care in the prehospital setting, eliminating the need to change medical techniques when the transport services arrive, and it gains public support for the fire department. The public tends to identify the entire emergency medical system with the agency that transports, just as the public identifies the fire department with the community's EMS when the fire apparatus is the first responder (6,13).

Transporting also can create some challenges as well, among them dramatically increasing the call volume. As previously mentioned, the public tends to abuse the system by using the transporting service for nonemergency functions such as for transportation to the doctor's office. These nonemergency calls tie up emergency vehicles and in some instances have been so significant that they have been cited as contributing factors to EMT/paramedic burnout (13,6).

The average time out of service is also greater for transporting vehicles than for nontransporting vehicles. Also, some departments may find it difficult to obtain the funds needed to buy, operate, maintain, and staff the additional apparatus and equipment needed for transporting (6).

A number of fire departments successfully provide transporting services, however. Among some of them identified in research conducted for the *Fire Service EMS Program Management Guide* for the U.S. Fire Administration in 1980[15] are the following. (This list is not meant to be all-encompassing, but is presented here to illustrate some of the characteristics of some departments that include transport services in their EMS systems.)

1. *Dual-role, cross-trained paramedics on transporting ambulances with engine or truck company first response:* The City of Miami (FL) Fire, Rescue, and Inspection Services—career firefighters; Palo Alto (CA) Fire Department—career; Shreveport (LA) Fire Department—career; Montgomery County (MD) Fire/Rescue Services—career and volunteer firefighters; and Prince George's County (MD) Fire Department—career and volunteer.
2. *Dual-role, cross-trained EMTs on transporting ambulances without engine or truck company first response (career):* Lexington (MA) Fire Department and Methuen (MA) Fire Department.
3. *Dual-role, cross-trained paramedics on transporting ambulances without engine or truck company first response:* Baltimore County (MD) Fire Department—career and volunteer firefighters, Brewster (MA) Fire Department—career and volunteer, Fairfax County (VA) Fire and Rescue Department—career and volunteer, Memphis (TN) Fire Department—career, and Tuscaloosa (AL) Fire Department—career.
4. *Dual-role, cross-trained EMTs in first response on transporting ambulances and paramedics in vehicles capable of transport:* Milwaukee (WI) Fire Department and Seattle (WA) Fire Department—both career departments.

Defibrillation   The AMA advocates that all firefighting units carry defibrillators and that personnel be trained in their use (10). This endorsement is based on research that has shown that using a defibrillator to shock a patient's heart back into a proper rhythm is the single most important factor in improving survival rates of heart attack victims. The International Association of Fire Chiefs has endorsed the concept of equipping every fire suppression unit in the United States with an automated external defibrillator (AED).[16] The ultimate goal of any EMS system, says the AMA, is that responders to cardiac emergencies be available to administer CPR and defibrillation within four minutes of the call to 911.

A number of fire departments have been providing or are planning to add defibrillation to their services, and a number of them providing the service have developed standard operating procedures (SOPs) to cover the procedure. Among fire departments having such SOPs are the Shreveport (LA) Fire Department, Fairfax County (VA) Fire and Rescue Department, St. Paul (MN) Department of Fire and Safety Services-St. Paul-Ramsey Medical Center, and the San Diego (CA) Fire Department.[17]

As fire service involvement in EMS continues to grow, increased demands will be placed on fire service care givers in the field as well as personnel in dispatch centers, note Richard A. Keller and Jamiel M. Yameen, authors of a three-part EMS-fire service survey report.[18] "The fire service's role in EMS is dynamic and continues to alter as departments explore new areas of involvement. With one-third of respondents providing dual-career tracking, it is obvious that the fire service has made a significant commitment to EMS as an integral element in its mission," they report.

The challenge for all EMS systems, point out the authors of the *JEMS* "200 Cities" survey, will be to demonstrate that EMS is part of the solution—not an impediment—to cost-effective health-care delivery.

Case Studies

Atlanta, Georgia[19]   In May 1993, the Atlanta Fire Department (AFD) implemented a new rescue-medical plan to supplement the city's existing EMS, reports Timothy R. Szmanski, public safety planner and public information officer. The 1,102-member department operates 36 fire stations and has 35 engines, 16 trucks, one advanced and four basic life support (BLS) rescue (nontransport) units, two advanced life support (ALS) ambulances, eight airport rescue firefighting (ARFF) units, and various other command teams and special squads and equipment.

Since 1970, the AFD has provided EMS services, including transportation, at Hartsfield Atlanta International Airport. In 1974, the service was upgraded to ALS. Two ECHO ambulances are on duty at all times and respond to all incidents on airport property and the area surrounding the airport.

Medical transport within the city is provided by 16 private and two public ambulance services. The city is divided into 11 ambulance zones, assigned to various EMS agencies. Many of the calls are received through the Fulton County 911 center.

In the late 1970s, the department became responsible for supplementing EMS with first responders and providing extrication and rescue services. Five two-member rescue units (one ALS and four BLS) were placed in service and respond to all sections of the city, sometimes increasing response time to some of the outlying areas. Engine and truck companies respond as first-responder units to medical emergencies.

Under the new plan, 21 engine companies throughout the city will be upgraded to BLS. Personnel assigned to the BLS engines will receive a two-step pay increase.

Three rescue units will be taken out of service; the remaining two will be upgraded to ALS and supplement the EMS engine companies. Eventually, automatic defibrillators will be added to the EMS companies. All EMS engines will carry a four-member crew, two members of which will be state-certified EMTs. Specially equipped truck companies trained extensively in extrication and rescue at the Atlanta Fire Academy will handle that work. These changes are expected to improve response times throughout the city and reduce costs.

Update (July 1994)   All new recruits are trained to the firefighter/EMT-A level. Classes for all fire department personnel currently are in progress. The department is studying the financial feasibility of upgrading the 21 engine companies to defibrillation units within five years.

Austin, Texas[20]   The total quality management BASICS Plan, implemented by the City of Austin, Texas, in 1991, established "customer service" as the city's top priority. Providing the best service to the citizen/customer in the most cost-effective manner, therefore, was the basis on which Division Chief James Fiero of the Austin Fire Department (AFD) proposed to city management that the Austin EMS Department be consolidated into the AFD. The fire department's involvement in EMS quality assurance has arisen primarily from the city's implementing a program that placed automatic defibrillators on all AFD engines and other selected fire companies.

Statistics   The Austin EMS Department operates seven full-time and one part-time BLS ambulances and four full-time ALS ambulances and two part-time ALS units. One of the full-time BLS units provides coverage to the county. All except four of the EMS units run out of fire stations. The closest fire department engine company, the closest ALS or BLS ambulance, followed by the ALS unit, and, as appropriate, an EMS supervisor normally are dispatched to a cardiac call within the city. These apparatus are staffed by five to nine people, depending on personnel levels and the number of units responding. Firefighters are pulled off their companies to provide the proper staffing levels to manage medical transports. During this time, these companies are out of service and unavailable for other calls.

The fire department trains its personnel to the emergency medical technician automated defibrillator (EMT-AD) level. The

EMT-ADs are first responders to all life-threatening medical calls, providing BLS in under four minutes and immediate automatic defibrillator services.

Proposal   Among the recommendations made by Fiero were the following:

- Establish 10 paramedic engine companies (creating the need for 30 personnel for the units). Engine companies currently have four members assigned but run with three; assigning a fifth person would allow the company to respond with four on duty at all times.
- Maintain and support the system with 12 BLS transport ambulances staffed by EMT firefighters who would rotate off their regularly assigned companies and work on the BLS transport ambulance about every 12 to 18 months. These 12 BLS ambulances would require 72 additional personnel over current AFD staffing.
- Dispatch the closest paramedic engine company and BLS transport ambulance to a cardiac call. If one of the "regular" BLS engine companies is closer, dispatch it as well, to provide the same BLS care furnished under the current system. Return that BLS engine to service as soon as a paramedic engine arrives on the scene. One or two of the paramedics assigned to the responding engine could ride in the transport ambulance if paramedic care is needed during transport.
- Retain 132 of the 153.5 full-time positions in the EMS Department. Even with the reduction in personnel, the new system would provide 10 instead of the present six ALS units (four full-time and two part-time) and allow the number to increase as the city's needs and demands warrant.
- Retain EMS personnel who do not want to become cross-trained as firefighters on one of the BLS or ALS ambulances or in a staff-support function during system implementation. When they leave or retire, fill the operational positions with cross-trained firefighter/paramedics. The paramedic engine company system could be on line within five years.

Costs would involve adding one person per unit per shift, their training, and equipment. Increasing the number of paramedic ambulances (as the medical professionals advocate) would involve adding three staff members per unit per shift (currently, the EMS Division personnel cannot take their earned vacation without the city's having to pay overtime to cover staffing levels), the necessary training and equipment, and the cost of another ambulance. Under a paramedic engine company system, the only additional cost involved in adding paramedic units is training personnel.

Austin's city management declined to study the consolidation issue, saying, "It can't be done."

Update (July 1994)   The AFD is in the process of hiring 100 to 140 new personnel, and the EMS Department is increasing its staffing to maintain coverage. "Now would be the best time to implement this enhanced system. It would save the city millions of dollars each year," Fiero maintains. Moreover, he reports that, when surveyed, Austin EMS Department employees asked why the department was attempting to duplicate many of the rescue operations already provided by the AFD and why EMS was not consolidated with the fire department to improve services.

The Austin Fire Fighters Association established a committee to study the issue of consolidation. That committee was joined by several members of the EMS Department also interested in this merger. Since then, the city manager has appointed her own committee to look into the issue. Both the fire and EMS departments are in the process of changing their department directors.

Fayetteville, North Carolina[21]   The City of Fayetteville Fire Department (FFD) undertook in 1989 a study to determine if switching from EMS BLS squads to engine companies would help curb the rising costs of providing EMS (personnel, vehicle maintenance and replacement, fuel, and training). The study included comparative analyses of engine company and squad runs, including the total and average number of runs, the average time spent on scene, mileage, maintenance costs, the average miles per gallon for each unit, and the average response time, as well as salary costs for personnel assigned to the squads.

Annual reports for the period from 1984 to 1988 showed that the squad companies answered 3.5 calls for every engine company call and that out-of-service time for the squads was about 33 percent greater than that for engine companies.

There also were some workload disparities. The per-year incentive pay for EMTs (all personnel below the rank of lieutenant are required to be certified as EMTs) assigned to squads or serving as alternates amounted to $19.58 (before taxes) per two-week pay period for the highest paid squad company member, or 58 cents per extra run. Yet, the firefighter assigned to a squad had the same rank and station duties as the one assigned to the engine company. Squads answer all fire calls along with engines and trucks, if available. In 1988, for example, Squad 1 answered 3,196 calls compared with 654 calls for Engine 2, which had the highest number of runs of all engines.

Statistics   At the time of the study, FFD operated eight engine companies, two truck companies, and five rescue squad units out of seven stations. The engine companies had crews of four, and each rescue unit had a crew of two per shift. Personnel assigned to the five rescue units provided BLS until the outside agency's ALS transporting service arrived on the scene. (Fayetteville transports only in extreme life-threatening situations; only one of the city's vehicles has transport capabilities.)

Findings   The study concluded that despite the experiences of other departments to the contrary, the FFD at that time would not have realized any significant savings by changing from squad to engine-company response, and response time might be slower.

Recommendations   Among the recommendations offered were the following:

- Continue to use squads for first-responder units with EMTs rotated onto the squads on a regular basis so they could remain proficient in their skills.
- Institute a policy that would dispatch the closest unit—squad or engine—to an emergency, reducing the number of times any unit would be out of its district. Maintain detailed records on response time, out-of-service time, and fill-in time for other units in these districts to assess the level of service.
- Consider dividing the territory of the busiest unit and assigning one of the least-busy squads to the central station and assign the personnel of squads scheduled for vehicle replacement to the engine companies that would absorb the squad's runs. Replacement should be done on a least-busy-company basis.

Update (July 1994)   At present, all FFD engines provide EMS at the basic EMT level. Deputy Chief James A. Hall reports that about a year and a half ago one squad that didn't have a high volume of calls was taken out of service and a second one was removed from service about a year ago. The personnel were moved to engine companies. The moves were instituted on a trial basis, and the squad vehicles were kept should they have to be reinstated. Since absorbing the two squads into the engine companies, the FFD has been able to maintain the same level of service. "Each situation is unique to the locale and its personnel," says Hall. "We don't know how much further we will go in instituting this change because of the high volume of calls: Eighty percent of the 12,000 calls received by the department are for EMS, and the engines would be on the road all the time."

Kane County, Illinois[22]   When one of the local hospitals gave notice in June 1982 that it would not renew its contract to provide ambulance service for the county, the fire chiefs of St. Charles, Geneva, and Batavia met with Batavia's mayor, J. D. Schielke, a member of the Batavia Fire Department, to explore the available alternatives. The result was the formation of the Tri-City Ambulance Service (TCAS), governed by a board comprised of two elected officials from each city, the three fire chiefs, and the Paramedic Services of Illinois (PSI, the paramedic/firefighter provider) area supervisor, with Schielke as board chairman. The board controls the budget and allows fire chiefs to control the service on a daily basis.

In December 1982, the cities of Batavia, Geneva, and St. Charles (Tri-Cities) and their surrounding fire protection district areas transferred operation of the paramedic ambulance service from the two local hospitals to the cities' three fire departments. The service was started with four paramedic/firefighters per 24-hour shift, backed up by two firefighter/EMTs staffing three ALS ambulances and with the same two ambulances operated at the hospitals and a fire department unit previously used as a BLS ambulance.

The 103-square-mile Tri-City area (30 miles west of Chicago along the Fox River), a combination of residential, commercial, industrial, rural, and agricultural developments, has seen explosive growth. Population has grown by about 25,000 people since 1982 and is approaching 100,000.

Update (July 1994)   According to Batavia Chief William J. Darin, some things have not changed since 1982. For example, the paramedic/firefighters continue to be an asset to the fire departments' day-to-day operations, in addition to carrying out their primary responsibility, EMS. In Batavia, an ambulance is dispatched to assist on all structural incidents. For a working fire, one of the paramedics is assigned as command aide until relieved by another officer; the other paramedic is assigned to the point of attack on the outside of the structure, in SCBA, to assist with getting the attack hoseline into operation and to monitor the actions of the attack crews. If necessary, of course, the duty paramedics immediately will assist with rescue and extinguishment, depending on the circumstances. The paramedics' first responsibility is to care for a patient; thus, when there are injuries in a fire incident, paramedics are assigned to treatment and other responding personnel are used as aides or entry-point monitors. Paramedic/firefighters assist with all regular station duties, and all have assigned districts within which to make routine fire and occupancy inspections.

Each department has a paramedic coordinator who directly supervises the paramedics in that particular contract. An overall coordinator oversees the entire three-city operation. The coordinators are appointed by PSI with the consent of the three fire chiefs.

Dispatching for TCAS continues to be provided by Tri-Com, which has been jointly serving the area's fire, police, and ambulance services since 1976.

Revisions However, many changes in service have occurred since 1982, including the following:

- Eight, instead of four, paramedic/firefighters are needed per day (two for each of the four front-line ALS ambulances).
- As of January 1, 1994, a fourth ALS ambulance with two additional paramedic/firefighters per shift was added, increasing the number of personnel provided by PSI from 12 in 1982 to 24 in 1994. The City of St. Charles, which has gone from one fire station in 1982 to its present three fire stations, received the fourth ALS unit.
- The City of Geneva will open its second fire station in 1994, while Batavia has relocated one of its two fire stations since 1982.
- In 1983, TCAS responded to 2,077 ambulance requests and transported 1,587 patients to their choice of area hospitals. In 1992, it responded to 3,120 ambulance requests and transported 2,400 patients. The ambulances also responded to approximately 1,000 fire-related and 667 change-of-quarters responses in 1992. Anytime three of the four ambulances at either the north or south end of the ambulance district go out of service on an ambulance response, the remaining unit is moved to the middle City of Geneva quarter, so it can be centrally located for a better response time.
- The first-responder program was expanded by sending the closest engine or squad company to assist. An engine or squad continues to respond to assist in most responses.
- The budget has increased over the years, but since the area is rapidly expanding, the cost to taxpayers has been negligible because of the increased assessed valuation of the entire Tri-City Ambulance District. The 1983 budget was $442,000 and the 1993-1994 budget, $1,056,938, minus $237,000 for the fees collected, leaving a total of $819,018 to be raised through the tax levy. This amount is divided among the three cities.
- User fees (for transport only) increased from $50 and $100 for patients living or working in the district and nonresi-

dents, respectively, in 1982 to $75 and $150 in 1993. The fee
is still lower than the $90 fee charged to residents prior to
1982.
- The fleet of ambulances has changed drastically since 1982.
  Five new ambulances were purchased between 1985 and
  1993. Budgeting will make it possible to rechassis or replace
  an existing ambulance in 1994-95, 1995-96, and 1996-97, resulting in a state-of-the-art fleet.

In 1994, TCAS is now able to serve its citizens from four ALS
ambulance locations and seven fire stations. Intergovernmental
cooperation has continued to work with regard to the dispatch
center, ambulance service, and automatic and mutual-aid fire responses, which this year may be expanded to include the concept
of sending the closest engine, not just the closest ambulance.

Phoenix, Arizona[23, 24]   During the summer of 1973, EMS requests approached 30 percent of all fire department dispatches.
No paramedic service was available. Several agencies (fire and
four ambulance companies) delivered EMS with very little coordination. The Phoenix City Council, the Phoenix fire and police
departments, and representatives of various health-care agencies conducted an in-depth evaluation of the need for and delivery of EMS.

Training at that time consisted of American Red Cross Advanced First Aid for fire department personnel and little or no
training for some ambulance company personnel. Ambulance response times were as long as 20 minutes. Medical equipment was
limited: all fire companies were equipped with a resuscitator and
first-aid kits.

Recognizing the need for improved EMS, the city council assigned to the Phoenix Fire Department (PFD) the responsibility
for EMS and directed it to develop and implement plans for upgrading the EMS delivery system.

Update (July 1994)   The PFD is the sole provider of EMS
within the City of Phoenix. Today, 26 of the department's 47 engines and two of its 11 ladders are paramedic, staffed with at
least four members, any two of which are paramedics. The paramedic engine concept was implemented in the late 1970s and is
being used also for two of the department's ladder tenders (five-
person, four-door medium-duty trucks with custom "rescue"
-type bodies; they carry most of the typical ladder company
equipment except ladders, including hydraulic rescue extrication
equipment, EMS equipment, as well as basic ventilation equipment, duplicate SCBA, and bunker clothing for each crew mem-

ber). The department has six additional ladder tenders that provide BLS service.

When the City of Phoenix chose to go to a single transportation service, the PFD successfully competed. In November 1985, the Phoenix Fire Department Emergency Transportation Service (ETS) was implemented. It consistently maintains a response time of under 10 minutes 92 percent or more of the time, a majority of the responses being under five minutes.

Ambulances are staffed with EMT firefighters responding from fire stations. The fleet includes 19 first-line vehicles and nine reserve Type II Ford 350 van conversions with diesel engines. Due to changes in van body design, the PFD began using Type 1 modular ambulances in 1993. A three-year replacement cycle is in effect.

According to Gary P. Morris, deputy chief of District 10, the closest available unit, including engines and ladders, is always dispatched to medical emergencies. On calls indicating a potential life-threatening medical emergency, a paramedic engine or paramedic ladder (the closer one) is always dispatched. If the closest unit is a paramedic engine or ladder, that unit along with an ambulance is the basic dispatch. If the closest unit is a BLS engine or ladder, it responds with the next closest paramedic company and ambulance.

For auto accidents with entrapment, a ladder company is also dispatched for extrication, along with a chief officer to command operations.

For multiple-patient incidents, the alarm room has the option of dispatching one of two levels of a predesignated major medical response—based on the number of patients reported or the seriousness of the incident.

Basic response includes three engines (two paramedic), one ladder company, one chief officer, and one ambulance. Initial response to a major incident includes six engines, (four paramedic), two ladder companies, two chief officers, three ambulances, and a command post vehicle. Engines and ladders carry four crew members each.

The department has a major medical plan and standard operating procedures defining a medical management command system. Incident management systems, including the major components of incident command and sectors for extrication, treatment, transportation, landing zone, and staging, are used routinely. These plans are exercised regularly.

Dual-role firefighters deliver fire and EMS. New recruits receive EMT certification. The first EMTs were certified in 1971; all members completed EMT certification in 1974. The first paramedics were certified in December 1974. About 900 firefighters are trained to the level of EMT and 241 as Certified Emergency Paramedics (CEPs).

The PFD conducts its own EMT continuing education and re-certification and paramedic training programs. Paramedic prac-tice is regulated by the Arizona Department of Health Services, and paramedics must be certified every two years.

Plano, Texas[25] Since 1980, Plano (20 miles north of downtown Dallas) has been developing a state-of-the-art EMS system as a means of coping with the city's rapid growth. Its population has grown from 100,000 in 1984 to 155,000 in 1993 and is expected to reach approximately 220,000 by the year 2003. Ten to 12 percent of the community's population turns over every year. The citizens are sophisticated and highly demanding of the services they want, says Fire Chief William Peterson.

Currently, 160 personnel, operating out of seven fire stations, provide EMS and fire services. An eighth station is under con-struction and is expected to be in service in October 1994. Sta-tions 9 and 10 are in the planning stages.

In August 1982, the fire department began delivering para-medic services; and in early 1983, it developed an EMS action plan that included specific objectives, some of which are listed below, with target dates. Updated information appears in italics.

- Train all fire department members to the level of EMT; select and train 36 paramedics. *New personnel now must be certi-fied as firefighters and EMTs before they can take the entry test. Since 1985, employees have been hired under the condi-tion that they become paramedics, if it is deemed necessary. The department now has 70 paramedics.*
- Train all paramedics as CPR instructors and develop an ag-gressive citywide citizen CPR-training program. *A group of six to 10 paramedics (certified as CPR instructors) has pro-vided CPR training in schools, fire stations, and businesses/industries since 1985. The department currently offers a monthly CPR course.*
- Train fire department dispatch personnel to the level of EMT and then implement an emergency medical dispatch system. *This has been "one of the most dramatic elements of the sys-tem in terms of performance," Peterson reports. Preinstruc-tions have averted tragedies, such as drownings, he adds.*
- Provide ongoing continuing education of EMT and paramedic personnel in the fire stations. *The medical director or his staff does this on a monthly basis.*
- Equip all fire department vehicles to provide BLS capability. *This was done some time ago.*

- Initiate paramedic capability on engine and truck companies. *Engines have had paramedic capability since 1985; trucks were upgraded in 1993.*
- Initiate a user fee to minimize system abuse and limit transport to the closest medical facility. *Initial billing in 1983 was $50 per run. Today, it is $250 for residents and $300 for*

Ambulance billing service

Through an innovative method of filing claims directly with insurance carriers for ambulance service fees, the fire department for the city of Plano, Texas, has recouped approximately $850,000 for fiscal year 1994-95 and projects to generate more than $1 million in revenue for FY 1995-96.

Fire Chief William Peterson said this method of seeking reimbursement from insurance companies will continue to have a great impact for taxpayers in Plano. "That basically will translate into more than a $1 million revenue and curbs the need to raise property taxes to run the fire department-operated ambulances," he said.

In order to increase service to customers and reduce the customer burden of filing paperwork with their insurance carriers, Plano decided early in 1993 to bill insurance companies directly for ambulance services.

The reason was clear: about 75 percent to 80 percent of Plano residents who were receiving ambulance services had medical insurance that would reimburse municipalities for costs related to their hospital transport.

"If we don't bill third party insurance carriers for ambulance services, it amounts to a taxpayer subsidy for insurance carriers," Peterson explains.

That year, Plano collected approximately $358,000 in ambulance fees. Fees were figured at $200 per person and $400 per family for residents and non-residents. The collection rate was 60 percent.

In August 1993, Plano contracted with a company to assume Emergency Medical Service billing operations for the city. This company was expected to file reimbursement claims electronically with insurance carriers. Prior to this, customers were billed directly for the service by the Accounting Department, and the customers, in turn, would have to contact their insurance company for reimbursement.

Bruce Testa, City Controller, said the decision to contract for billing and collection was a matter of cost-avoidance. "The EMS

nonresidents, plus $4 a mile for transporting to a hospital. Peterson estimates that revenues will approach $600,000 within the next year. A certain percentage of citizens feel the service should be free because they pay taxes, Peterson explains; but "if we do this," he says, "we're subsidizing third-party payers."

had grown so much that the Accounting Department couldn't handle the increased claims without upgrading a computer system and adding staff members," he said.

In 1993-94, more than $669,000 was generated through ambulance services. Fees were raised to $250 for residents and $300 for nonresidents, in addition to a $4 per mile charge. The collection rate continued to increase that fiscal year to 65 percent.

In 1994-95, the plan has generated more than $850,000 in revenue for ambulance services, with a more than 70 percent collection rate. Per-person fees remained the same, however, the per-mile charge was increased to $5. The collection rate reached 70 percent and Peterson said it continues to show signs of improvement.

The city also incorporated a fee structure for services.

"Basically the purpose of the fee change was to maximize recovery of amounts from third party insurance carriers," Peterson said. A $30 fee was charged for administering oxygen and $25 for a second attendant where cardiovascular pulmonary resuscitation was performed, where the patient weighed more than 300 pounds or had to be carried up and down stairs.

In addition, Peterson said, the patient delivery area was expanded to meet requests by customers who preferred to be transported to area hospitals that are within their insurance network and may be outside of Plano. The fire department expanded the number of hospitals to which it would transport patients from two local hospitals to 10 area hospitals.

The fire department is projecting revenue in excess of $1 million for the next fiscal year (1995-96), Peterson said. Service fees will be raised to $275 for residents and $330 for nonresidents. The per-mile charge will be $7. Other fees will remain the same.

This approach to insurance reimbursement for ambulance services is on the cutting edge of maximizing revenue potential, Peterson said. "Very few municipalities recognize the potential here," he said.

Contact: Rachel Welch Gomez, Public Information Coordinator, City of Plano, PO Box 860358, Plano, TX 75086-0358; (214) 578-7307.
Source: Government Information Services.

San Jose, California[26, 27, 28]   In 1989, the fire department provided first-responder BLS services, and a private ambulance company under contract with the County of Santa Clara provided paramedic services.

Believing that the fire department could provide more efficient paramedic services at a lower cost, the fire department at that time proposed to city management that the department take over the paramedic program. Questions relative to the appropriate role of the fire department in the city's EMS system and the basis for allocating fire department resources had been raised when the city's Office of Management and Budget reported to the city council that while the number of fires had not increased during the preceding 10-year period, the total number of fire department emergency responses had steadily increased. The city initiated a study of the EMS system.

Richard D. Wattenbarger, who last year retired from his position as deputy chief of the fire department and is now a teacher of fire science at Mission College in Santa Clara County, originally proposed to San Jose's city managers that the fire department assume responsibility for the city's paramedic services. The city denied the fire department the authority to assume the paramedic function.

Update (July 1994)   EMTs are trained at the academy to EMT-I and EMT-D standards as mandated by the state of California. EMTs provide first responder BLS, and defibrillation services are available on all first-response vehicles, reports Fire Captain Bill Mayes, who manages the department's EMS program.

"Over the past 20 years, our workforce has had a total changeover. Department members are younger and highly educated. There isn't the resistance to EMS there was 20 years ago. Seventy percent of the department believes the department should increase service to the paramedic level even though they all may not want to be paramedics," observes Mayes.

Members of the San Jose Firefighters L-230 and the administrative staff worked together to bring forth a department initiative, with the city manager's approval, to the city council requesting approval to once again study the feasibility of instituting an ALS/Transport program in the fire department.

The proposal was presented on November 9, 1993. The city council authorized the study and provided $25,000 for the hiring of a professional consultant. The department formed a paramedic team and named Jeff Clet, a battalion chief, project director. The team and consultant are working together to prepare another proposal for providing ALS/paramedic services through the fire department. It was anticipated that the proposal would be submitted to the city council by the end of July 1994.

The experiences of the departments profiled above and other fire organizations show that an EMS system must be dynamic and efficient if it is to meet the needs of the community it serves. Proactivity, sound management, and evaluation are as vital to EMS organizations as they are to fire-suppression organizations.

Note: Numbers in parentheses within the text of the article denote subsequent references to the endnotes.

1. Phone interview with Deputy Chief Gary Morris, Phoenix (AZ) Fire Department, Aug. 4, 1993.
2. Cady, G.A. and Scott, T. "EMS in the United States: A Survey of Providers in the 200 Most Populous Cities." *JEMS,* Jan. 1993, 71-76,83.
3. Morris, G.P. "Fire Service EMS: Living Up To Standards." *JEMS,* June 1987, 51-55.
4. Phone interview with Mary Beth Michos, chief of EMS and specialties teams coordinator, Montgomery County (MD) Department of Fire EMS and Rescue Services, March 1993.
5. Fiero, J. "Refining Fire and EMS Services Using Paramedic Fire Companies." Research project, National Fire Academy, Aug. 1990.
6. Smith, B.H. "Profiles Defining Fire Service EMS." *JEMS,* June 1984, 75-76.
7. Butler, T. "Call the Fire Department." *Emergency,* Dec. 1989, 45-47.
8. Alguire, W.J., Cosby, J.C., Jackson, D.B., et al. *Patching up the marriage between fire service and EMS.* Research project, National Fire Academy, April 1988.
9. McKeen, D.K., Rynning, N., Weaver, B.J., Smith, K.M. "The Illusion of Gorgeous Uniqueness of the Fire Service Toward EMS." Research project, National Fire Academy, Jan. 1991.
10. "Guidelines for Cardiopulmonary Resuscitation (CPR) and Emergency Cardiac Care (ECC)." *JAMA,* Oct. 28, 1992, 268:16, 2289-2295.
11. Harley, G., Johnson, D., Kantak, G., et al. *"Fire / EMS"—A Marriage in Trouble.* Research project, National Fire Academy, Aug. 1990.
12. Gratz, D.B. "EMS in the fire service TIME OUT!" *Fire Chief.* Nov. 1983.
13. MacCallum, D.S., Loyal, V.T., Nye, N.P., et al. "Alternative EMS Delivery System Profiles for the Fire Service." Research project, National Fire Academy, July-Aug. 1986.
14. Phone interview with Ricky Davidson, Chief of EMS, Shreveport (LA) Fire Department, Jan. 25, 1993.
15. Pringle, Jr., R.P. "Fire Service EMS Profiles," *Implementation of EMS in the Fire Service: Challenging the Fire Service,* International Association of Fire Chiefs, 1991. The profiles were formulated by the Advanced Coronary Treatment Foundation for the U.S. Fire Administration's *Fire Service EMS Program Management Guide,* 1980, and updated by the IAFC in 1991 through its "Current Issues in Fire Service EMS" survey.
16. Murphy, D.M. "Rapid Defibrillation: Fire Service to Lead the Way." *J Emerg Med Serv,* 1987; 12:67-71. In *JAMA* Oct. 28, 1992; complete citation in Endnote 10.
17. *Implementation of EMS in the Fire Service: Challenging the Fire Service,* Appendix E.
18. Yameen, J.M. and Keller, R.A. "EMS in the Fire Service: Operational Characteristics: EMS/Fire Service Survey Report: Part two. *Fire Chief,* Sept. 1991, 63. This is

the second of a three-part survey series conducted by the consulting firm Fitch & Associates in conjunction with *Fire Chief* magazine. The other segments were Part one: "Defining the EMS Role of the Fire Service," published in *Fire Chief,* May 1991, pages 45-49, and Part three: "How Fire Departments Administer Emergency Medical Services, published in *Fire Chief,* Nov. 1991, pages 53-56.

19. Szmanski, T., press release June 7, '93; phone Sept. 4, '93 and Jan. 14, '94.

20. Fiero, J., "Refining Fire and EMS Services Using Paramedic Fire Companies," NFA Exec. Fire Officers Program, June '89; phone Sept. 7, '93; letter Feb. 3, '93; faxes Sept. 3, '93 and Jan. 13, '94.

21. Hall, J.A. "Engine Company Emergency Medical Response: It Works for Others, Will It Work for Fayetteville?" NFA Exec. Fire Officers Program, June '89; phone Sept. 7, '93 and Jan. 12, '94.

22. Darin, Wm. J., "Tri-City Ambulance Service Staffed by Paramedics/Fire Fighters," *FE,* Nov. '83, 52-54; fax: "Tri-City Ambulance Service 10 Years Later," Sept. 10, '93; phone Jan. 12, '94.

23. Morris, G.P. "EMS Is Not a Fire Department Stepchild." *F Com,* Aug. '77, 32-35; letter Sept. 16, '93; fax Jan. 14, '94.

24. "Phoenix Fire Department Profile," undated.

25. Peterson, Wm. "Improving Public Support for the Fire Service Through EMS,'" *FE,* Nov. '83, 55,56; phone Sept. 7, '93; fax Jan. 14, '94.

26. Wattenbarger, R.D. "A Paramedic Program Research Project," NFA Exec. Fire Officers Program, Nov. '89; phone Jan. 27, '93.

27. Mayes, Wm., phone Aug. 13, '93; fax Sept. 2, '93.

28. Clet, Jeff, phone Jan. 18, '94.

Fire Investigation: Advances in Science and Technology

James H. Shanley, Jr.

The science of fire

The basic goal of most fire investigations is to determine the origin and cause of the fire. The origin is the place where the fire started. The cause is the reason for the initiation of the fire—i.e., the circumstances or agencies that brought fuel and an ignition source together with air or oxygen. The origin may be a general area, such as "the southwest bedroom," or it may be very specific, such as "the electrical outlet in the north corner of the third floor near column H-5." Often, the terms *area of origin* and *point of origin* are used to make the distinction between the two types of origin areas. Each fire scene must be carefully and methodically evaluated to determine the origin. The fire investigator strives to pinpoint the point or area of origin, but often the scene does not permit such precision.

Fire dynamics   One of the most useful tools for determining a fire's origin is the fire pattern. Fire patterns form by the growth and spread of the fire from the point of ignition to extinguishment. To understand fire patterns and how they are produced requires an understanding of how and why fire grows and spreads. This field of study is known as fire dynamics.

The application of heat to a combustible solid causes vapors and gases to be released, a process known as pyrolysis. We refer

Adapted from James H. Shanley, Jr., "Fire Investigation Change and Evolution, Part 2: Understanding the Science of Fire," *Fire Engineering* (May 1994) and "Fire Investigation Change and Evolution, Part 3: New Tools and Old Myths," *Fire Engineering* (June 1994). Reprinted with permission of James H. Shanley, Jr., and *Fire Engineering*.

to materials "burning," but it is the vapors and gases given off by most solid materials that actually burn. The solid itself is chemically changed by the application of heat. These changes may be visible as patterns on the material after the fire has been extinguished.

Ignition of the pyrolysis products will occur if sufficient oxygen and ignition heat energy are available. Once ignition has occurred and the fire is self-sustaining,[1] a portion of the heat energy released will go to preheat and pyrolyze more fuel, which causes the fire to grow. As the fire grows, its need for oxygen increases.

Combustion of the pyrolysis products can produce gases such as carbon dioxide (CO_2), carbon monoxide (CO), and water vapor (H_2O); solids such as carbon soot (C); and some heavy, tar-like liquids. The mixture of these items is commonly called smoke. Smoke also may contain unburned pyrolysis products. The products of pyrolysis become heated by the fire, rise, and collect at the ceiling of the room, forming a hot upper layer while the lower layer remains relatively cool.

As a fire in a room grows, products of combustion are given off in greater quantities and begin to fill the room from the top down. Hot gases can build up to the point where they can ignite and burn in the upper layer. This phenomenon is called *flameover* or *rollover,* not to be confused with *flashover.* Flashover occurs when most, if not all, of the exposed combustible materials in the room ignite virtually simultaneously. This usually includes exposed surfaces of the floor—especially if it is carpeted, furnishings and other contents, and walls, in addition to the hot upper layer gases. The rapid increase in the fire's intensity often results in flame coming from openings (windows) and fire spreading to adjacent rooms. The thermal and toxic atmospheric conditions produced by flashover are rarely survived by anyone in the room or nearby, including fully protected firefighters.

Fire patterns   If the room opens to fresh air, the fire as it grows will draw air into the room through these openings. This air flow causes patterns to form on surfaces in the room, especially around the openings to the room such as the windows and doors. Typically, when there is an opening to the fire room, the relatively cool fresh air will be drawn in at the bottom of the opening as the hot fire gases leave the opening from the top. This causes heat damage in the form of charring, burning, or blistered paint to the upper portion of the opening, while little or no damage is caused to the bottom of the opening. It is often possible to discern from this pattern the direction from which the hot gases came, which in turn points back to the area of origin. Examining all available openings for these patterns can be very helpful in understanding where the fire started and how it spread to adjacent rooms.

If a room has no openings, the oxygen available eventually will become depleted and the intensity of the fire will decrease. A fire is said to be *ventilation-controlled* when its growth is controlled by the quantity of oxygen available to it. A *fuel-controlled* fire, on the other hand, has unlimited oxygen; but its growth is controlled by the quantity of fuel available. A ventilation-controlled fire produces a greater quantity of carbon monoxide and soot as its oxygen is depleted. Under certain conditions, these and other combustion products may fill the room and, with the sudden introduction of fresh air, can burn very rapidly or explode. Such an explosion[2] is called a *backdraft* or *smoke explosion*. Fires that become ventilation-controlled are common, but backdrafts are not very common. Flashover, the much more common occurrence, is the real threat to occupants and firefighters.

Fire plumes   A basic fire pattern is the one produced by the fire plume. The fire plume is the area above the flame shaped roughly like a cone. This area is composed of the hot gases (smoke) that rise from the flames and spread out as they rise. As they rise, air is drawn into them by a process known as entrainment. If this cone comes in contact with a vertical surface such as a wall, it is truncated (cut) vertically and a fire pattern in the shape of a "V" will be produced. If the plume comes in contact with a horizontal surface such as the ceiling or the underside of a table, the plume cone is similarly truncated by the horizontal surface, and a circular pattern will result on the surface. The diameter of this circular pattern will increase as the distance from the fire increases. These patterns form because the fire plume is hot and contains smoke particulates that, when they come in contact with a clean wall, cause heat and smoke damage to the surface. Smoke patterns are formed by the condensation of smoke on the surface of ceilings and walls, which often are cooler than the plume. This also may happen on glass windows or other surfaces.

These truncated cone patterns may, and often do, remain after the fire is extinguished. The base of the truncated cone (the vertex of the V) will indicate the location of a heat source and may assist in origin determination. A circular pattern will be almost directly over the fire and also can assist in origin determination.

If the flame itself comes in contact with a noncombustible wall surface such as gypsum or plaster, the flame can burn off any soot or condensed smoke that was there. This pattern also will be in a truncated cone pattern. It is called a *clean burn* pattern and also may be V-shaped. The V may be right-side-up or upside-down, depending on the size of the fire and the distance between it and the wall surface. A clean burn pattern is a definite indication of flame or a high-temperature plume.

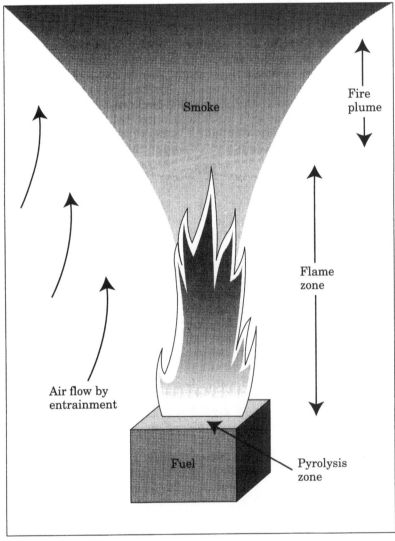

Figure 1. A fire has three zones: the pyrolysis zone, the flame zone, and the fire plume. Each of these zones can produce patterns that may be helpful to the fire investigator.

If flame comes in contact with a combustible wall surface such as wood paneling, it may leave a pattern as charred material, or the fire may consume part of it. Material that is missing because it has been consumed by the fire is also a fire pattern.

Lowest burning: A note of caution   Using patterns, it often is possible to find an area in the room of origin where the fire was at its lowest point. This may be the point of origin but is not by definition the point of origin. Before the point of lowest burning is declared the point of origin, other reasons for low burning and the patterns that indicate it must be eliminated. When materials in the room, such as curtains, burn and drop down, they can produce areas of low burning. Such "drop-down" easily can be mistaken for a point of origin. The fire investigator must carefully examine all areas suspected of being places of origin.

The lowest point of burning is associated with the point of origin because after the fire starts, it and its products spread upward and outward. However, fire burns downward as well, just at a much slower rate than it burns upward. This holds true unless an unusual circumstance makes it easier for the fire to burn downward. Unusual circumstances include the influence of ventilation; plastics that melt, burn, and drip; and ignitable[3] liquids, such as gasoline or kerosene, that promote rapid fire spread over their surfaces.

Unusual circumstances should not automatically prompt the fire investigator to call a fire incendiary. An incendiary fire is one that has been deliberately set to cause damage or injury. The circumstances and patterns discussed above can be indicators of incendiary fires, but the investigator must carefully consider and rule out natural, nonincendiary causes before jumping to conclusions.

In a cause investigation, the investigator considers specific fuels that may have been brought to the place of origin deliberately. The cause investigation should always follow the origin investigation. Before determining how and why a fire started, the fire investigator must be reasonably sure of where the fire started.

First material ignited   An investigation is not complete or adequate if the investigator identifies only an area of origin and a source of heat. Identification of the first material ignited is key if the investigator's theories of how and why the fire started are to withstand scrutiny. The investigator must be able to prove that there was a fuel present at the point of origin capable of being ignited by the heat source. A heat source is said to be competent when it is capable of causing ignition of a fuel. The first material ignited may be bed clothing, curtains, a cardboard box, or an ignitable liquid.

Ignition of any material requires that it be brought to its ignition temperature. There are two types of ignition temperatures—autoignition and piloted ignition. A material's *autoignition* temperature is the temperature at which that material ignites without the presence of flame. Its *piloted* ignition temperature is the temperature at which it ignites in the presence of a flame, which acts as a pilot to the ignition of the pyrolysis products. For this reason, a material's piloted ignition temperature is always lower than its autoignition temperature.

Ignition requires a specific amount of heat energy, determined by the condition and composition of the fuel. For example, it takes less energy to ignite a piece of paper than to ignite a piece of wood, despite the fact that paper and wood are essentially the same material and have similar ignition temperatures. The heat source must be substantial enough to provide to the fuel the minimum amount of heat energy required to cause ignition. When small globs of molten copper from an arcing electric circuit land on a solid piece of wood, they will not ignite the wood even though the temperature of the liquid copper (1,981°F or higher) far exceeds the ignition temperature of the wood (600°F or higher). The reason is that the small globs of copper do not contain sufficient heat energy to ignite the solid piece of wood. The molten copper is not a competent ignition source for the wood. However, if the small copper globs were to land on some paper or cotton or pass through an ignitable mixture of propane and air, ignition would be more likely. These materials require less heat energy to bring them to their ignition temperatures than the solid piece of wood does. The difference between temperature and heat energy is very important in fire cause and ignition source evaluation and must be understood by investigators.

The first material ignited can be determined by examining the area of origin for any remnants of the material or by looking for patterns produced by the burning of it. Information provided by people who were familiar with the area of origin before the fire might be useful in making this determination. Examining similar areas of the room or building also may help determine what comprised the area of origin before the fire.

Flashover and accelerants: A closer look   The phenomenon of flashover is very important in fire dynamics. It can occur in most room fires when sufficient fuel and oxygen are present. When flashover occurs, it produces heat and smoke patterns on many of the unprotected surfaces of a room, including low areas of walls and the floor. These patterns are a result of the great quantity of heat energy and smoke found in a room that has flashed over.

Fire investigators must consider low patterns carefully to ensure they are not mistaken for the low patterns produced by the burning of an ignitable liquid on the floor. The investigator must evaluate from the condition of the room and its contents whether flashover occurred and, if so, what its result on the room was. If an ignitable liquid is used to intentionally start a fire in a room, it most likely will produce patterns on the floor where it burned. However, if the room subsequently flashes over, the liquid burn patterns may be obscured by those produced by the flashover. For this reason, the investigator must rely on other tools to determine cause.

If it is suspected that an ignitable liquid was used as an accelerant, the investigator can collect a debris sample and have it chemically analyzed for such a liquid. The best places to collect such samples are from areas where the liquid may have flowed and collected and that may have been protected from the fire. The collection of any sample for chemical analysis also should include a control sample, for use by the analytical chemist to determine what materials may have been present in the debris as a result of the fire, or even prior to the fire, and which are not related to the use of an ignitable liquid to start the fire. When many synthetic materials (including ordinary carpet) burn, they may produce pyrolysis products that appear in the analysis to be very similar to materials normally present in ignitable liquids such as gasoline and kerosene. The control sample should be the same material as the evidence sample, but it should be from an area that could not have come in contact with the ignitable liquid.

The intense fire conditions of flashover are possible with almost any type of fuel. A fire in a typical living room couch of mostly polyurethane foam can flash over a 10- by 12-foot living room in five minutes or less. Witnesses and firefighters may describe such a fire as one that grew very quickly and was very intense. The investigator should be careful not to associate such fire growth and intensity with an incendiary fire. Fire research, fire investigation, and computer fire modeling have shown that such conditions can develop rapidly within rooms where no accelerant is present.

Fire investigation is a complex science that draws from many other scientific fields. Today's fire investigator has the difficult job of staying current in applicable technologies and applying them to fire scene investigations. This article covers only a small part of this technology. Additional information and training can be obtained from textbooks; seminars; and materials such as NFPA 921, *Guide for Fire and Explosion Investigation,* which is published by the National Fire Protection Association. The National Association for Fire Investigators [(312) 427-6320] produces two training seminars for fire and explosion investigators per year.

Computer-based models

Computer-based fire models, which became available for general use only within the past 10 years, have been widely accepted in the fire safety field for predicting conditions within a room during a fire. Previously, such conditions could be determined only by conducting actual fire tests and measuring the desired parameters. Fire researchers, engineers, and computer programmers developed these models by analyzing large quantities of data obtained through fire tests. Analyses of these tests showed that the various parameters associated with a room fire under specific physical conditions could be predicted and evaluated mathematically. The parameters of greatest interest were those that would assess the survivability chances for an individual in a particular room. These parameters include the temperatures in the room of fire origin and adjacent rooms, the concentration of several products of combustion (carbon monoxide and carbon dioxide, for example), incident radiant flux on objects in the room, and the thickness of the hot layer that forms during a room fire. The models are designed so that these parameters are given at regular time intervals during the modeled fire, making it possible to predict the fire conditions in each specified room at any given time. This information, combined with that known about humans' tolerance levels of fire products, presents a method for assessing survivability.

A variety of computer fire models developed for specific purposes and applications are available. The models most useful to fire investigators are those that specifically model room conditions, generally known as "compartment" models. Some are designed to model a single compartment and others, multiple compartments. An example of a single-compartment model is the FIRST model, one of the earliest models, developed from the Harvard Computer Fire Model. An example of a multiroom model is FAST (Fire And Smoke Transport), which predicts fire and smoke transport in multicompartmented enclosures or structures. Both models are available from the National Institute of Standards and Technology (NIST).[4]

Each model has its limitations, which users must continually keep in mind. Some models, for example, do not handle areas with a high length-to-width ratio, such as corridors or rooms with high ceilings. The danger of misapplication is not that the models will refuse to run but that they will run and generate erroneous results. A basic tenet of fire modeling is "garbage in equals garbage out," a reminder that the user must be careful when selecting input data. Most models will accept any data, right or wrong, and will not warn the user about data that are beyond the capacity of the model. Fire investigators should seriously consider pursuing training in the use and application of computer fire models, since most investigators may find many of the concepts and terminology foreign, which will make independent study difficult at best.

Hazard I and FPETool The NIST-developed HAZARD I computer-based fire model, available through the National Fire Protection Association (NFPA), probably is the "best seller" among fire models.[5] It incorporates the FAST model to perform the fire calculations and generate the results. HAZARD I also contains other models that can be used to predict evacuation times from the room(s) and evaluate tenability within the rooms.

Another fire model gaining in use is FPETool, also developed by the NIST. Because this model, which is actually a collection of models and correlations—some of which are customized to specific applications and others of which can be applied to most fire situations—was developed under contract with the General Services Administration (GSA), it is distributed by the NIST without charge.

One of the models included in FPETool is ASET (Available Safe Egress Time), a room model that can be used to predict the time to the onset of hazardous conditions and the time available for occupants to escape. Also included in the FPETool are correlations (a simple model generally developed directly from experimental data to help predict such things as time to flashover), the quantity of fuel needed to flash over a room, detector activation times, and other tools useful to the fire investigator.

Input data For all these models, the user must input basic data that describe the compartment, the fuel, and the fire. The most important, and usually the most difficult, component of the input data is the heat release rate data for the fuel being considered. [Heat release rate (HRR) is the quantity of energy given off by a fire per unit time and typically is measured in kilowatts (kW)]. The information needed includes a profile of the growing intensity of the fire and the heat release rate as a function of time. The best source for this data is actual burn tests of the fuel involved; the heat release rate is determined from this experimental data. An example would be burning a polyurethane couch in a furniture calorimeter, measuring the weight of the couch as it burns and the quantity of oxygen consumed. The heat release rate can be determined from this data. Since most people do not have access to the equipment needed to conduct these kinds of tests, the next best source of the data is reports and other published material. Often, data related to an item similar to the one being sought will be found and can be used in the model.

Another approach would be to select fire growth curves the investigator knows represent an upper and a lower boundary to possible values. The results obtained will also present a boundary of possible results. This method makes it possible to do sensitivity analyses—the analyses of the effects of the choices on the results. These data use what is referred to as a "t-squared" fire, one that grows exponentially—that is, the heat release rate is a function of the square of the time, t^2. The different input fires range from "ultrafast," such as that involving a pool of gasoline or a pile of thin cardboard boxes, to "slow," such as that involving a fire retardant-treated mattress or a box of books (see Figure 2).

The user supplies the data related to the specifics of the room or rooms being studied, such as the length, width, and height of the room(s); the finish materials of the interior walls, ceilings, and floors; and the size and placement of openings between the rooms. The remainder of the input data needed are physical properties for the specific fuel being considered, including heat of combustion and weight.

Figure 2: A graphical representation of typical fire input data for fire models. Growth rate ranges from ultrafast to slow.

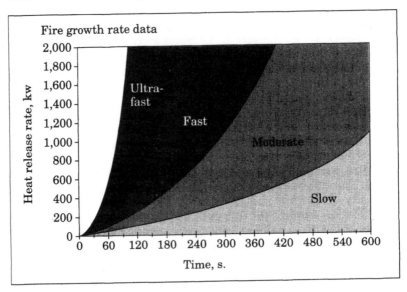

Fire model output   Most fire models yield numerical information, which the individual running the model must organize into a useful form. HAZARD I contains a routine that graphs data such as temperature or oxygen concentration as a function of time. Such a graph makes it possible to see how these variables change through the course of a fire (see Figure 3).

The investigator using computer fire modeling must keep in mind that the model is only a tool and should not be used by it-

Figure 3: Sample output graphs from HAZARD I computer fire model. Shown for three rooms are the upper layer temperature in degrees C, carbon monoxide concentration in parts per million (ppm), fire size in kilowatts, and the layer height in meters.

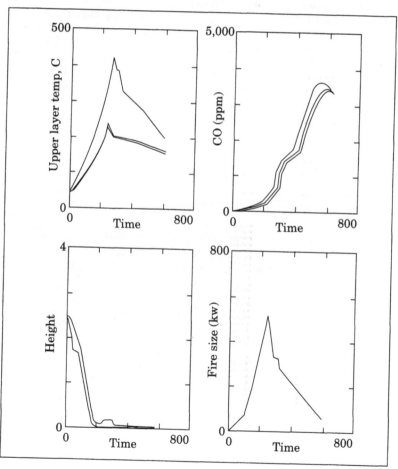

self to make decisions. The model must agree with the evidence, observations, and determinations made at the fire scene—not the other way around. Determining origin and cause are the primary duties of most fire investigators, and computer fire modeling can make these tasks easier and increase investigators' confidence.

Other new tools

Among some other new tools being used by fire investigators are dogs, electronic sniffers, and portable gas chromatographs.

Dogs   Able to detect accelerants, these dogs are trained in a manner similar to dogs used to detect explosives and drugs. They can indicate the location of these materials at a fire scene. California has completed its first certification test of accelerant-detection dogs. This new fire investigation tool may enable investigators to find accelerant evidence in circumstances where it previously would have been impossible. Confronted with a completely burned-out building, also known as a "black hole," it is very difficult to determine where the fire started and the areas from which to take evidence samples. Reports show that accelerant-detection dogs have been able to detect accelerant residues in these "black holes," enabling the investigator to collect samples.

Electronic sniffers   Although they have been around for a while, they have not been used much on the fire scene until recently. They are able to detect small concentrations of many different hydrocarbons and other compounds.

Portable gas chromatographs   They permit on-scene chemical analysis of evidence samples at the fire scene, which may improve the results because the samples are "fresh" and the possibility for contamination is reduced.

Old fire investigation myths

Fortunately, most of the many myths related to fire investigation have gone the way of leather hose and back steps on fire apparatus. However, those that still exist are being used by the ignorant fire investigator who has not kept up with the training and education that are so necessary. NFPA 921, *Manual for Fire and Explosion Investigation,* was written in part to refute these myths and provide the investigator with a credible reference. NFPA 921 discredits the myths by presenting the scientific explanations of the phenomena involved. Most of the myths were started based on observations made after fires. After investigators had ob-

served these phenomena a number of times, they began to associate the observations with their determinations of origin and
cause. These observations in time came to become direct "evidence" of a particular fire cause, and investigators would ignore
indicators that were contrary to this "evidence."

Spalling of concrete One fire investigation myth still widely
held in some circles is that spalling of concrete indicates an incendiary (arson) fire. Spalling is a process wherein pieces or sections of concrete break loose from the floor or walls, leaving
behind shallow craters. The exact mechanism for spalling is not
precisely known, but what is known is that it is a reaction of concrete to heating at its surface. When an ignitable liquid is burned
on a concrete surface, radiant heat energy from the fire plume
may cause the concrete to spall. However, radiant energy from
other fuel sources, such as that from a polyurethane couch or automobile tire burning near a floor, also may cause the concrete to
spall. The radiant energy produced after flashover may be intense enough to cause spalling.

The fire investigator, when confronted with spalling, must
consider the kinds of fuels that were available in the areas and
the intensity of the fire. For spalling to be determined an indica-
tor of accelerant use, the fire investigator must establish that one
was actually present and, if so, that it was intentionally used to
start the fire. The investigator should take fire-scene samples
from the area where spalling occurred and from other areas as
well to determine through laboratory analysis that these ignitable liquids were present. In many cases, ignitable liquids can
be present at fire scenes for very normal reasons. Gasoline
residue in a garage, for example, should be expected. Determining that a fire was incendiary solely on the basis of spalled concrete is totally invalid and will not hold up under scrutiny.

Depth of char A fire investigation myth that has been fading
is that the depth of char on a piece of wood found at a fire scene
indicates how long that wood has burned and the location at
which the fire burned the longest is the site of the fire's origin.
Fire research and testing have shown, however, that the burning
rate of wood is highly variable and depends on many factors,
such as moisture content, wood type, wood finish, fire ventilation, and radiant exposure of the wood.

Color of flames and smoke In the days of wool and cotton
furniture, the color of smoke generated from fires that originated
in these furnishing was a little more gray than black. During
those times, black smoke with yellowish flames at a fire scene

was one of the indications of an incendiary fire, and an investigator would ask witnesses and firefighters at the scene whether they saw black smoke with yellowish flames. Today, however, a great deal of the furnishings in residences and businesses are made of polymers (plastics) derived from the same hydrocarbon raw materials found in gasoline. When these materials burn, they give off very black smoke and their flames tend to be yellowish. Observing these factors at a fire today, therefore, provides the fire investigator with little or no information related to the fire's cause. Yet, some investigators still ask, "What color was the smoke?"

Low burning   This myth holds that because a fire generally burns upward, the lowest point of burning is the site of the fire's origin. The problem with this myth and misapplication of fire dynamics is that low burning may result from other causes. In many cases, for example, fire spreads downward due to natural and expected causes such as the falling of burning material from above, melting and dripping of burning plastics, radiant ignition of materials, and effects of ventilation. The fire investigator should consider all these patterns in the room under investigation—not rely on just one—before determining the fire's site of origin.

Multiple origins   According to this myth, establishing that there were multiple and unrelated points of origin proved the fire was incendiary. The fire investigator should understand that nonincendiary fires can produce patterns that may give the appearance that there were multiple points of origin. Cursory examination of or reliance on other myths such as low burning or spalling concrete may indicate that there were multiple origins and prompt the investigator to make an incendiary determination. A careful examination of all of the patterns and correctly attributing them to their sources often reveals that there was only one point of origin. At this point, careful investigation must rule out all accidental fire causes, and evidence that may support the cause determination must be collected. It is inadequate to make an incendiary determination based only on origin determination. A careful origin determination that does not rely on myths or invalid assumptions may reveal multiple points of origin. If the investigator has ruled out nonincendiary reasons for these patterns, then the possibility that the fire had multiple points of origin because it was an incendiary fire should be considered, and the investigator should proceed with the cause determination at each of these points.

The future

Fire investigation is changing more now than ever before. Much of the art is being replaced by science. The myths are steadily dying, some faster than others. New tools will help the fire investigator to do a more accurate job. The ultimate purpose of fire investigation is not to determine origin and cause but to reduce and eliminate death, injury, and destruction of property caused by fire. When we fully understand how and why fires start, only then can we take steps to prevent them from happening again. Better fire investigation done by competent and properly trained fire investigators will result in fewer fires.

1. A *self-sustaining* fire will continue to burn without outside influence. Some fuels will ignite and burn in the presence of a heat source but will self-extinguish if the heat source is removed.
2. The explosion usually is a deflagration, which is characterized by slower reaction and pressure front speeds than a detonation.
3. *Ignitable liquid* is used here to indicate a flammable or combustible liquid that is capable of being ignited. If the liquid has a flash point at or below room temperature, then vapors from the liquid can be present in sufficient quantity to be ignited.
4. The NIST can provide ready-to-use fire models with supporting documentation. The Building and Fire Research Laboratory (BFRL) at the NIST is a government research facility dedicated to providing help to the fire service, fire protection, and fire investigators. To learn more about the NIST, write to NIST, Building and Fire Research Laboratory, Gaithersburg, MD 20899; (301) 975-6850.
5. Contact the NFPA at 1 Batterymarch Park; Quincy, MA 02269; (617) 770-3000.

Child and Juvenile Firesetters

Jessica Gaynor
and Daniel Stern

David likes to play with his mother's cigarette lighter. Every day he watches the flame burn. David's mother noticed burn marks on the carpet underneath David's bed and on some of the furniture in his bedroom. She became fearful and insisted that David light matches in front of her or light her cigarettes, after which she would yell at him and spank him. Two days after one of these incidents, while David was trying to burn his mother's bed, the flame from the lighter lashed out at him causing first degree burns over 90% of his hands and arms. David is five years old.

David is one of the approximately 4,000 children injured annually in the United States as a result of fireplay. Of every 100 people who die each year in child-set fires, 85 are children. Playing with fire is the leading cause of death for preschoolers in the United States and the second leading cause of accidental death for five to 14-year-olds. The tragedy is that fire experts at the United States Fire Administration estimate that for every 10 fires set, eight are preventable.

Who are these children who play with fire? Why are children at such high risk for fire injury or death inflicted by their own hand? How widespread is this problem? And what, if anything, can we do to help them before they hurt themselves or others?

This article explores the psychological profiles and high risk level for child and adolescent self-inflicted fire injury and death and methods of clinical intervention.

Adapted from Jessica Gaynor and Daniel Stern, "Child and Juvenile Firesetters: Examining Their Psychological Profiles," *Firehouse* (September 1993) and "Juvenile Firesetters: Part II: Effective Intervention," *Firehouse* (October 1993). Reprinted with permission of *Firehouse* magazine.

Psychological profiles

The U.S. Fire Administration's Juvenile Firesetter Programs estimate that about half of child-set fires are the result of single-episode, careless or accidental fireplay activity. Children involved in this type of firestarting are typically young boys between the ages of five and nine, most of whom express remorse for their firesetting. Short-term educational intervention has been demonstrated to be effective in preventing the recurrence of firestarting behavior in these youngsters.

Children involved in repetitive, deliberate firesetting are responsible for about one-third of juvenile fires. Recurrent firesetters can be divided into two major age groups: younger children, averaging eight years; and adolescents 13 years and older. There are specific psychological features which distinguish these two classes of firesetters.

Young firesetters   Research confirms a definite psychological profile for young firesetting children. They are mostly boys coming from mixed socioeconomic backgrounds, ranging in age from as young as three through preadolescence. They have a greater number of physical illnesses, with many of them reporting histories of sexual abuse. They are of average intelligence, with a large number having learning disabilities. Emotionally, they experience overwhelming feelings of anger and aggression coupled with an inability to express these emotions in socially acceptable ways. Their general behavior is characterized as overactive, impulsive and mischievous, and they are prone to temper outbursts which frequently result in the destruction of physical objects or personal property.

Socially, these children are isolated, detached and alone. They have poor academic as well as behavioral records at school. They come from single-parent homes, where the father is absent. If both parents live in the same house, there tends to be a high degree of marital discord, with an overprotective mother and a father who administers harsh methods of punishment. One or more family members also may carry a psychiatric diagnosis, with the most common being alcoholism.

Environment can play a significant role in reinforcing the firesetting behavior of young children. When specific environmental stressors occur, such as a recent divorce or geographic move, they trigger emotional reactions in these children which lead to firesetting. Firesetting releases feelings of anger or resentment which are lying just below the surface. These children frequently set fires in and around their homes, often igniting a room or object that is associated with the source of their feelings. They set their fires alone, and they immediately run from the scene without intending to extinguish the fire. They may, however, return to the fire shortly after ignition or within several hours, either to watch the fire burn or to view the damage. If the behavior of firesetting remains undetected, it becomes a positively reinforcing event in the lives of these children because it serves to satisfy their emotional conflict.

Firesetting adolescents   The profile of firesetting adolescents is different from firesetting children primarily because they are at different phases of psychological growth and development. It is 10 times more common for adolescent boys than girls to firestart. The majority of these boys are white and range in age from 13 to 15. They have a higher than average number of accidents resulting in physical injury and they demonstrate higher levels of risk-taking behavior. In addition, these boys experience sexual and gender conflicts and are frequently involved in sexual misbehavior. They are angry, defiant and lacking in emotional depth and display clinical features consistent with antisocial and delinquent personality patterns.

The home and school environments of these adolescents are troubled. A significant number of these boys have histories of physical abuse and come from homes where physical violence is common. They often are disruptive in class and engage in fights with their peers. They have long histories of behavioral and academic failures, including expulsion from more than one school setting. These boys have experienced violence, abuse and failure early in their lives.

As with the behavior of normal adolescents, peer group activity greatly influences the behavior of firesetting adolescents. Adolescent firesetting is done in small groups, in which firestarting frequently is accompanied by other antisocial behaviors. These boys typically engage in alcohol or other drug use just prior to a firestart, and they may participate in activities such as petty theft or vandalism during or after firesetting. Once they set the fire, they will not attempt to extinguish it or go for help. They may feel excitement, pleasure and defiance at watching the fire burn. They rarely show remorse or guilt for their actions. For many adolescents, firesetting is their first successful criminal activity which becomes socially reinforced because they have gained attention, acceptance and recognition from their peer group.

During the last decade, the U.S. Fire Administration has taken a leadership role in designing and implementing an early warning system to identify those youngsters who are at significant risk for becoming involved in fireplay, firesetting and arson-related activities. This early warning system was developed by a multidisciplinary team of professionals from the fire service, medical and mental health field, the schools, law enforcement and juvenile justice. It consists of an interview and evaluation package designed to assess the level of risk or severity of firesetting behavior in youngsters and their families. Documented in a three volume series entitled, *Juvenile Firesetter Handbooks,* it is the most widely accepted system utilized by fire departments for evaluating the risk level of juvenile firesetters.

There are three levels of designated risk—little, definite and extreme—each representing successively more severe degrees of firesetting. From interview questions and a brief written questionnaire, using children and their parents as informants, data is gathered regarding family history, the child's physical and psychological make-up and previous and current firesetting incidents. The little risk level represents children who have set one or two fires out of experimentation or curiosity; the definite risk level describes children who have been involved in repeated firesetting episodes that may reflect underlying psychological conflicts. The extreme risk level designates youngsters whose repeated firesetting is a signal of serious behavioral or emotional disturbances. This system of identification and classification is an important screening tool for fire departments because not only does it enable them to identify high risk youngsters and their families, but it also allows them to triage these families to a variety of intervention programs tailored to meet their specific needs.

Conclusion

Child and adolescent firesetters have two different personality profiles. In addition to their psychological profiles, they can be classified according to their risk of setting fires. Low risk youngsters involved in single episode fireplay incidents must be evaluated and educated with respect to the dangers of firestarting. Utilizing the U.S. Fire Administration's *Juvenile Firesetter Handbooks,* fire departments can provide front-line evaluation and education services to their community. It is urgent that high risk firesetters and their families be identified, evaluated and given access to mental health interventions designed to control firestarting and adjust underlying psychological conflicts.

Intervention

The problem of juvenile firesetting extends to all types of children, from young, healthy pre-schoolers to disturbed adolescents. The U.S. Fire Administration's Juvenile Firesetter Programs show that the greater percentage of fires are set by young children in the five to nine age group. In addition, these programs indicate that five- and six-year-olds may not be capable of understanding the concept that a single match can destroy a house. Therefore, not only do young children represent the highest risk group with respect to their involvement in firestarting, but they also are the most likely victims of fire injury and death.

A significant number of elementary school children are involved in unsupervised fireplay. It is estimated that 40% to 60% of these school children have participated in at least one unsupervised firestart, while 58% to 77% have witnessed an incident and at least 75% have known someone who played with matches. Luckily, less than 3% of these fireplay incidents require fire department intervention.

Approximately 2% of children carrying a psychiatric diagnosis present with the primary problem of firesetting. The most frequently occurring psychiatric diagnosis for these children is Conduct Disorder. This diagnosis is characterized by a persistent pattern of behavior that either violates the rights of others or breaks societal laws. Unlike elementary school children who may be involved in only one or two unsupervised firestarts, psychiatric patients are more likely to be involved in several incidents of firesetting behavior. In addition, the fires set by children with psychiatric diagnoses are more likely to cause serious damage requiring firefighter suppression.

Approaches   There are three general intervention approaches aimed at reducing the number of youngsters involved in firesetting. They are primary prevention, early intervention and core intervention.

Primary prevention   Primary prevention programs are designed to communicate fire safety and survival skills to children. They operate under the assumption that fire interest is a natural curiosity which emerges in most youngsters as early as three years of age. Prevention programs teach children how to master and control their curiosity through learning the rules of fire safety. Schools and the fire service are the predominant community agencies involved in primary prevention. There are several excellent school-based programs, targeting the entire age range from pre-schoolers to adolescents. In addition, the fire service offers a variety of prevention approaches, from national media campaigns to resources on how to operate local fire education programs. If prevention programs are successful, the majority of children will develop the necessary knowledge and skills to demonstrate competent fire safety behavior.

Early intervention   Early intervention programs represent the most recent and innovative attempt to combat the problem of juvenile firesetting. The goal of these early intervention programs is to identify children and families at risk and to help them access services designed to eliminate problematic firesetting behavior and prevent its recurrence.

The U.S. Fire Administration has assumed the major leadership role in developing these programs for juvenile firesetters. The most widely implemented early intervention program model is one in which fire departments offer three types of services: screening and evaluation; fire safety and education and referral. Typically, youngsters and their families will be interviewed and assigned a level of firesetting risk. If there is little risk, they will be asked to participate in a brief fire education program designed to prevent further fireplay. If there is definite or extreme risk, youngsters and their families will be referred to additional intervention services, which may include medical or mental health, social services, law enforcement or juvenile justice.

Early intervention is the cornerstone of the National Juvenile Firesetter/Arson Control and Prevention Program cosponsored by the U.S. Fire Administration and the Office of Juvenile Justice and Delinquency Prevention. The Institute for Social Analysis, in collaboration with The Police Executive Research Forum, designed a national effort to help communities develop and implement effective intervention services for juvenile firesetters. The centerpiece of this program is a compendium of training and technical assistance materials intended to help local jurisdictions select, design and operate their own juvenile firesetter and arson prevention program. These materials, collected in a series of manuals, entitled *The National Juvenile Firesetter/Arson Control and Prevention Program* are available from the Juvenile Justice Clearing House and offer a comprehensive guide to building effective community intervention programs for juvenile firesetters.

Core intervention Core intervention programs are the direct services designed to stop recurrent firesetting and help adjust the underlying psychological conflicts. Mental health programs utilizing individual and family psychotherapy are the primary core intervention approaches. Cognitive-emotion and behavior therapy are the most highly developed individual psychotherapies used in the treatment of juvenile firesetting.

The major goal of cognitive-emotion psychotherapy is to teach youngsters how to recognize their urge to firestart, interrupt their behavior before it starts and substitute socially appropriate types of behavior. The primary therapeutic mechanism is the construction of a written graph by youngsters, with help from their parents and their therapist. Both the feelings and the specific events leading up to and following the most recent firestart are graphed. The assumption of this graphing technique is that there is a typical pattern of feelings which accompany the urge to firestart. Youngsters can be taught to recognize these feelings, and they also can be taught not to act on them. Instead, they are taught to substitute alternative, socially appropriate behaviors.

Behavior therapy techniques also are effective in treating firesetting youngsters. Most of the behavioral methods, such as punishment, negative practice and satiation, employ the use of threats or aversive consequences to eliminate firestarting. Critical to this type of treatment approach is the cooperation of parents in helping to carry out specific exercises in the home utilizing these various procedures. In a relatively short amount of time, normally six to twelve sessions, behavior therapy methods can stop as well as prevent the recurrence of firesetting behavior.

Family psychotherapy has been successful in the treatment of firesetting behavior. While one objective is to stop firesetting, the primary therapeutic goal is the restructuring of family communication and interaction patterns. The premise is that if the dysfunctional patterns of relationships within the family are corrected, then overt symptoms, such as firesetting, will diminish.

Although outpatient psychotherapy is the treatment of choice for the majority of firesetting youngsters and their families, if clinical evaluation reveals the presence of severe psychopathology, an untenable home or family environment, or if a child is considered to be a significant danger to themselves or others, then inpatient or residential intervention must be considered.

There are two types or therapeutic philosophies which drive inpatient treatment programs. The first is a more traditional psychodynamic approach where the treatment emphasis is on the nature of the therapeutic alliance formed between youngsters and program staff. Both individual and family psychotherapy are employed, and the treatment program is long-term, ranging from six months to two years. The second approach is behavioral, where specific behaviors are identified for change, and discrete interventions are designed to adjust these behaviors. The firesetting youngsters are the primary focus of the behavior change methods, with parents and family members included in the therapy once the firesetting behavior has been eliminated. Behavior therapy programs are relatively short-term, lasting from four to eight weeks, and are currently the most widely offered inpatient treatment for firesetting youngsters.

Conclusion

Selecting the best intervention strategy depends primarily on the nature of the firesetting problem. All children can benefit from primary prevention efforts. The U.S. Fire Administration offers a variety of approaches which are presented in their publication, *Public Fire Education Today.* The cooperative effort between the U.S. Fire Administration and the Office of Juvenile Justice and Delinquency has produced an integrated community approach, documented in the National Juvenile Firesetter/Arson and Control and Prevention Program manuals, which provides guidelines for establishing an effective service delivery system for juvenile firesetters. However, the essential element in treating serious firesetting behavior in youngsters is the availability of mental health programs designed to adjust the underlying psychological conflicts and social conditions which so often accompany firesetting. Identifying the best fit between the nature of the firesetting problem and an effective intervention approach is the key to the successful elimination of juvenile firesetting behavior.

PART 3

Improving Firefighter Safety and Training

Perspectives on Training

George Oster

There's safety in training, not in numbers. For some time now, this simple sentence has fueled a fire so intense that none of us has been able to knock it down: "Fire officers should not begin structural fire attack until a minimum number of firefighters are on the scene."

Sides have been taken. Gauntlets thrown. Stands assumed. Some would apply standards to uncontrolled fires while others specify simple numbers. Still others oppose minimum staffing altogether.

From a review of the yearly fatality reports, it's clear that firefighters are not killed because there aren't enough of them on the fireground, but because the ones who *are* there haven't had proper physical conditioning or fireground training. These problems will not be overcome by the sheer application of mass. Said quite bluntly, firefighters die most often not because there are too few, but because they are out of shape or because someone screws up.

Wellness

This poses a couple of issues for the trainer: firefighter wellness and the application of training principles and techniques to the fireground.

There has been much discussion regarding firefighter fitness. This emphasis on "fitness" has generally highlighted only physi-

---

Adapted from George Oster, "Training Perspectives," *Fire Chief* (January 1994). Reprinted with permission of *Fire Chief* magazine.

cal conditioning aspects. Some discussion has drifted into a debate of validity, an examination of whether physical tests mirror actual physical exertion on the fireground. Others have hyped the "challenge" or competition-type activities, which often encourage less-fit individuals to overexert themselves.

Truly physically conditioned firefighters and officers are those who have prepared themselves through a total wellness program. The five principles of wellness encompass important aspects of a person's complete being: fitness, exercise, nutrition, stress management and biomechanics.

Most importantly, a total wellness approach helps ensure physically conditioned fire officers and firefighters who are prepared to face the challenges of the emergency scene.

Training

The application of training to the fireground has also been skewed by the minimum-staffing controversy. Some would advocate applying training standards to the fireground. In particular, NFPA 1403, *Live Fire Training Evolutions in Structures,* has been suggested.

But automatically applying training standards ignores one of the prime objectives of those standards and of training itself—the development of firefighters and fire officers who can make reasoned judgments.

Training, based on standards, should prepare officers to evaluate fire in terms of existing resources and the resources required to neutralize it, or defend it if resources are inadequate. It prepares the officer to make decisions. It shouldn't make the decisions for the officer.

Much of the debate about minimum staffing, which ignores the on-scene officer's responsibility to make judgments, reminds me of the fire chief who read the latest research concerning use of fog nozzles to attack fires. The research indicated that 30° fog was the most effective pattern for many applications. "Good enough for me," thought the chief, who immediately ordered his mechanic to weld all fog nozzles to a 30° angle!

This, of course, removed any possibility of the nozzle operator or the officer in charge making any error in judgment when attacking the fire, because it prevented them from making any judgment at all.

By the way, that was 1955.

Will applying training standards or minimum staffing to the fireground "weld" fire officers in place, removing their decision-making authority and responsibility? Are we back in 1955, or have we never left?

Developing good judgment

There are some very effective ways to train firefighters and officers to make good decisions on the fireground.

At the firefighter level, a relatively new concept is "training in context," developed at the Montana State University's Fire Training School. When using TIC, the entire context of an evolution is taught, from donning protective clothing and response, to skill application and post-application routines. Rather than learning one skill at a time, the firefighter learns each task as part of an entire, structured process and is much better able to make decisions on the fireground.

Boone County (Mo.) Fire District has been using TIC for the last two years. Fireground crews don't have to worry about the "little decisions," such as which line to pull or tool to carry. These little decisions have been made on the training ground and are performed automatically on the emergency scene.

This frees up the crews to concentrate on the more important tactical decisions, such as how to safely approach the fire, where to attack and when to ventilate. In Boone County, the result has been better decisions made on the fireground.

At the officer end of the spectrum, the Executive Fire Officer Program at the National Fire Academy helps officers learn the best ways to gather data, synthesize it and draw conclusions. This lays the groundwork for the officer who must evaluate an emergency scene and available resources, and make decisions based on those evaluations.

Accountability and liability

I offer a caveat to all fire department trainers and others who read these words. There are two other interrelated issues often encountered in the fire service today: accountability and liability.

Actually, my definition of accountability and liability are the same—both mean taking responsibility for our actions. The difference is that when you're talking about accountability, you're in the stationhouse. When you're talking in terms of liability, you're in the courthouse.

Accountability or liability, or both, often drive behavior, particularly on the fireground. They both imply greater responsibility, which most people want, to a certain extent. I have seen fire officers hiding behind SOPs, standards and requirements when simple evaluation, judgment and action was all that was needed—because they knew they would be held accountable, and maybe liable, if they made a mistake.

An innovative fire chief and department in Iowa have taken a clue from the latest computer application, fuzzy logic. Fuzzy logic does not program a computer to control, say, your refrigerator's cooling cycle by a strict schedule based solely on temperature. Rather, the computer learns from the pattern of cooling needs, door openings and other data it gathers, and cools the refrigerator more efficiently.

This innovative department is using what I call "fuzzy procedures." These fuzzy procedures are general operating guidelines for various fire department duties. They allow officers to make decisions based on their evaluation of the event, the needs compared to the resources and the expected outcomes.

Of course, the chief expects that the officers will make decisions using their good judgment. Empowering officers on the scene to make decisions based on resources, needs and allocations is critical.

One image I conjure when thinking about applying training standards to an uncontrolled fire, or not preparing and empowering fire officers to make reasoned judgments, is an engine company reporting arrival, establishing command, setting up—and then watching the building burn! This may not be so far removed with minimum staffing.

In summary, here is a training perspective for the minimum-staffing issue. The trainer should remember:

- Firefighters die because they are not physically fit or trained well enough to be on the fireground, not because staffing is inadequate. The sheer application of mass won't prevent firefighter fatalities.
- Assuming they are trained to do so, fire officers and firefighters must have the authority to call the shots on the fireground. This power implies accountability for judgments and actions.
- Minimum staffing offers a new opportunity for firefighters and officers to use their evaluation and decision-making abilities: They will have to balance the resources required and the resources available on the scene to do the best job possible.

Training in Context

Brian Crandell

Under stress, firefighters will perform as they learned. Based on this premise, the training environment should re-create the context and content of the environment in which firefighters are expected to perform. This is what training in context does.

Training in context involves training in tactical or strategic wholes, not in parts, by re-creating operational conditions as closely as possible. In fact, it has been called "on-the-job training without the risk."

Another way to explain it is that training in context is "tactical training," not "topical training." The skills to be taught are done in logical sequences, the way they would be encountered during fireground operations.

Training in context does not have to be adopted all at once, or for everything at once. Organizations that have made training in context work for them have done so by taking a chance initially.

Any one of its elements can be tried out by itself. If it works for you, when the time is right, try another element.

If you were the learner, what would you consider the ideal conditions under which to learn something new?

- A training setting just like the environment you'll experience on the job.
- Clear expectations of what to do and how to do it.
- Lots of practice with an experienced instructor right beside

Adapted from Brian Crandell, "Training in Context: Tactical Training in Tactical Settings," *Fire Chief* (March 1993). Reprinted with permission of *Fire Chief* magazine.

you to coach you and make sure you don't fall into bad habits you'll both have to fix later.

Training in context includes all of these elements. Any skill, whether psychomotor (pulling hose, for example) or cognitive/affective (the customer service approach), will be learned more effectively and efficiently if it is learned in context.

What is a good place to start? Say the training goal is the evolutions for car fires. One way is to have separate evolutions, not necessarily in this order, covering: donning personal protective equipment, mounting and riding apparatus safely, donning SCBA and activating PASS device, locating and deploying tools and hoselines, deploying as a team, operating nozzles and hand tools, forcing entry into a passenger compartment or under the hood, fire attack, overhaul, repacking hose, cleaning and checking hand tools, changing SCBA tanks, rehab, and cleaning and checking turnout gear.

All these skills, which will be performed in a set, logical sequence on the fireground, could instead be combined in a single basic exercise. The exercise's central prop could be an old car, maybe one already cut up from extrication practice, with several straw bales inside.

The exercise would begin with the learners donning their PPE, mounting and riding the apparatus (maybe just once around the training grounds), and going through each of the steps in sequence, though obviously at something less than full speed, depending on their skill level.

Once they had mastered the car exercise, the next evolution might be an interior structural attack. This would reinforce almost all of the skills from the first exercise, and it would add several more skills, such as staying oriented inside a building, maneuvering hose lines through doorways and pulling ceilings.

The next exercise might have a patient in the building, instead of or in addition to the fire. This adds primary search skills, while again reinforcing everything from donning PPE to rehab.

Montana's Fire Training School uses a training-in-context system with four major components:

1. Clearly defined operations that describe the activities delivered by the organization. A clearly defined body of knowledge gives learners a performance goal to work toward.
2. A training environment that consists primarily of coaching learners while they look at the activity and then perform repetitions of it.
3. A coaching methodology designed to support the learners' performance and personal growth.

4. Identification of learner behaviors that contribute to an effective learning experience.

These four components mirror the three points above, about the ideal conditions in which to learn. This system uses "clearly defined operations," for example, to define for learners what and how they are expected to perform.

Clearly defined operations

Operations are defined in terms of the organization's values, the community's service needs and what firefighters know works. Run and incident histories are good sources for determining what types of activities the organization carries out regularly and thus what skills members need to provide those activities.

Preparing members for all service needs is a difficult process at best. Defining operations attempts to concentrate on those skills needed to meet highly critical, frequently occurring service needs. "Critical" here includes anything that affects firefighter safety.

The skills required for these core service needs will often meet the skill needs of more unusual service demands. Solid training in the basics, applied creatively by members, is the foundation from which unusual service needs are met.

The issues are "How frequent is an operation, regardless of how critical it is," and "How critical is an operation, regardless of how frequent or infrequent." To return to the example above, if personnel can fight a care fire, they can handle a lawnmower fire.

As part of the training-in-context approach, defined operations include tasks that occur prior to the focal task set of a tactic and those that immediately follow the focal task set.

If the tactic is roof ventilation, for example, the focal task set would be cutting the hole in the roof. The defined operation would include every step from responding from the station, through placing the ladder, sounding the roof and cutting the hole, to safely exiting the roof.

And because of the way it defines where a training operation begins and ends, training in context gives continual support to those skills that should be essentially automatic, such as donning PPE and SCBA.

The operations being taught should be fail-safe in outcome. Fail-safe means that if the incident turns into a worst-case scenario, the operational system performs safely with few or no changes needed.

For example, if people are trained to always don SCBA, they will be spending a small amount of time that might not always be necessary. They will, however, also be protecting themselves, and the overall operation, in case the incident turns out to be more serious than usual.

Training and operating in a fail-safe manner means taking "extra" steps when you have time, so you don't have to take extra steps when you don't have time. This way, every routine incident becomes practice for the big one.

Operations that are defined so as to never underestimate a situation are winners, and so are the firefighters at the incident, and so is the public.

The training structure

The training-in-context structure is based in large part on recreating the elements of an operational environment and providing lots of coached practice in that environment. The training environment, including the setting, people, procedures and equipment, should be as close a recreation as possible of the setting before, during and after the service is delivered.

Fire service instructors should act as if training and performance at incidents were identical. For example, firefighters should be trained on pumps by actually driving and operating a pumper. Ladder raises should be taught using the same number of crew members that will perform them during operations.

In addition, the environment for training in context should include only one variable member group. If a training program's goal is to train crew members, all other personnel involved in the activity should be able to perform the defined operation to standard.

Specifically, new crew members should work with crew leaders (company officers), driver/operators and command officers who perform to standard. Competent personnel in these roles are a major part of recreating the operating environment as you want it to occur at incidents. These personnel do not directly assist the coaches, other than by competently performing their jobs.

With other members not performing to standard, new crew members may see a skill incorrectly performed. Any exposure of a new member to the incorrect performance of a skill results in additional training effort to correct any mislearning that may take place.

The operations developed from defining services should be arranged as they occur tactically, not topically, as in the car fire example given earlier. A curriculum should take advantage of the cumulative effect of past learning as the foundation of new learning, as in the transition from the car fire exercise to interior attack.

Building on past learning this way helps members view new learning as supported, achievable and sensible.

The coach-to-member ratio varies with member need. When a member's performance requires repeated coaching of the same quality indicators, the coach can effectively work with only one member.

"Quality indicators" define time and correct procedure. A common training objective is "Don an SCBA," while a QI would be to complete the donning in 60 seconds. Within that time, the member would meet at least four more QIs:

- have all straps and buckles attached per the manufacturer's instructions,
- perform a five-second seal check,
- have no exposed skin between the hood and mask, and
- have his or her helmet back on snugly.

When members are making progress toward standard, a coach can effectively coach two members (firefighters). A coach can coach three members when they are near or to standard, such as during in-service training.

Crews should be composed of members at a similar skill level. Crew members thus start at roughly the same place and are ready for the same material at roughly the same time.

During a training session, a strong sense of community (identity, mutual support, respect, trust, understanding) generally evolves among the members of a crew and between them and their coach. This sense is significantly enhanced by leaving crew composition and coach assignment intact (assuming appropriate skill development) for the duration of the training.

Once the members' performance meets the standard, mixing crew members is acceptable. In organizations where crew composition will vary, mixing members who have met the standard is desirable.

Several steps are used in training in context.

1. *Explanation* of the operation, while providing members with a *vision* of the tactic being performed excellently.
2. *Perfect process practice* with coaching.
3. *Rehabilitation,* including pre- and post-performance mental rehearsals.

Vision with explanation   The vision provides members with a picture to imitate, a clear picture of the operation as performed to standard. The emphasis should be on:

1. The tactic's objective.
2. Task activity that makes up the tactic.
3. Safety issues, such as paying close attention to footing when ventilating a pitched roof.

The vision may be shown through a video or an actual performance to standard. Of the two, video provides a higher degree of consistency, increases the ability to reproduce all or selected parts of the vision and reduces time between visions.

If an actual performance is used, it should be performed by personnel who meet the standard, in an environment closely recreating one likely to be found surrounding the same service in the real world.

Members should be grouped by role and provided with a coach who will interpret and highlight parts of the tactic and/or skill. As the vision is presented, members should focus on the role they will play in performing the tactic.

Coaches should alert members to a few important activities to watch during the vision (for example, crew integrity, radio at the crew leader's ear, sounding the roof, rolling a rafter with the saw, and so forth).

The vision should be repeated as often as necessary, to reinforce lessons and communicate expectations. A highly effective method is to present a vision, then have members practice the same sequence. When the vision is presented again (a process we call "reflection"), members will see more than they did the first time, because they are much more familiar with the operation and aren't overwhelmed with details.

It is important that the participants begin the next step, perfect process practice, with a clear vision of performance to standard and a high degree of awareness of their role as members of the crew.

Perfect process practice

"Practice doesn't make perfect, perfect practice makes perfect."
Vince Lombardi

"Perfect process practice" means that the member meets all sequence and technical skills quality indicators with or without the assistance of a coach, in whatever time is necessary to complete the tactic. Perfect process practice is the method used to help members reach the standard.

"Perfect product practice" means that the member meets all sequence and technical skills quality indicators, without a coach's assistance, in the time the standard calls for. Perfect product practice is a training system's desired outcome.

The major portion of learning occurs during the coached repetitions of perfect process practice. The primary element of perfect process practice is the correct performance (sequentially and technically, but not time standard) of a complete tactic.

The coach provides immediate corrective feedback in a positive and supportive manner. Members are stopped as soon as the coach recognizes an error. The member should physically, emotionally and mentally recover from the error or setback and continue with the tactic. Recovery from tactical and strategic setbacks is a critical part of doing everything right (surviving) when everything is going wrong.

The crew's performance ability should determine the number of reps they attempt. Crews should continue to perform a tactic until an error-free performance occurs.

Experience indicates that about seven reps are necessary for a crew to meet a performance standard. Early reps may take as long as 10 times the standard time to complete.

When members switch firefighter position assignments within the same crew, experience indicates that another five reps are necessary to bring the members with new assignments to standard.

Coaches should move to the next tactic as soon as a crew meets standard. When a crew develops a level of frustration that blocks further progress on a tactic, coaches may wish to move to another tactic temporarily and return to the initial tactic later.

Perfect process practice involves executions of a complete tactic. There are three types of perfect process practice repetitions, used in the order given:

1. Practice for sequence   The purpose of practice for sequence is to give members an opportunity to learn the activity sequence of the parts of the tactic and the operational relationships (IC, driver/operator, etc.) affecting the tactic. During practice for sequence, members, as a crew, literally walk through the physical movements of the tactic and talk through the cues supporting the task parts. Practice for sequence is performed as a crew, but off the prop, and without PPE or SCBA.

The members and the coach provide corrections as needed to assure perfect process practice. Members should take as much time to complete the practice for sequence as necessary to perform a tactic's sequence correctly. Experience indicates that on average two repetitions of practice for sequence are needed.

When members have demonstrated the tactic in the correct sequence, continue with practice for technical skills.

2. Practice for technical skills   Practice for technical skills builds on the foundation of correct sequence. It focuses on technical competence developed within the framework of correct sequence. As member and crew competence increase, speed should also increase, but members and crews should increase speed only when correct sequence and technique are demonstrated.

Practice for technical skills should be performed in context, and coaching should occur as often as member skill requires.

3. Practice for standard   When members perform all technical skills correctly, in the proper sequence, the time to complete the tactic should approach the standard time. Practice for standard is accomplished when all sequence and technical skill quality indicators are met, no coaching is necessary, and the time meets the standard (perfect product practice).

Members should be encouraged to recognize that frequent practice is necessary to retain tactical skills for *on-demand, to-standard* performance. If the members can perform the sequence and technical skills correctly, but do not meet the time standard, coaches may ask the members to add some zip (*safe* zip) to their next performance.

Making apparatus available is an operationally driven outcome to all tactics. Crews should be assigned to making their apparatus available prior to being sent to rehab (with the exception of cases of extreme exertion, sensed by the coach or reported by the crew).

Rehabilitation   Coaches and members should remember that participants performing physically demanding tactics in context are subject to considerable physical stress. Safe performance requires adequate rest and rehydration following activity.

The amount of rehab necessary to assure recovery varies with the type and amount of activity in which the member engages. Experience indicates that practice for sequence requires about 10 minutes of rehab for 50 minutes of activity.

The amount of rehab time necessary will increase as member performance approaches standard, because the physical demands are becoming more severe. Activity to standard generally requires rehab time at least equal to the time used during the activity.

Coaches and crew leaders should remain sensitive to the crew members' rehab needs and requests. Members are encouraged to be aware of their rehab needs and communicate them to their crew leader and coach.

There is an increased level of awareness among athletes and the medical community of the need to remain adequately hydrated during physically demanding activity. Members are encouraged to take as much fluid as they are comfortable taking during each rest period. Cool and cold weather activity requires special attention to hydration maintenance, as felt thirst is generally less than during similar exertion in warm weather.

Rehab periods can be used effectively to enhance member performance through the development and application of six psychological skills:

- Positive mental attitude.
- Goal-setting (achievable, adaptive, positive performance).
- Positive affirmations.
- Stress control, through breathing and visualizations.
- Mental rehearsals, using a crew-based, internal perspective.
- Mental conditioning (situational awareness, predetermined responses to significant circumstances).

Each skill is used as a foundation from which each member may choose to build more psychological skills. The psychological skills are important, simple areas addressed consistently during the instruction.

The first enhancement technique is the use of relaxation exercises and mental rehearsals. Rehabilitation is more effective when members are relaxed. Mental rehearsals reinforce past learning, prepare members for future reps and build awareness and confidence.

Relaxation and mental rehearsals are only effective when members want them to be effective. Coaches are encouraged to become fluent in these techniques and educate members about their benefits before asking members to try them.

Mental rehearsals are only slightly less effective than actual physical performance of skills. They are very effective coaching tools, considering that they do not generate physical stress and take less time to complete.

Macros   During rehab and other periods when time is available, coaches may find the use of information "macros" useful. Macros fill in many of the "Whys?" members ask during tactical drills.

Since training in context does not necessarily include lecture as a separate component, lecture-type material, such as the rationale for a specific action or standard, can be addressed with macros. Coaches should have at least a mental list of material that should be talked about, in case members' questions don't cover everything.

Use macros at the time the member asks the question, except when answering would interrupt performance of a tactic. The member's question "Why?" indicates that he or she wants to learn and is ready to learn right then.

Use macros in whatever order members bring questions up. Documenting the content and application ideas for each macro helps the coach and member remember the information and improves consistency between coaches.

Topics for macros are as varied as the information presented during the drills. The list of macros is probably very large. Useful topics have included:

- Flashover prevention, cues and consequences.
- PPE performance during flashover.
- Collapse prevention, cues and consequences.
- Heat stress prevention, cues and consequences.
- Fire flow calculations.
- Hose selection, capabilities and limitations.
- Driving safety.
- Physical fitness assets, programs and cautions.
- Relating individual member activity to crew tactics.
- How crew tactics fit into operations.
- Customer service perspectives.
- Prevention as part of the service.

The goal of training in context is not so much to teach people *subjects* as it is to teach them to respond to *situations*. And if firefighters have been trained to respond with a logical sequence of actions, their performance on the fireground will be prompt, expert and confident.

Where Tools and People Meet

John LeCuyer

More than one out of three firefighters was injured in the line of duty in 1992, according to the International Association of Fire Fighters' Death and Injury Survey. Overall, the "incidence" or frequency of firefighter job-related injuries is 4.3 times that of the average worker in private industry, as reported by the U.S. Bureau of Labor Statistics.

In both private industry and the fire service, musculoskeletal disorders and injuries are the leading cause of work-related disability. Reducing injuries depends on reducing risk factors, and that is the principal goal of ergonomics.

Ergonomics is the science that addresses human performance and wellness in relation to the job, equipment, tools and environment. It draws on a wide range of disciplines, including anatomy, physiology, kinesiology, behavioral science and psychology.

Although ergonomics knowledge has been traditionally used to improve the design and use of consumer products, the work setting has spurred new applications. Ergonomics has grown explosively in recent years as work-related injuries have been better recognized, and as improved methods of identifying and abating hazards have become available.

Workplace ergonomics

Applied in conjunction with injury analysis, ergonomic principles bring problem areas in the workplace into clearer focus, leading to improved performance, health and safety. Prevention is the

Adapted from John LeCuyer, "Where Tools and People Meet," *Fire Chief* (February 1994). Reprinted with permission of *Fire Chief* magazine.

key, and it relies on reducing workplace stressors, such as fatigue of a specific muscle or muscle group because of overuse or overexertion, through ergonomic controls.

There are two types of ergonomic controls: administrative and engineering. Administrative controls are used to minimize exposure to stressors and require supervisory monitoring to ensure compliance. Some examples relevant to the fire service are:

- Proper work methods.
- Exercise programs.
- Training programs.
- SOPs.
- Assignment of personnel.

Engineering controls are used to modify the workplace, tools or job design. Chapter 4, Section 4-5.1 of NFPA 1500, *Fire Department Occupational Safety and Health Program* states: "The fire department shall consider safety and health as primary concerns in the specification, design, construction, acquisition, operation, maintenance, inspection, and repair of all tools and equipment."

An awareness of the effects that tools and equipment have on the performance of firefighting tasks and on any subsequent injuries is crucial. Obviously the firefighter's most dangerous workplace, the emergency scene, cannot be controlled completely, but the inherent hazards can be minimized. The work methods (administrative controls) and equipment used at the scene (engineering controls) can be modified to reduce the dangers present at emergency incidents. The same approaches can also make firefighters safer in other workplaces.

Implementing ergonomic principles in the workplace begins with a workplace assessment that includes an injury analysis. It is best to address as many ergonomically incorrect issues as possible, even if a major problem has not yet developed. The point of prevention is to intervene before a problem occurs.

Engineering controls should be emphasized initially, because they have the greatest effect on a firefighter's behavior and performance. The most obvious engineering control in the fire service involves the specification of equipment, especially apparatus, but knowing your workforce and who will be using this equipment is critical. Hiring smaller people, but then purchasing larger equipment, might literally spec a firefighter out of a job, or at least his or her ability to perform it satisfactorily.

Newer isn't always better

Comparing an old piece of apparatus with its replacement purchased by a local department graphically depicts several problems

(Figure 1). The new rear-engine configuration was a tradeoff: a more spacious and quieter cab for a less-than-desirable rear work area and compartment design.

The upper compartment latch is 13 inches higher on the new rig. The increase from 65 to 78 inches will still be in reach for the average firefighter (5′ 10″), but out of reach for many.

An easy overhead grasp-type reach distance was prescribed to be about 77 inches (195 cm) in some earlier design books that considered only men, but now about 73 inches (185 cm) is recommended to accommodate 95% of women. The newer apparatus does not meet this criterion.

If the handle were lowered to accommodate more firefighters, there would still be the question of whether they could reach in and retrieve tools safely once the door was opened. Along with a lower latch, slide-out shelves might have to be installed.

Another problem is the hose bed height: 63 inches on the old one and 81 on the new. That same average firefighter who could reach the hose from the ground when catching a hydrant now has to step up on the tailboard for access.

That task, however, is more difficult and less safe. The step up is 4 inches higher (pull up those baggy bunker pants), and the tailboard is only 12 inches in depth, 8 inches less than the old one.

This translates to a balance problem, which requires one hand to grip a safety bar and the other to pull hose. Then it's a matter of "falling off" to complete the motion, but don't forget the extra 4-inch drop when you do.

One solution for this apparatus would be a return to the old donut on the tailboard for catching hydrants.

Yet another problem is the location of ladders. The difference between ladder mounts on these two rigs is 12 inches, and that's significant. Removing a 24-foot ladder used to be a one-person evolution. Now it requires two people, and tall ones at that.

Specifying a ladder lift to lower the ladder might be the best solution here; an electric lift can be retrofitted for less than $2,000. You will still need two people to retrieve any ladders, though, because the ladders are getting heavier.

In terms of administrative controls, staffing and assignments might have to be reviewed. The transition from old rig to new rig in this example required one back injury and two knee injuries before those adjustments were made.

Ergonomic resources

To prevent injuries in cases like those above, practical recommendations must be made and implemented. This provides management with some understanding of the cause-and-effect relationship between the workplace and injuries and the cost

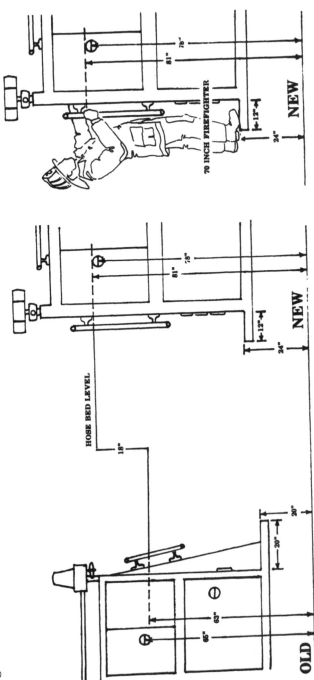

Figure 1. When the truck gets taller.

benefit of implementing a preventive program. Simply returning an injured firefighter to the environment that created the injury without evaluating and correcting the problem is poor injury management.

Assessment and consultation services are available from a variety of vendors, particularly therapy groups that provide rehab services to your injured firefighters. They should be included in the investigation of accidents as part of the treatment process.

I recommend use of a Field Investigation Report that displays a simplified graphic describing the accident (Figure 2). This provides therapists with some very useful information that could prevent further accidents.

If budget constraints prohibit consultation or expensive diagnostic procedures, there is still an alternative. Use the ergonomic experts you have working for you: firefighters.

Your in-house experts study their job every shift and most likely have the best ideas for improving safety. An outside consultant who is unfamiliar with firefighting will use this resource, so why don't you? The ergonomic ideal may not be achieved, but the basic principles can be applied.

Ways to lighten the load

Based on work experience, for instance, a firefighter will know that it's easier to push a heavy weight than pull it, and to slide a weight rather than carry it, although he or she might not know that in theory the force needed to lift a weight is about 32 times that required to slide it. Anyone involved in heavy manual labor quickly discovers an easier way if he or she expects to endure, and firefighters are no exception.

Supervisors must be receptive to firefighter feedback and provide alternatives when possible. Human behavior plays a large role in causing accidents, and it's important to actively involve everyone in the safety process.

An effective injury-investigation procedure combined with firefighter feedback will help identify some key stressors in your environment. A simple, inexpensive example of an ergonomic intervention that can be introduced at any department involves the common tool box or trauma kit.

More than one firefighter has carried a 50-pound tool box through an apartment complex to discover they needed only one tool. Change requires that management allow a firefighter to decide what tools are most commonly used and then provide a separate smaller kit for them.

This simple idea was implemented in our department for $150. Reducing the weight of heavy boxes (those weighing more

Figure 2. Documenting injuries.

FIELD INVESTIGATION REPORT
AURORA FIRE DEPARTMENT

NAME: *JOHN DOE*   AGE: *46* HT. *70"* WT. *185*

POSITION ASSIGNED *DRIVER- E-1* ACCIDENT LOCATION   *S*

FITNESS LEVEL   *3*   PHYSICAL PERFORMANCE SCORE   *P*

INJURY DESCRIPTION:
*THE FIREFIGHTER WAS RETRIEVING A TOOL BOX FROM THE TOP COMPART-
MENT OF ENGINE 1 AND STRAINED HIS LOWER BACK.*

GRAPHIC:

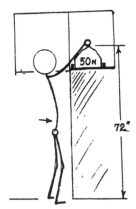

RECOMMENDATION:

*THE TOOL BOX WAS WEIGHED AT 50 LBS. THE HANDLE WAS LOCATED 72"
ABOVE GROUND AND AN ADDITIONAL LIFT OF 2" TO CLEAR BRACKET WAS REQUIRED.
THE KEY CONTRIBUTING FACTORS ARE WEIGHT AND LOCATION OF TOOL BOX. THE
HEIGHT OF ORIGIN CREATES A LUMBAR ARCH. PLACEMENT OF EQUIPMENT IN
EXCESS OF 25 lbs. SHOULD NOT ORIGINATE ABOVE THE SHOULDER LEVEL.
THE LOAD SHOULD BE REDUCED OR RELOCATED.*

---

than 50 pounds) by splitting the load between two smaller units
will remove the contribution to injury associated with handling
such loads (Figure 3).

A single heavy box is a problem for another reason, too.
Asymmetrical loads, those carried in one hand, can create a
spinal curvature that can accelerate the process of disc degenera-
tion over the long term. And people usually carry a heavy load in
the same hand, time after time.

Figure 3. A balanced load.

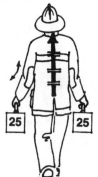

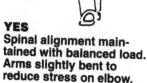

NO
Asymmetrical load forces a spinal curvature, pinching discs. Straight arm creates stress on elbow joint.

YES
Spinal alignment maintained with balanced load. Arms slightly bent to reduce stress on elbow.

Just because an injury doesn't manifest itself in association with a specific task doesn't mean it's a sound practice, so it's essential to remove potential risk factors that are easily corrected.

For example, research has reported 45% to 60% declines in grip strength when wearing fire-resistant gloves. Adequate grip strength and hand dexterity are essential for safe handling and operation of tools and equipment, so substituting a lightweight glove for work that doesn't require thermal protection makes sense from both safety and economic standpoints. Work gloves can be purchased for a fraction of the cost ($6 a pair vs. $60 a pair), reserving the fire gloves for their intended use.

Another easily overlooked problem is the practice of lining compartment floors with a non-skid material that prevents equipment from sliding when the apparatus is in motion and also provides drainage. The problem is that this material prevents a firefighter from sliding a heavy piece of equipment for retrieval, forcing a lift with extended arms that places tremendous stress on the lower back (Figure 4).

Biomechanical studies have shown that it's not unusual for the lumbosacral disc (L5/S1) to be subjected to 800 pounds of compressive force while the individual is lifting a 35-pound load (a smoke ejector, for example). If the load is heavier, or can't be held close to the body as it's lifted, forces on the spine can exceed 2,000 pounds.

The National Institute of Occupational Safety and Health recommends that jobs requiring compressive forces on the L5/S1

Figure 4. A safer compartment.

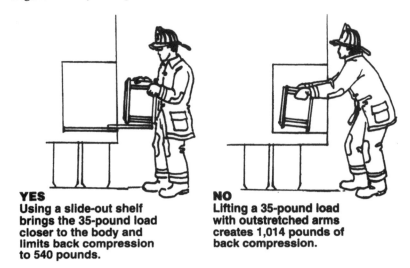

YES
**Using a slide-out shelf
brings the 35-pound load
closer to the body and
limits back compression
to 540 pounds.**

NO
**Lifting a 35-pound load
with outstretched arms
creates 1,014 pounds of
back compression.**

greater than 770 pounds should be monitored, and that jobs involving forces in excess of 1,430 pounds be redesigned.

The solution is to provide slide-out shelves to eliminate lifting with outstretched arms. That way the advantage of using the decking material is not lost, but neither are body mechanics compromised.

When 'cures' cause harm

When implementing solutions, caution must be taken to avoid a misdiagnosis that could create another problem or accentuate the one that exists, such as in the apparatus comparison (Figure 1). In an effort to reduce cab noise on apparatus, manufacturers installed rear-mount engines, which required a new design that led to other problems previously discussed.

Another example would be the blanket use of back-support belts. Some firefighters have made this change based on observing workers in other fields. Unfortunately, says Dave Harberson, an Arvada, Colo., sports therapist, routine use of back-support belts can lead to a weakening of the torso musculature and literally create back problems.

There are situations in which this device is appropriate, but one should consult with a therapist before using a belt. Remember that there are no ergonomic cure-alls and that each solution is situation-specific. The back belt does not increase the ability to lift and can not overcome muscle inadequacy, to which 90% of back pain is attributed.

Cadaver studies, which measure the spine's own strength separate from its supporting musculature, have reported disc fractures occurring at 600 pounds of compressive force. An individual's ability to repeatedly and safely tolerate forces up to or beyond the NIOSH limit (1,430 pounds), therefore, depends primarily on the strength of the back muscles.

Developing and implementing a personal fitness program is encouraged to improve strength, muscular endurance and flexibility in the muscles and joints that support and align the spinal column. The best approach for "in-house experts" is to keep it simple and address the obvious based on personal experience.

The new firefighters

Firefighting is and probably always will be a physically demanding occupation. It is unrealistic to think that all task loads can be reduced or simplified, yet it makes even less sense to knowingly contribute to their difficulty.

New legislation and the removal of discriminatory barriers such as height and weight requirements and age have changed the fire service's demographics. Larger anthropometric variations exist in the workforce today, for example in reach capability, particularly with shorter-statured, older or physically limited employees.

The design and specification of apparatus require great concern to ensure that people can physically reach all tools and equipment to perform their jobs. The average male can lift 100 pounds for a few seconds when the hands are close to the shoulders. This capability is reduced to 40 pounds when the hands are 20 inches in front of the shoulders, such as reaching into a compartment. The height of a compartment and the weight of the objects stored there are important safety concerns.

Mismatching a worker's strength when compared to job requirements has been shown to greatly increase the risk of future musculoskeletal problems and injuries.

In 1981, NIOSH recognized the growing problem of work-related back injuries and published the "Work Practices Guide for Manual Lifting." The WPG was based on the theory that "overexertion injury is the result of job demands that exceed a worker's capacity."

The guide employs a somewhat complex formula that identifies acceptable load weights for select populations and tasks. (This formula was revised in late 1993 to provide a greater safety margin, but the WPG had not been updated yet.)

Ergonomics of a ladder raise: Why taller is easier

Raising portable ladders is a vital ladder company function, and the ability to effectively perform a ladder raise depends on the firefighter's skill, training and physical ability.

The physical demands imposed by a given ladder, however, are not the same for everyone, but vary with individual size. This lends support to the historically common practice of assigning the "big guys" to the truck. Not only is physical strength a factor, but stature is, too.

The following analysis of a ladder raise graphically defines the physical requirements relative to body stature. To determine the physical requirements to perform a ladder raise, it's necessary to record the weights and dimensions of the various ladders and the height of the individual performing the task.

The force (F) is a resultant of two components: The vertical force (Fv) required to lift the ladder, and the horizontal force (Fh) required to push it forward. Calculations were based on the impulse/momentum formula: $M = F \times L$ (moment equals force times lever arm).

Initially, the moment (or torque) of the 28-foot (108-pound) ladder at rest is 108 pounds $\times$ 8 feet, or 864 foot-pounds (8 feet because the center of gravity is where the weight lies).

To lift the ladder from the top rung, the lever arm becomes 16.5 feet, so the force required to initiate the movement to head height is 864 ÷ 16.5, or 52.4 pounds. The remaining angles and forces were similarly calculated with height measures in increments of 2 inches. (See table. Note that samples of direct force measures were taken using a push tensiometer, and the resultant values were consistent with the mathematical model.)

As shown, a 60-inch person raising a 108-pound, 28-foot extension ladder must apply a force of 86 pounds at the heaviest point in the raise (rung 8 at 44.2°), lifting about 80% of the ladder's weight.

In comparison, a 72-inch person raising the same ladder must apply a maximum force of 72 pounds (rung 7 at 46.1°), lifting 67% of the ladder's weight. The shorter person must lift an additional 14 pounds to accomplish the same task and therefore works harder.

This is a relatively light ladder at 108 pounds, and the difference may not appear great at first glance, but *is* significant when

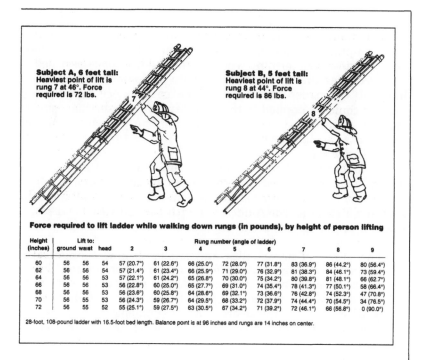

Subject A, 6 feet tall: Heaviest point of lift is rung 7 at 46°. Force required is 72 lbs.

Subject B, 5 feet tall: Heaviest point of lift is rung 8 at 44°. Force required is 86 lbs.

Force required to lift ladder while walking down rungs (in pounds), by height of person lifting

Height (inches)	Lift to: ground	waist	head	Rung number (angle of ladder) 2	3	4	5	6	7	8	9
60	56	56	54	57 (20.7°)	61 (22.6°)	66 (25.0°)	72 (28.0°)	77 (31.8°)	83 (36.9°)	86 (44.2°)	80 (56.4°)
62	56	56	54	57 (21.4°)	61 (23.4°)	66 (25.9°)	71 (29.0°)	76 (32.9°)	81 (38.3°)	84 (46.1°)	73 (59.4°)
64	56	56	53	57 (22.1°)	61 (24.2°)	65 (26.8°)	70 (30.0°)	75 (34.2°)	80 (39.8°)	81 (48.1°)	66 (62.7°)
66	56	56	53	56 (22.8°)	60 (25.0°)	65 (27.7°)	69 (31.0°)	74 (35.4°)	78 (41.3°)	77 (50.1°)	58 (66.4°)
68	56	56	53	56 (23.6°)	60 (25.8°)	64 (28.6°)	69 (32.1°)	73 (36.6°)	76 (42.8°)	74 (52.3°)	47 (70.8°)
70	56	55	53	56 (24.3°)	59 (26.7°)	64 (29.5°)	68 (33.2°)	72 (37.9°)	74 (44.4°)	70 (54.5°)	34 (76.5°)
72	56	55	52	55 (25.1°)	59 (27.5°)	63 (30.5°)	67 (34.2°)	71 (39.2°)	72 (46.1°)	66 (56.8°)	0 (90.0°)

28-foot, 108-pound ladder with 16.5-foot bed length. Balance point is at 96 inches and rungs are 14 inches on center.

considering body motion. The lift is basically an incline press, and the weight is substantial for this type of motion.

Adding to the difficulty, the process of "walking" the rungs requires that the press be performed with one arm at a time, pressing single-handedly a weight that would be excessive for most people by NIOSH standards. Larger or heavier ladders, such as the 35-foot extension, could generate a 30-pound difference between the two heights. It's no surprise that shoulder problems and injuries are common among firefighters.

Assigning firefighters to ladder company operations should be done with consideration to matching the work to the worker. The smaller person will have to work harder at a higher level of intensity, increasing his or her risk of injury. To compensate for the natural disadvantage, they must be stronger. It makes more sense to employ administrative controls and assign firefighters appropriately.

The guide was intended for use in industrial settings, but has some application to the fire service. For example, using specialized equipment found in the therapy setting, a firefighter could be evaluated to determine whether the ladder raise described in the accompanying sidebar was within his or her safe lift zone limits. If the stress was found to be excessive, ergonomic intervention could be applied to reduce or avoid overexertion injuries, such as administrative controls focusing on personnel and assignments, assigning two personnel to the task or assigning taller personnel.

Ergonomic modification of the workplace will help reduce injury risks for all firefighters in the current workforce, while also providing the "reasonable accommodation" mandated by such legislation as the Americans with Disabilities Act. From a safety standpoint, departments must be ready to take appropriate action.

The study of ergonomics and safety is now sophisticated enough to have a significant effect on the prevention and cure of the most prevalent worker injuries. As the costs of workers' compensation escalate, the best approach is an effective prevention program. Proper workplace ergonomics supplemented by a sound fitness program can play a key role in an injury-prevention program.

As former NIOSH director Donald Miller said, the greatest occupational safety and health problem today is blindness to the benefits of prevention.

Chaffin, D.B. and G.B.J. Andersson, "Occupational Biomechanics," 2nd. ed., J. Wiley and Sons, N.Y., 1991.

Chaffin, D.B., Occupational Health and Safety, Jan. 1992, Vol. 61, No. 1.

International Association of Fire Fighters, Death and Injury Survey, 1992.

NFPA 1500, Fire Department Occupational Safety and Health Program, 1992 ed. National Fire Protection Association, Quincy, Mass.

National Institute for Occupational Safety and Health. "A Work Practices Guide for Manual Lifting." Tech. Report No. 81-122, U.S. Dept. of Health and Human Services (NIOSH), Cincinnati, 1981.

Rasch, Philip, Ph.D., and Roger K. Burke, Ph.D., "Kinesiology and Applied Anatomy." Lea and Febiger, Philadelphia, 1960.

Salvendy, Gauriel. "Handbook of Human Factors." John Wiley & Sons, N.Y., 1987.

Ulin, Sheryl and Thomas Armstrong. Journal of Occupational Rehabilitation. Vol. 2, No. 1, 1992.

When OSHA Comes Knocking

Jack Abraham

You might have heard the joke that you know you're going to have a bad day when you get to work and see a "60 Minutes" news crew waiting outside your office.

There is another, more frequent event for chiefs that bears some resemblance to that image: coming to work and finding a car marked "Occupational Safety and Health Administration" in the parking lot.

An OSHA compliance inspection is serious business. As employees, firefighters are entitled to a workplace free from recognized hazards. Chiefs, in turn, have the right to expect their personnel to follow established safety laws and regulations and standard operating procedures (SOPs) implemented by the department.

And OSHA? Well, they have the legislated responsibility and authority to enforce occupational safety laws adopted as part of the Code of Federal Regulations.

Applicable portions of OSHA standards

It came as a surprise to many fire service managers in the early 1980s when we realized that our occupation had been subject to occupational safety laws since 1970. We quickly became schooled in Subpart L of 29 CFR 1910 and acknowledged the requirements for training, protective clothing and physical fitness for firefighters.

Adapted from Jack Abraham, "When OSHA Comes Knocking," *Fire Chief* (April 1993). Reprinted with permission of *Fire Chief* magazine.

What chiefs need to realize is that all sections of the OSHA regulations that apply to general industry also apply to protecting career and volunteer firefighters. Note that a few states exclude government workers from their state OSHA plans, which would leave the fire service work force in these instances unprotected by federal OSHA standards. There are, however, legislative efforts currently under way to extend OSHA protection to all government employees.

One of the aspects that makes firefighting difficult for OSHA compliance officers to regulate is defining the workplace, but there are three sources that can be examined for compliance:

1. Required written safety records and training records
2. The fire station, facilities and firefighting equipment and
3. Interviews with department's personnel.

In other words, the compliance officer does not have to follow you to alarms to cite the department for unsafe acts or conditions.

Written documents are required, including a safety plan for employees, a written Incident Command System (at least for hazmat response) and an Infectious Disease Control Plan. The number-one OSHA citation in 1990 for general industry (this includes the fire service) was a lack of an adequate and functional written Hazard Communication program.

How are the exits at your station? Locked? Blocked? Adequately marked?

What about your portable fire extinguishers? 29 CFR 1910.157(e) specifies monthly and annual inspections, hydrostatic testing, and six-year inspections for aluminum cylinders. Documentation is required.

More than 4,000 times a year, employers are cited for failure to display the required OSHA poster at a place accessible to all employees. That means each fire station, too.

How does the compliance officer (CO) verify what he or she is told by the chief? By reading the records and talking to the firefighters. If the CO is told that the fire department is equipped and prepared for confined-space rescue, the trained personnel had best be lined up outside the office. Their answers about training and practices need to be consistent.

One more important point about applicable portions of the standard: There is a paragraph in the Occupational Safety and Health Act of 1970 called the "General Duty Clause." Because it would be impossible for every possible safety deficiency to be written into law, the lack of a specific law prohibiting an unsafe condition does not relieve the chief from providing a safe and healthful workplace. In the absence of a specific law, the General Duty Clause is cited as the source for a violation.

I am sure you get the picture: Your fire department and my fire department are no different from any private place of business when it comes to complying with OSHA regulations.

When to expect an OSHA inspection

You can plan to be inspected if your department has experienced the tragedy of a firefighter killed on duty. You can also put the coffee on and buy donuts to impress a compliance officer if five or more personnel have been hospitalized as the result of a single event.

If OSHA receives a written complaint from a firefighter describing what the agency's area director deems to be an imminent danger to personnel, the chief will be contacted so as to facilitate rapid correction of the deficiency, and an OSHA compliance officer can be expected within 24 hours. Otherwise, you will probably not have prior knowledge of an inspection.

OSHA is required to respond to a signed written complaint by an employee. Depending on the severity of the alleged violation, you might receive a telephone call inquiring about the violation and asking you to respond in writing. Or the CO may drive up to the door of the fire station with the complaint in hand.

The individual who contacted OSHA has the right to remain unnamed and is protected by law from discrimination or retaliatory action by the employer. Some OSHA programs have an entire division that follows up on nothing but employee claims of retribution.

Your department may have been selected at random for an inspection, or the CO may have witnessed unsafe acts or conditions while driving to work one day and scheduled an inspection. The likelihood of a random inspection is increased if the department has a higher-than-average reportable lost-workday injury rate. Lastly, if your department has a history of previous OSHA citations, follow-up inspections can be expected.

What happens during an inspection A compliance officer is required to identify himself or herself to the officer in charge of the station. Subordinate officers at headquarters or a substation should immediately call the chief, or his or her representative.

Request that the inspector come to your office, if you are the chief. This is your home turf and an environment that should put you at ease. Close the door and stop all phone calls or interruptions; give this meeting your full attention. Smile and greet this new friend warmly.

The compliance officer is required to display his or her credentials. Call the Department of Labor if you have any doubt about the validity of these credentials. Under no circumstances should an OSHA official attempt to collect fines from anyone during a field inspection.

You will be told the reason for and the scope of the inspection. If the inspection is the result of a complaint, you will be given a copy of the complaint, with the complainant's name deleted upon request.

At this point the chief has the legal right to deny access to the property to the OSHA inspector. But you can expect your new friend to return with a document wrapped in blue: an administrative search warrant. Game's over, OSHA wins. The employer also has the right to stop an inspection at any time and ask the compliance officer to leave the property, but the administrative warrant will prevail.

It would be prudent for the chief to advise his or her immediate supervisor about the impending inspection before making any decisions.

An opening conference is held before the inspection with the chief, any other local official, the compliance officer and an individual representing the firefighters. Unionized departments will probably have a designated representative. Nonunion departments may have preselected an employee representative from the department's safety committee, or the employees can spontaneously select a representative. Under no circumstances can the chief or the employer appoint the employee representative.

If no employee representative can be designated in a timely manner, the compliance officer is required to consult with firefighters during the inspection. These discussions can be held in private.

The opening conference basically restates the initial information given to the chief by the CO. Then the inspection begins with all those attending the conference walking with the inspector. The OSHA representative observes, talks to employees or volunteer firefighters, and takes photographs of selected potential violations.

Here is an important point to remember: The violations that an OSHA compliance officer may cite become the basis for future litigation, either through an appeal to abate the citation(s), civil liability or future OSHA inspections.

If you are the chief, document everything that transpires during the inspection. Openly tape record all relevant conversations or take complete notes. If the CO takes a picture, you take a picture from the same perspective illustrating the same subject. If there is going to be sampling (noise, SCBA air quality, etc.), the CO is obliged to allow the department opportunity to secure sampling equipment of its own for simultaneous testing. The chief should collect the same evidence of violations that the OSHA representative collects.

Records are of special interest to the compliance officer. Commonly reviewed are the department's OSHA 200 Injury Log, first Report of Injury forms (or Workers' Compensation Injury Reports), documentation of exposure to chemicals or body fluids (which must be maintained for 30 years), training records (which must be maintained at least one year following termination of a firefighter), and the hazard communication training documentation for each member of the department. Photocopy any records that the compliance officer wants to take off the premises.

A closing conference is convened from all those present at the opening conference. This is an opportunity for open discussion on cited violations, for questions and for the chief to make a positive impression about the safety of the department's personnel. Any detail that can be documented that illustrates an effort to provide a workplace free from recognized hazards should be brought forward.

A certified letter containing the "Citation and Notification of Penalty" can be expected within six months. Even if corrections are made during the inspection, such as refilling a half-full SCBA air bottle on an engine, the department will still receive a citation for that violation.

A copy of the notice must be given to the employee representative. It must be also be posted in each station for a minimum of three days and until all citations are corrected.

OSHA's Field Operations Manual stipulates that violations be categorized as "non-serious" or "serious." These are defined as follows: A *non-serious* violation has a direct relationship to job safety and health, but probably would not cause death or serious harm. A penalty can range from nothing up to $7,000 for each violation. A *serious* violation exists when there is substantial probability that death or serious injury could result. A mandatory penalty is required and can be up to $7,000 for each serious violation.

Other types of violations, each of which could be serious or non-serious, include:

1. *Willful violation:* A violation that the employer knowingly and intentionally commits, or that a "reasonably diligent" chief should have known of. This is the type of violation where the chief has fielded and not taken corrective action on verbal and written complaints from firefighters about an unsafe condition in violation of an OSHA standard. Frustrated, the firefighters write a complaint to OSHA and then talk with the compliance officer during the inspection. Up to $70,000 can be assessed for each willful violation.

There is a trend in the private sector for OSHA to involve the Justice Department in a criminal investigation if a willful violation contributes to the death of an employee. The federal OSHA program stipulates a $250,000 fine, or six months in jail, or both. A second conviction for a willful violation doubles the penalties.

2. *Failure to correct a prior violation:* Up to $7,000 per day per violation. An abatement period is established that allows the department a specified amount of time to correct deficiencies. Failure to make progress on corrections is not taken lightly.

3. *Repeated violations:* Previous citations that were once corrected can also bring a fine of up to $70,000.

4. *Posting violations:* Each fire station is required to have a poster displayed explaining employer and employee responsibilities regarding complying with safety and health legislation. Failure to post can result in a penalty up to $7,000 per failure.

To complete the array of potential occupational safety and health violations that can cost, the penalty for falsifying records or reports is $10,000 and/or six months, and for assaulting a compliance officer, up to $5,000 and imprisonment for three years.

The area director of the OSHA office with jurisdiction makes the final decision about citations and penalties. The compliance officer who conducted the inspection does not have that authority.

The area director can use adjustment factors that reduce penalties by as much as 25% for a good-faith effort by the fire department to provide a safe workplace. To qualify for this reduction, the department must have had a written safety and health program in effect at the time of the inspection. An additional 10% reduction can be achieved by having no OSHA citations for serious, willful or repeat violations in the previous three years.

Administrative options

After receiving the "Citation and Notification of Penalty" and posting the notice, as required, the chief has basically three options: comply; comply, but ask for an extension of the abatement period; or contest the citation(s) or penalty(s). If you are the chief, these alternatives should be discussed with your jurisdiction's upper management and legal counsel.

The chief should be aware that not appealing is an acknowledgment of failure to comply with OSHA standards, and the citations become permanent in the department's OSHA file. That may not sound too bad, but consider that any future OSHA inspection or litigation concerning the fire department can reference those citations.

A previous history of citations could be construed by a jury in a civil or criminal lawsuit as showing an inattentive attitude by management toward the firefighters and their safety. A previous history also brings OSHA's attention in the form of follow-up inspections.

Compliance means correcting the citation within the specified abatement period and certifying correction to OSHA. Compliance also means paying the penalty within 15 days. It may require the repair of a grounding plug on an extension cord, the hydrostatic testing of fire extinguishers on the apparatus or the purchase of protective clothing in compliance with OSHA standards.

Compliance may mean establishing written procedures or training firefighters on a subject cited by the compliance officer. Compliance may cost nothing but time, or it may cost thousands of dollars.

After compliance is obtained, written verification is sent to OSHA and the posted "Citation and Notification of Penalty" can be removed.

As mentioned earlier, an abatement period is allowed for compliance. If for logistical, financial or other reasons compliance cannot be obtained within that period, an extension should be sought. The department has 15 days from the date of receipt of the citations to make a written request for an extension of an abatement date.

An extension can also be sought if progress is being made, but it has become apparent that good-faith effort will not meet the deadline. Remember that each day a violation continues past the established compliance date can result in a $7,000 fine.

Petitioning OSHA to extend an abatement date is one step. Posting that petition for 10 days for all affected firefighters to review is also required. Any employee has 10 days to file an objection to the requested extension with the OSHA office.

If the petition is uncontested, the OSHA area director acts on it and renders a decision. If firefighters object to the area director, a hearing is held with all concerned parties before a decision to extend compliance dates is rendered.

Fifteen postmarked working days are permitted for the fire department to file a notice that some or all of the citations will be contested. The filing of an appeal delays the requirement for the employer to correct the contested citations. Proposed penalties must also be contested within the same 15-day period. The written "Notice to Contest" sent to the OSHA office that issued the citation must state specifically which citations or penalties are being contested.

An informal meeting to discuss the citations and differences of opinion may be requested with the area director. This officer has the authority to adjust the severity of the citation, penalty or abatement date.

Here, too, the designated employee representative must be permitted to attend any meeting that may influence a decision to change the original Citation and Notification of Penalty. At this informal meeting, employees can object only to changes in the abatement period.

If an informal meeting is not desired, or an agreement cannot be reached informally, the OSHA area director refers the case to the appropriate Occupational Safety and Health Review Commission, which in turn assigns the case to an administrative law judge. The hearing is usually conducted close to where the citations were noted, minimizing inconvenience to the employer or employees attending the proceedings.

OSHA has the burden of proof. The fire department does not have to be represented by an attorney, but may be if it chooses. The strict rules of evidence do not apply in administrative hearings, and the judge will base his or her decision on whether the compliance officer can prove noncompliance with the applicable standard.

If the fire department loses the case, there is a specific sequence of appeals available that can lead to the U.S. Supreme Court.

The final decision can lead to the citation being vacated, reduced in severity, reduced in penalty or upheld in its entirety. If the fire department is successful in having the citation vacated, all or part of the legal expenses associated with the action may have to be paid by OSHA under the Equal Access to Justice Act. Such entitlement is not automatic.

Defense strategies

If the fire department chooses to contest a citation, a defense strategy must be established that will cause OSHA to fail in its burden of proof. Based on an extensive review of contested cases in general industry and the construction industry, the following strategies are suggested:

Unpreventable employee misconduct If you, the chief, have done everything in accordance with the OSHA regulations and an employee violates the standard, the citation can be vacated by proving the employee was at fault. This defense may be the most difficult of all.

Suppose one of your firefighters is seen by a compliance officer entering a burning building without using available respiratory protection. You are subsequently cited for a serious violation of 1910.132(a) and assessed a $7,000 penalty.

To appeal the citation based on employee misconduct, you must be able to document that before the citation:

- The fire department had a written safety policy requiring the use of respiratory protection
- All personnel were trained in the policy and proper use of SCBA, including when the individual seen performing the unsafe act was trained, by whom and the training outline used during that training session
- Progressive discipline had been taken against firefighters who had not worn SCBA in the past, unless you can provide witness testimony that this was the first time in history that someone in your department failed to use an air pack.

The compliance officer did not witness the violation   COs have been known to mistakenly use circumstantial evidence as the basis for a citation. Earlier I mentioned a half-full SCBA bottle as being a violation.

Suppose the bottle for which the fire department was being cited was on the work bench and not a piece of apparatus. Your defense could be that the bottle was out of service for maintenance, therefore not a violation. You may be asked to explain why the bottle was not tagged Do Not Use and removed to a place inaccessible to personnel, but you may still be successful in this defense.

The fire department has complied with industry standards   If you use water to hose out your apparatus bay, the fire station must have ground fault interrupters on electrical outlets in the bays. Suppose the station does have GFI, but upon testing by the compliance officer, they do not work. A successful defense may be that the fire department has complied by providing GFI, but it is not an industry standard—nor is it required—to routinely check GFI to determine its operational status.

Pertaining to firefighting, the national consensus standards adopted by the National Fire Protection Association will likely be the basis for deciding what is considered industry standard.

The OSHA compliance officer lacks expertise in the field
This is one reason why COs probably do not hang around the fireground with notebooks and sharpened pencils. If your department is cited and you as the chief outright disagree with the compliance officer, get an expert or two to testify at the hearing contesting the citation. If your experts are more convincing than the compliance officer, your department may be successful in having the citation vacated.

Small employer defense   This may work once for the small department to reduce the penalty when the citation has been corrected. OSHA's mission is to achieve safe working environments for workers, not generate revenue.

For example, your department has corrected a citation for failure to hydrostatically test fire extinguishers on the fire trucks, but the proposed $7,000 penalty would be catastrophic to the department. The OSHA area director or commission judge may sympathize and reduce or eliminate the penalty. I know of no circumstances where this defense has been successful more than once for a particular employer.

Citations can also be vacated due to clerical error or technical error in citing the wrong section of the standard, inadequate detail on the Citation and Notification of Penalty, or other bona fide reason.

If your department cannot comply

OSHA regulations make provision for special hardships or alternative means of providing for employee safety. If there are unusual circumstances in your department and you can prove that safety is not compromised by an alternative approach, then a variance obtained before a citation can eliminate a lot of time and hassle.

The OSHA office should be contacted in writing requesting the variance. There will be a hearing, which employees are allowed to attend. The likelihood of a variance being granted is greatly increased by employee support for the measure.

One word of caution about variances: They only apply to the department to which they are granted. I am aware of a fire department that was granted a variance to 1910.134(d)(5)(i), the regulation against facial hair when respirators are used. No other fire department can use that variance as protection from being cited for its firefighters having facial hair that can compromise a tight seal while using SCBA.

Things to do

- Become knowledgeable about occupational safety, then do what a "reasonably diligent" chief would do to provide a workplace free from recognized hazards.
- Determine the responsible agency for enforcing occupational safety standards in your state. Determine its authority over your department. Display the required bulletin board poster.
- If you are confident that your safety program is in compliance, you may request an advisory inspection by OSHA. While the findings are not citations, you will be required to

correct all noted deficiencies. Another alternative may be to ask your insurance carrier or a consultant to perform an advisory inspection. Again, once you have knowledge of a deficiency, failure to remedy it is "willful."

- Respond to concerns from personnel about safety, and work through those personnel to achieve safety, for everyone's benefit.

Cross, James R. "OSHA Inspections," Rescue-EMS Magazine (May–June 1992), p. 20.

Henry, Vic H. "Employer must study financial factors before challenging an OSHA citation," Occupational Health and Safety (May 1992), p. 36.

Sheridan, Peter J. "OSHA calling," Occupational Hazards (Sept. 1991), pp. 129–131.

Sheridan, Peter J. "How to handle an OSHA inspection," Occupational Hazards (Sept. 1991), pp. 132–133.

U.S. Department of Labor, Occupational Safety and Health Administration. "Employer Rights and Responsibilities following an OSHA inspection," Pamphlet OSHA 3000 (1990, revised), Washington, D.C.

U.S. Department of Labor, Occupational Safety and Health Administration. "OSHA inspections," Pamphlet 2098 (1992, Revised), Washington, D.C.

Infection Control

Murrey E. Loflin

OSHA's Occupational Exposure to Bloodborne Pathogens standard has been in place for about two years now. Since that time, how well have the fire and emergency medical services done at developing, implementing and managing infection-control programs? What have we learned from ironing out the kinks in infection-control programs? What has worked for other agencies, and what has failed?

The Virginia Beach (Va.) Fire Department's infection-control program has been in effect for about a year and a half, and we can look at the long-term successes and pitfalls the department has encountered.

The provisions of 29 CFR 1910.1030 have forever changed the way public-safety workers deliver emergency medical care. Firefighters, police officers and EMTs confront a significant health risk because of occupational exposure to bloodborne pathogens, including the hepatitis B virus and the human immunodeficiency virus, which causes AIDS. OSHA has set the following requirements to minimize or eliminate bloodborne pathogen occupational exposure hazards:

- All personnel must receive annual training and education on the 29 CFR 1910.1030 mandates.
- Each agency must develop a written infection-control program.
- All personnel must wear the proper personal protective clothing and use the proper equipment.

Adapted from Murrey E. Loflin, "Infection Control: Nothing to Sneeze At," *Fire Chief* (February 1994). Reprinted with permission of *Fire Chief* magazine.

- Medical insurance must cover health maintenance needs for the emergency responder, including exact procedures in the event of an occupational exposure.
- A hepatitis B vaccination must be offered to all personnel who could possibly be exposed.

What do these requirements mean to fire and EMS management from moral, legal and financial standpoints? As the requirements of the standard have been applicable during the last two years, have we taken the opportunity to better protect personnel and provide adequate service to our customers? Does the fire service view this standard in the same light as, say, NFPA 1500? How often have we heard the phrase, "I'm not required to comply with this standard, because I'm not governed by a state OSHA program"?

This directs us back to moral responsibility. Though a fire department may not have to comply with OSHA or even NFPA standards, from a moral standpoint a chief must take steps to ensure that his or her personnel are adequately protected by a proactive infection-control program. I know departments that think they are in compliance with 1910.1030 by simply providing personnel with the hepatitis B vaccination. If only it were that easy!

The price of infection control

There are costs involved with implementing an infection-control program. For example, the series of hepatitis B vaccinations costs about $120 per person. Personal protective clothing is another expense.

The philosophy that we have taken is that any piece of equipment, vaccine or procedure that protects our personnel is a good investment. It may cost money, but it's small change compared to the possible alternatives.

What if an employee contracts hepatitis B or HIV from an occupational exposure? What will it cost to provide medical treatment, not to mention salary and other benefits, possibly for the remainder of the infected employee's life? And what about the costs that aren't measurable, like the pain and suffering of the employee and his or her family, and the loss of morale in the department? Could your department afford these costs simply because it failed to develop, implement and manage an effective infection-control program?

As with any new standard, there's bound to be some resistance, whether from those who think it's too expensive or those who like doing things the way they've always been done. Are your department's infection-control procedures being followed? If not, why? Does the infection-control policy need to be reviewed and revised?

With the implementation of this program in our department, I have witnessed a wide range of attitudes, from "Who cares, it's part of the job" to the individual who completes paperwork as if he or she was in the same building with an HIV-positive patient. As the infection-control officer, you must be able to find a happy medium while maintaining credibility.

As mentioned earlier, the procedures or methods for delivering emergency medical care have completely changed. Hopefully, we're operating under the philosophy that the firefighter's, EMT's or paramedic's health and safety is as important as the patient's. If we want to stay in this business as public-safety workers, we have to think about our personal health and safety at each incident.

Unfortunately, the communicable disease problem in this country and throughout the world is going to worsen, regardless of what actions we take. Public-safety workers must take this opportunity to strengthen their defenses against occupational health exposures.

Writing a program

How do you write an infection-control program? Who has the information you need to develop and implement an infection-control program?

The first step is to contact your local OSHA compliance officer and ask for assistance. OSHA has developed sample programs that can help get you started on an effective infection-control program.

Many other resources are available. The USFA's "Guide to Developing and Managing an Emergency Service Infection Control Program" offers information about communicable diseases, sample SOPs, OSHA and Centers for Disease Control and Prevention regulations, and resource contacts. In conjunction with this guide is the National Fire Academy's "Infection Control for Emergency Response Personnel, The Supervisor's Responsibility" course, which teaches the basics on implementing an effective infection-control program.

Another valuable resource is NFPA 1581, *Fire Department Infection Control Program* (1991), which provides information on implementing an infection-control program from both emergency and non-emergency standpoints. The standard is currently going through the revision process to remain current with OSHA and CDC procedures.

One resource I found especially helpful when writing our department's SOPs was the CDC "Guidelines for Prevention of Transmission of HIV and HBV to Health-Care and Public-Safety

Workers." These guidelines provide information on cleaning and decontaminating equipment and clothing.

Training and education

Training and education are critical in infection control. The Virginia Beach Fire Department's 1993 annual in-service infection-control training was conducted by a nurse, which proved to be essential because of past problems with personnel not understanding disease transmission. The training enabled our personnel to better understand how various airborne and blood-borne diseases are transmitted. It also covered the employee notification process: who was to be notified if an employee was exposed to a bloodborne or airborne pathogen, and how the employee would receive test results.

This in-service seemed to be extremely successful in arming personnel with the facts about disease transmission and dispelling many misunderstandings. Plus, personnel were retrained on the reporting procedures and the notification process.

The single toughest issue to sell to our personnel has been personal protective equipment. Deciding what equipment to use requires constant evaluation because of changes in standards, costs and availability.

The use of latex gloves is not a difficult issue, except that personnel want a glove that won't tear and that covers the whole arm. The problem is getting personnel to use eye and face protection and, if needed, complete body protection.

We opted for the combination mask/eye protection. They were placed on each piece of apparatus, but it has taken time for personnel to remember to wear them. In the department SOPs, the mask/protective eyewear are required when suctioning or CPR is being performed.

Several months ago, a firefighter was suctioning a patient who had suffered a severe head injury. The firefighter did not have the mask/eyewear on. The patient vomited, getting body fluids in the eyes and mouth of the firefighter.

As I was investigating this exposure, I asked the firefighter why he wasn't wearing the mask. His response? He didn't have time to put it on. Fortunately, all the tests on the patient came back negative, but I made sure the firefighter knew what a risk he had taken, simply because he hadn't taken a few extra seconds to properly protect himself.

After reviewing protective clothing, I found a gown that can be slipped over the head and tied in back. This seems more practical than the disposable suits we initially used. The gown and booties are to be worn at all trauma situations, such as shootings, childbirth, vehicle accidents or any situation where blood or body fluids might be an issue. We placed four of these suits on each piece of apparatus, up from two. We made more suits available after an incident that occurred about a year ago, when we responded to a shooting with four victims.

The key to PPE is that it is correctly used, accessible, comfortable and durable. As a commitment to infection control, each VBFD member was issued two glove pouches (one for station/work uniform and one for turnout gear) and a disposable CPR mask for use off-duty.

Another point we stressed during training is to have the company officer size up each incident. What PPE will be needed? It is imperative that this is done on *each* call.

We also try to limit the number of personnel who might be exposed to bloodborne pathogens. In the past, everyone wanted to rush on to the scene to see what was happening. If we limit the number of personnel to the minimum required to adequately work the incident, we limit the number of potential exposures.

Reducing employee risk

If a true exposure does occur, such as blood in an EMT's mouth or eyes, it is imperative that the employee be given timely medical treatment. If hepatitis B is suspected, the employee must have a titer taken to determine the antibody level, if he or she has had the vaccination. If not, the employee should be given the hepatitis B immune globulin.

Another very important part of this process is the counseling the employee or member should receive if an exposure occurs. This can be a very difficult time for an employee, especially from a personal and family aspect. A place to go for help should be made available.

Proper decontamination of first aid and personal protective equipment is imperative to the safety and health of employees and the customers we serve. For most items, cleaning with soap and water and disinfecting with chlorine bleach is sufficient, but cleaning turnout gear and station/work uniforms is more difficult. NFPA and CDC both have guidelines for decontaminating these items. The first and most important rule to follow is the manufacturer's cleaning requirements.

NFPA 1581; NFPA 1971, *Structural Fire Fighting Clothing;* and CDC "Guidelines for Prevention of Transmission of HIV and HBV to Health-Care and Public-Safety Workers" have instructions for cleaning turnout gear. The VBFD has identified several key pieces of equipment for clothing decontamination:

- a commercial front-loading washer,
- a commercial dryer,
- a stainless steel sink,

- stainless steel drying racks, and
- a shower for quick cleaning of gross contamination.

We are specifying that the washers be equipped to automatically dispense the appropriate cleaning agents. This eliminates the firefighter "if-a-little-soap-is-good-a-lot-is-better" formula for cleaning clothing. Although front-loading washers are more expensive than top-loading machines, they make up for it in greater capacity, less water used, better cleaning (spinning vs. agitation), more options of garments that can be washed and programmable cleaning cycles.

Per OSHA and department policy, personnel must wash station/work uniforms at the fire station rather than take them home; each station has a residential-type washer and dryer for such purposes.

Police personnel do not have adequate facilities for cleaning and decontamination in the precincts, but while on patrol they are usually close to a fire station, and we have spill kits for police to clean their cars or for EMS personnel to clean ambulances in the event of a blood or body-fluid spill. Each station is also equipped with disposable garments for police or EMS personnel to don if their station/work uniforms become contaminated.

The infection-control officer

As discussed above, personnel must know the infection-control reporting and notification procedures. For starters, personnel must have a contact person, usually the infection-control officer, to notify if an exposure occurs.

Of course, personnel must know what constitutes an occupational exposure. If a firefighter gets blood on his or her intact skin, is this considered an exposure? No, because intact skin is a barrier, just like medical gloves.

If a firefighter has cut his or her arm and then gets a patient's blood or body fluids in this cut, that would be an occupational exposure, and the notification process should begin—and the sooner the better, because the patient needs to be tested. If the firefighter waits, the patient could be treated and released or pass away before the request can be made.

The final rule of the Ryan White Comprehensive AIDS Resource Emergency Act of 1990, scheduled for release early this year, requires that emergency response employees be notified following transport of a patient with certain airborne diseases, and be notified whether victims have certain bloodborne diseases, should an occupational exposure occur.

In the past, using our department as an example, the infection-control officer would notify the hospital of any exposure, and the hospital would report the results of the patient's test back to the infection-control officer, who would pass them on to the employee. The CARE Act requires that the test results go directly to the employee.

Also, we had departmental procedures that required an employee to notify his or her supervisor of an off-duty exposure to a communicable disease. The CARE Act prohibits this.

Infection control has become a top concern for public-safety agencies across the country. The communicable disease issue is not just an urban problem; there is no discrimination among the population of a community. The principal issues are the safety, health and welfare of personnel and proper and appropriate emergency medical care.

Infection control is not something a department or its personnel can take lightly. An effective and efficient infection-control program takes time to develop and implement, and must be managed every day and on every incident.

PART 4

Improving
Productivity

Lessons in Productivity

Improving productivity is no longer just a fashionable concept—it's now a political and economic necessity. Tax and expenditure limitations, lower sales and property tax revenues, less federal aid, and the public's demand for better service and reduced costs add up to one pressing challenge for the modern fire service: improve productivity.

Productivity is the measured result of a triad of components common to any workplace: workload, efficiency, and effectiveness.

Workload is the amount of work performed within a standard time period. Examples of workload measures include the number of fire prevention inspections completed each day, the number of arson arrests each year, or the number of training academy instructional hours each week.

Efficiency is most often expressed as an input/output or output/input ratio. The cost for each fire prevention inspection, arson arrest, or hour of academy instruction are all efficiency measures.

Effectiveness is the assessment of a specific program or an organization's success in achieving desired results. Several effectiveness measures might include reducing fire deaths through a public education program, reducing arson fires by improving investigation techniques and increasing the rate of convictions, or state certification for a predetermined number of firefighters after academy instruction.

Adapted from Joe Schumacher, "Lessons in Productivity," *Fire Engineering* (February 1989). The author extends special thanks to Shelly Cook, City Manager's Office, Aurora, Colorado, for her generous research assistance in preparing this article.

Increasing productivity requires improvements in workload, efficiency, and effectiveness; it's not, however, reduction of the Insurance Services Office rating. Surprisingly, the ISO never originally intended for its esoteric evaluation of the reliability and adequacy of a community's fire defenses to be used by any fire department as a self-selected measure of organizational effectiveness and improved productivity.

Furthermore, improving productivity isn't necessarily providing more bang for the buck. Some departments equate more "bang" with building another fire station or hiring additional firefighters. In most jurisdictions, this isn't the kind of bang the public desires. Most citizens are satisfied with the present level of fire risk, fire losses, and response times. The public wants more tax dollar utility and greater efficiency, which means better use of existing resources.

Productivity improvement program

A formal, organization-wide productivity improvement program is one way to enhance fire department operations. Typically, a PIP examines both the technical and the human sides of an organization. Productivity improvement areas could include work standards and measurements, planning and scheduling, work simplification, greater employee participation, improving motivation, and job enrichment.

The City of Aurora (Colo.) Fire Department, for example, critically examined its organizational structure, personnel, technologies, procedures, policies, and processes in response to a 1983 citywide PIP. Its improvements in efficiency, effectiveness, and workloads included:

- combining several rescue squads into paramedic engines, saving $200,000 per year per rescue squad,
- replacing one engine and ladder company with a "quint" (or combination engine and ladder truck), saving $400,000 initially and $80,000 per year thereafter;
- centralizing staff and firefighter assignments. A suppression division staffing captain now controls all firefighter and equipment assignments; this has significantly improved coordination and reduced overtime costs;
- providing a "roving" microcomputer for suppression division firefighters. One paramedic lieutenant entered the department's entire equipment inventory using a database software package that tracks the location and status of all firefighting equipment;
- computerizing the annual fire and life-safety business inspection process;

- involving suppression division and rescue division firefighters in the annual building inspection process;
- replacing fire prevention bureau uniformed firefighters with nonuniformed civilians;
- using individual activity logs and reports to more accurately track and compile fire prevention bureau inspectors' workloads and to evaluate the efficiency and effectiveness of inspection activities.
- signing mutal aid and overlapping response agreements with the Denver Fire Department and the Cunningham Fire Protection District. This eliminated the need to build at least one $650,000 fire station; and
- merging the training division staff with the Denver Fire Department, creating the Rocky Mountain Fire Academy. This agreement saved Aurora about $7,000,000 (the department would have had to start from scratch) and is the first of several possible joint ventures, including a fire apparatus repair facility, selected hazardous materials responses, and a common dispatching center.

Coproductivity programs

Did you know that taxpayers regularly help their local government deliver public services, which in turn improves productivity? Examples of such coproductivity include placing trash containers or piles of leaves near the street curb for city pickup; not parking on snow-removal routes and fire lanes; and installing security locks, lights, alarm systems, and smoke detectors.

The City of Detroit and the fire departments of Aurora and Colorado Springs all enlisted their citizens to help deliver fire protection services. Each city, using a special coproductivity program, significantly improved its productivity and, surprisingly, enhanced its organization's image, too.

Detroit, Michigan   Detroit's successful efforts to reduce the number of fires during the city's infamous Devil's Night (Halloween night) firesetting and vandal spree is a dramatic coproductivity case study. Mayor Coleman Young and his staff successfully convinced the public to help itself solve a communitywide arson problem.

Detroit's comprehensive campaign, which began in the mid-80s, mobilized 17,000 concerned citizens and city workers dedicated to one common cause—reducing Devil's Night fires. This community's concerted effort included:

- 1,500 neighborhood watch groups and block clubs looking for arsonists and suspicious characters;

- special citizens-band patrols and student volunteers with portable fire extinguishers and mobile radios;
- 20 Domino's Pizza car and van patrols;
- an elementary and junior high school poster/essay contest designed to get youngsters involved and concerned about the damage and dangers of arson and starting fires;
- a public information program encouraging homeowners to leave porch lights on, maintain a local fire watch, and impose a dusk-to-dawn curfew for their children; and
- generating cooperative media support. Most newspapers and television stations agreed to "low-profile" Devil's Night stories, thereby reducing its destructive glamour and macabre mystique.

Additionally, the city reduced the number of arson targets by demolishing 675 vacant buildings and emptying large trash containers just before the long holiday weekend. Detroit also distributed 250,000 informational brochures encouraging homeowners to wet down their garbage and service station operators not to sell gasoline in portable containers. Detroit's mayor also placed city trash collectors, dog catchers, and street sweepers on arson and fire patrol.

The success of this creative and innovative program is readily apparent from the drastic reduction in fire calls during the three-day holiday period.

Aurora, Colorado   The City of Aurora Fire Department developed two programs that place a share of fire prevention and life-safety inspection responsibilities with selected business owners.

Aurora requires child-care center operators to conduct daily, weekly, and monthly inspections of their facilities' fire and life-safety components. Using a diplomatic approach and a special self-inspection form, Aurora's firefighters convinced child-care center managers to participate in this program. A self-inspection form, the centerpiece of the program, is displayed near the alarm panel or on a readily visible bulletin board.

Statistics show that Aurora radically reduced child-care center fire code violations by almost 80% in the first six months of the program.

Aurora's second self-help program requires owners of high-rise buildings and other target hazards to inspect quarterly and test annually their automatic sprinkler systems. An inspection and activity log is prominently displayed near each building's main water control valve for quick code-compliance evaluation by firefighters.

Prior to implementing both programs, Aurora firefighters constantly reminded building owners and managers to inspect and test their building's life-safety systems. This often irritated the owners and placed the department in a strict code enforcement role.

Through these two Aurora programs, business owners and managers become personally responsible for a larger share of

---

Benchmarks of fire protection excellence

Several progressive productivity improvement measures might include:

- drastically reducing the frequency and severity of firefighter injuries and smoke inhalation cases by implementing a department-wide safety program including a mandatory turnout gear and SCBA policy for at least all structural fires, car fires, and haz-mat incidents;
- reducing fires and fire deaths within the jurisdiction by sectioning the city into grids and assigning fire management areas to local station officers;
- developing a descriptive and inspirational mission statement for each division of the department;
- setting realistic yet challenging performance objectives for each division of the department and every program of the fire department's budget;
- establishing individual performance and workload criteria (especially at the senior command and staff level) based on members' knowledge, skill, ability, job maturity, and career aspirations;
- combining selected staff and line positions;
- using a citizen satisfaction survey to assess division or departmental effectiveness;
- using containment or fire control time to assess suppression division efficiency;
- using postfire analysis sessions as a learning activity and training needs assessment tool—not as a medium to attach blame;
- merging the building department's inspection responsibilities with your department's fire prevention/inspections bureau;
- hiring a fire protection engineer as the fire marshal;
- developing a career plan for each department member;
- implementing an officer development program;
- developing a mentor system for firefighters and junior officers; and
- using state certification guidelines as the minimum training and competency criteria.

---

code activities within their structures. Aurora's firefighters can advise and diplomatically sell fire prevention rather than mandate code enforcement.

Colorado Springs, Colorado   The Colorado Springs Fire Department also uses a self-help inspection program—this one targeted at low-hazard (B-1 and B-2) business occupancies such as doctors' offices—that is impressively successful. During annual fire and life-safety building inspections conducted by the department's suppression firefighters, B-1 or B-2 business owners are asked to inspect their own facility. If agreed upon, the department provides both verbal and written instructions, including a detailed explanation of its self-inspection form. An addressed, stamped envelope accompanies the form to help ensure an acceptable rate of return.

The Colorado Springs Fire Department reports a remarkable 98% return rate over the past two years for the inspection program, with no significant problems in getting people to comply.

Coproductivity programs illustrate the public's willingness to assist local governments in delivering municipal services. They also reduce a community's fire risk and generate significant community support. Most business owners will not only readily accept a greater share of code enforcement responsibility, but often genuinely welcome the opportunity to fulfill code requirements. This kind of fire department/citizen interaction can significantly enhance the fire department's image within the community.

Volunteer and self-help coproductivity programs can help us get through financially turbulent and demanding times and better the quality of services in good times as well. Hence, fire chiefs can simultaneously do more with less in their jurisdictions by implementing innovative and exemplary productivity improvements similar to Detroit's volunteer program and the self-help inspection programs instituted by the Colorado fire departments of Aurora and Colorado Springs.

CITY OF COLORADO SPRINGS
FIRE DEPARTMENT

SELF INSPECTION REPORT

Issue
Date _____

Inspection
Number _____

Business Name _____   Street Address/Number _____   Business Telephone _____

Principle Business Activity _____   Responsible Party _____   Responsible Party Telephone
(For Emergency Contact)

DIRECTIONS

1. Walk through your business with this form in hand. Answer all questions listed below.
2. You have until _____ to complete this form. If you need assistance, check the box below or call 578-7040.
3. When inspection is completed and corrections made, sign and date the form below.
4. Enclose the white copy of this form in the mailing envelope which has been provided. Keep the yellow copy for your records.

★   ★   ★   ★   ★   ★   ★   ★   ★   ★   ★   ★   ★   ★   ★   ★

		YES	NO	Not Applicable
1.a.	Are the address numbers facing the street of address?	___	___	
b.	Are they visible and legible from the roadway?	___	___	
2.	Does your building have fire lanes, and if so, are they kept accessible and unblocked?	___	___	___
3.a.	Are all exit doors kept unlocked and openable from the inside during business hours?	___	___	
b.	Are exit corridors, stairways and hallways leading to exits unobstructed?	___	___	
c.	Are illuminated exit signs in working order?	___	___	___
4.	Are fire extinguishers hung on the wall, checked at regular intervals, and inspected annually? Indicate last inspection date. _____	___	___	
5.	Are all electrical cords and extension cords in good condition? (Insulation not frayed or broken.) Note: If extension cords are placed under rugs, please remove them immediately.	___	___	
6.	Are boiler, furnace, or water heater rooms kept clear of flammable or combustible liquids?	___	___	
7.	Are other combustible materials kept a minimum of five feet away from boiler, furnaces, and water heaters?	___	___	

★   ★   ★   ★   ★   ★   ★   ★   ★   ★   ★   ★   ★   ★   ★   ★

THANK YOU FOR YOUR COOPERATION

Richard C. Smith
Fire Chief

Responsible Party Signature _____   Date _____

Check this box if you need Fire
Prevention assistance or call 578-7040.   ☐

From Hoselines to Online

John A. Granito

It's a cold, rainy night. A wide-bodied jet overshoots the airport runway, crashing into a busy highway. The plane completely destroys two cars. A tanker truck loaded with gasoline slams on the brakes and jackknifes, narrowly avoiding the aircraft. Surviving passengers jump onto the plane's evacuation slides as a fire begins in one of the port engines.

Over the next several hours, the responding fire officer will be tested to the limit as he manages men, women, and equipment from many fire stations in the metro area. And during the entire session, he will remain at his duty station, available to respond to a real emergency. The aircraft, the tanker, and the 20-mile traffic backup exist only in a simulation.

Welcome to the wonderful world of computers.

Computers and training

Of all the questions that cause me to break out in a cold sweat, the most frightening is "Are you computer literate?" Everyone, including my youngest grandchild, knows more about computers than I do. It'll come as no surprise, then, that I leaned on friends and colleagues when preparing this article describing some of the ways in which computers are changing how the fire service trains personnel, conducts inspections, develops master plans, and communicates.

The question I asked was pretty straightforward: "For your type of work, how are computers making a significant, positive difference?"

Reprinted with permission from *NFPA Journal*® (January/February 1995, vol. 89, no. 1) © 1995, National Fire Protection Association, Quincy, MA 02269.

The first area I looked at was training.

Training on real equipment will always be an important part of a fire fighter's work. But computer training systems add an extra dimension by allowing fire fighters to handle incidents that are too hard, too expensive, or too dangerous to set up in a training facility.

Using a standard desktop computer, fire officers can practice the command and control decisions they would make during real emergency responses and disaster recoveries. Users can rehearse an infinite variety of incidents, including fires, haz-mat spills, and natural disasters, whenever there is a spare moment. This lets students work at their own pace and ensures that each student receives the same information.

Best of all, traditional computer-based training with boring text screens has been replaced by multimedia training, which uses sophisticated graphics, as well as sound, animation, and photographs. According to Philip DiNenno and Geoff Snowman of Hughes Associates, Inc., in Columbia, Maryland, a typical multimedia training system consists of a 386 or 486 computer, with a keyboard, monitor, mouse, and CD-ROM drive.

Unlike some office software, training programs are usually easy to use, so that a minimal amount of time is spent learning to use the training system itself. Typically, multimedia training programs on IBM compatibles run in Microsoft Windows. Apple Macintosh computers are also widely used.

A typical example of a multimedia project is the carrier deck fire fighting curriculum that Hughes Associates is currently developing for the U.S. Navy. This curriculum consists of five CD-ROMs that familiarize the user with the carrier deck, flammable materials and ordnance, fire fighting team organization, fire fighting incidents, and crash and salvage procedures. During each scenario, the student fire fighter plays a variety of roles and makes the crucial decisions needed to bring the incident under control.

The curriculum CD-ROMs store full-screen, full-motion videos of equipment, personnel, and techniques. They are narrated and contain actual sounds from the flight deck. An optional program tracks the student's progress, meeting the Navy's need for detailed training records.

Another multimedia training program developed by Hughes Associates allows fire fighters to practice the basic skills that the driver and crew of an engine company need when responding to a haz-mat incident. This program teaches a wide variety of tasks, ranging from high-level command and control to basic skills such as equipment operation.

Virtual reality multimedia systems increase the quality of the illusion by creating a world that exists only within the system. The student wears a special headset with goggles that provide a three-dimensional view of the computer's world. As the student looks in different directions, the computer senses head movements and changes the view in the goggles. This gives the student an extremely realistic impression of a fictional world in which he or she can pick up objects using a glove that senses hand movements.

Virtual reality can give a novice fire fighter the experience he or she needs in an environment in which one mistake in the real world would lead not to a chance to try again, but to injury or death. Currently, virtual reality techniques need expensive workstation computers. According to DiNenno and Snowman, however, virtual reality will probably be available on any desktop system in 2 to 4 years.

Multimedia training is becoming widely accepted in government and industry to deliver high-quality, consistent training wherever and whenever needed. The fire service's training needs are unique, but multimedia training can fill the gaps in most traditional training approaches and contribute to the ultimate goal of producing well-trained, highly skilled fire service personnel.

Virtual reality demonstrates exactly how the power and versatility of desktop computers can take us a giant step forward in providing realistic and interesting training—and it points toward the next giant step in that area.

Immersive virtual environments

The problems of live fire suppression training are certainly well-known. As John Cater, principal engineer of Advanced Simulation and Training Concepts at the Southwest Research Institute in San Antonio, observes, "fire fighting training in most fire schools is still provided by setting fires in specialized burn buildings, an expensive undertaking. The buildings are constructed of high-temperature concrete blocks or bricks, and the flames are fueled by gas and diesel fuel to create realistic heat and dense smoke. The Occupational Safety and Health Administration and the Environmental Protection Agency are actively working to eliminate the personal and environmental hazards of staging these real fires, and alternative methods of fire protection training are being pursued by leading training facilities around the world."

One of these alternative methods is called "virtual environments," a concept with which Cater is very familiar. He heads a research and development program whose goal is to produce a system called the Advanced Virtual Environment Real Time Fire Trainer.

In an article entitled "Deep Immersion Virtual Environments" that appeared in *Technology Today* in March 1994, Cater described how "the sights, sounds, smells, and other sensations contributing to these lifelike experiences are created with electronic sensors, microencapsulated odor chemicals, various environment-altering equipment, three-dimensional sound systems, and computer-generated images."

In the article, Cater notes that "a description of any virtual environment system must consist of at least three components. The first is the experience that the user has while linked with the computer. The second is the hardware linking the human and computer into one large, closed-loop feedback system. The third is the software that generates the imagery and acoustic responses sensed during the experience.

"The experiences encountered in virtual environments are often described by such phrases as 'the human and the computer have fused,' or 'you have the feeling of being there.' However, there are different virtual environment paradigms under development at computer interface laboratories around the world, each designed to induce sensory experiences appropriate to particular applications. The most prevalent ones are immersive, through-the-window, and second-person systems."

Working with the State Fire Training Directors Association at the Southwest Research Institute's Deep Immersion Virtual Environment (DIVE) Laboratory, Cater's team examines applications for immersive virtual environments, which he describes in *Technology Today* as "those that use the . . . goggle displays with three-dimensional sound provided by high-quality headphones." Cater's team involves as many senses as possible, having employed sight, hearing, smell, touch—everything but taste—to date.

In addition to images and sound, the system generates radiant heat and smoke odors to more closely replicate an actual fire environment. The user actually feels that he or she is performing the task being presented by the computer.

A second type of virtual environment paradigm is the through-the-window environment, best illustrated by an interactive video game. In these systems, says Cater, "another environment exists within the computer, but the user must view it through the computer monitor screen."

The third type of system is the second-person system, in which the user is photographed with a video camera and his or her likeness is superimposed on a computer-generated scene. The computer interprets the movements and gestures the overlaid figure makes, using them to modify the underlying environment accordingly.

Conceptually, computer-based virtual environments are more than 30 years old, but it is only in the past 5 years that affordable technology has been developed. The hardware used in these virtual environments is still not cheap, however. The systems include transducers, which transform the user's head and body positions into computer data, as well as displays and image generators, which produce visual representations of the data collected by the transducers. According to *Technology Today,* such computers typically cost $25,000 to $50,000 per eye—and one computer is often needed for each eye to provide real-time imaging speeds in three-dimensional systems.

Computers make inspections easier, too

Not all computer advances depend on such complex systems, however. Assistant Chief Richard Carman, Fire Marshal of the Puyallup, Washington, Fire Department, has been very successful using a second-generation fire inspection management system with a write-on, clipboard-based computer.

"For many of us, springtime brings warm weather, vacations, and maybe even a family visit to the fair," says Carman. "To the Puyallup Fire Department, the state fair means much more than hot dogs, cotton candy, and midway rides. It means hard work, and lots of it. Consider a population more than tripling in one evening, hundreds of new businesses opening in only a few days, and your jurisdiction growing instantly by 60 acres. As the fire marshal in Puyallup, it's my job to provide fire and life safety services to the fair, without increasing personnel.

"The biggest impact on the bureau is the increased inspection workload—500 inspections in 3 days! But in the spring of 1994, a single inspector completed all these inspections and reinspections in a few days. What made this possible? Computer technology!"

Carman says that the work that once took a small army of inspectors and data-entry staff to complete was handled by a lone inspector armed with a pen-based computer and a ballpoint pen. He inspected every tent, helium tank, flammable decoration, electrical panel, fire extinguisher, and kitchen hood at the fair, then electronically revised the bureau databases and prepared summary reports for the fire chief.

Until this year, the bureau sent its inspectors into the fair carrying a stack of multipart forms, code books, and form letters. When the inspectors finally returned to the office, they placed their reports on the top of a growing mountain of forms for the data-entry personnel to transcribe into the department database. A day of inspections translated into 40 hours of laborious data entry, and incomplete forms slowed the process and weakened the value of the database. The inevitable word-processing errors further reduced the accuracy of the data.

Today, the inspectors' handwriting is instantly turned into typed text.

"The first time you see this," says Carman, "you'll be amazed. Since this essentially eliminates all typing, the errors that used to be made during this step are gone forever. And it's not just the errors that are gone: Overtime for data-entry personnel is now a thing of the past. Inspectors simply touch an icon on the screen, and the data collected are electronically transferred to the department computer system. What used to take a week to enter is now completed in minutes, 100 percent error-free. And since the pen computers know when an inspection form is not completed properly, incomplete forms cannot be saved in the field."

On-screen prompts help the inspector fill out the necessary forms correctly. And code books are no longer needed, since the pen-based computers contain reference databases that allow the inspector to locate code sections and requirements easily. Training is simple, and after a half-hour of classroom orientation and an hour or two in the field, inspectors are on their own.

Although gathering inspection data is important, useful reporting of these data is critical.

"Paper forms with manual data entry just don't allow for detailed reporting," Carman notes. "This is why, in the past, we tracked only essential data, such as business names and emergency contact numbers.

"That has changed dramatically. With the pen computers routinely tracking the smallest detail, comprehensive reporting is now simple. After the fair, we produced a lot of reports, most of which would not have been possible previously. One of these reports includes data on specific violations, which will help us prepare our pre-event requirement literature in the future."

Carman says that the fair was a test for the Puyallup Fire Department pen computers. Because the department knows that the computers worked under the extreme demands of the fair, they are confident that the computers will also work well during routine inspections—which is a boon for this growing city. In the past 10 years, occupancy inspections in Puyallup have doubled. A building boom is in full force and is expected to continue for many years. As the city strains to provide services to the expanding area, the fire department is challenged to control ongoing costs. Fortunately, its one-time capital expenditure of $3,450 for a hand-held "clipboard" computer will result in savings year after year—and will improve the service being provided, too.

Computing a department's needs and capabilities

Many fire departments call on outside organizations to help them update master plans and assist with station location and relocation calculations. Mark Morse, vice president for Public Safety Programs at MMA Consulting Group, Inc., in Boston, uses

A computer review of existing fire station locations determines whether desired coverage and response objectives are being met. It is even possible to determine how long it takes to reach a target area.

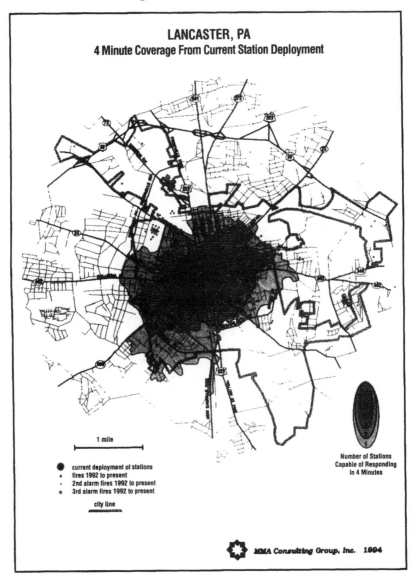

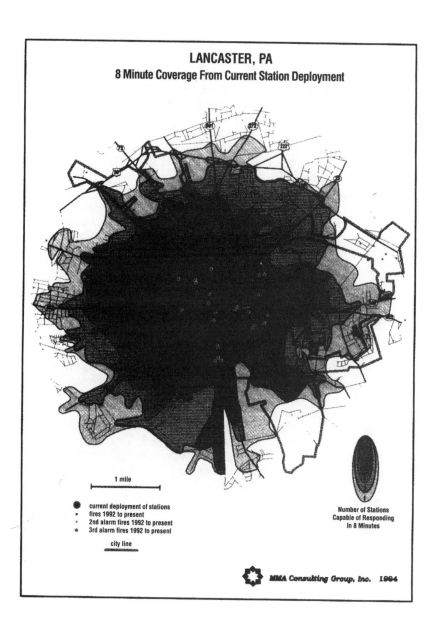

LANCASTER, PA

8 Minute Coverage From Current Station Deployment

1 mile

● current deployment of stations
· fires 1992 to present
· 2nd alarm fires 1992 to present
✦ 3rd alarm fires 1992 to present

city line

Number of Stations
Capable of Responding
In 8 Minutes

MMA Consulting Group, Inc. 1994

computers to provide answers and alternative responses to these key issues.

"Computers have changed the way we evaluate fire, rescue, and EMS services enormously," according to Morse. "Consultants have always relied heavily on expert observations and opinions supported by available data, but sometimes it's difficult to support consulting analysis with realistic alternative strategies, given the countless variables that often are present. Using geographic information systems (GIS), plus complex data analysis and sophisticated costing analysis—all done with computers—we've expanded tremendously the quality of consulting reports, of the analysis, and of the judgments, as well as the availability of sound alternatives."

Fire departments often call on consultants to analyze station location or relocation issues, personnel deployment strategies, cost of services, and a host of other issues which would be almost impossible to understand and analyze without sophisticated computer programs. Fire station location or relocation studies are a perfect example of the way computer analysis strongly supports final recommendations.

Using a GIS-based system, consultants can review a range of alternatives for a selected level of coverage and see those alternatives on a map. A computer review of existing station locations determines whether desired coverage and response objectives are being met. It is even possible to determine how long it takes for a full alarm assignment to reach a target area, factoring into the analysis one-way streets and varying the speed of response by street or even by time of day to reflect traffic conditions. The location of past incidents, housing characteristics, and target areas can be "overlaid" so that the analysis is more complete. Thus, an entire array of possibilities may be examined. The more reasonable the possibilities and approaches considered, the more likely it is that the decisions ultimately made will reflect the true conditions and needs of a municipality.

"Let me give a good example of how a computer software program we use is making both problem analysis and solution-path identification easier," says Morse. "This example is from a project we've just completed involving more than 40 fire departments that protect a very large county."

While parts of the county are urban, most of it is suburban and rural, and a good portion of it has no municipal water supply. Working with a consultant, county officials and fire department officers designed a plan to improve the ISO/CRS public protection classification for structures that are located within 5 miles of a fire station but have no water main service.

The fire suppression rating schedule now credits the delivery of water to an incident, not just through a pressurized hydrant system, but also by tanker shuttle or relay and by drafting from certified sites. A department's ability to deliver a sustained, specified fire flow for at least 2 hours may—with certain detailed stipulations—result in significant insurance savings.

"Using our computer program," Morse says, "officials easily identified all structures within 5 road miles of an existing station, plus areas where a new or relocated station might be possible. Still using the computer, we then hypothetically redeployed existing tankers and portable tanks to key stations, taking into account the certified year-round drafting sites and hydrants already in place and the ISO-required fire flows."

In such situations, the computer reveals that a redeployment of existing resources among departments willing to engage in a detailed "functional consolidation" program may give property owners impressive savings. As Morse notes, "the beauty of the computer is that it enables us to play out this scenario long before a department has to agree to move a tanker, or buy large-diameter hose, or identify rural drafting sites that meet the specs."

GIS-based computer analysis is the type of analysis most frequently discussed by departments undertaking a master plan, analyzing staffing, or locating or relocating a station. However, other tools are just as valuable.

Spreadsheet and data-based computer applications allow for a more thorough analysis than would have been thought possible 20 years ago. And as a result of this analysis, fire departments are often able to accurately measure their activities and service delivery or capacity, to reconsider the conventional wisdom, and to develop more appropriate strategies.

It is important in this era of cost consciousness to be able to determine the true costs of services. How much does the department's public education program cost? What is the price of enforcement? How much do volunteers cost? Valid cost data often provide the documentation fire service administrators need to make informed decisions or persuasive arguments to local legislators.

It is clear that fire departments expect sophisticated reasoning and justifications for major recommendations, especially when those recommendations have substantial cost implications. The use of advanced computer software programming greatly enhances a department's ability to analyze and understand program inputs and outgoing services.

Enhancing communications systems

Edward Olmstead, also an MMA Consulting Group staff member and a director of the New York State Association of Fire Chiefs, uses computer communications equipment every day.

Computer modeling

Fire departments are not the only fire protection practitioners using computers to enhance their effectiveness. Fire protection engineers are also taking advantage of the computer to model scenarios that will help them understand fire behavior and human behavior in fires, and allow them to design more efficient fire protection systems. Two examples of such computer models are FPEtool and HAZARD I.

FPEtool is a computerized package of relatively simple engineering equations and models, using calculations based on established engineering relationships which are useful in estimating the potential fire hazard in buildings. The package, developed by the Building and Fire Research Laboratory at the National Institute of Standards and Technology with extensive support from the U.S. General Services Administration, addresses problems related to fire development in buildings and the resulting conditions and response of fire protection systems.

FPEtool expresses hazardous conditions in terms of the temperature, location, visual obscuration, latent and potential energy, oxygen content, and carbon monoxide and carbon dioxide concentrations in the smoke and hot gases a fire produces. FPEtool also includes the means for estimating egress time; the ignition of exposed items; smoke flows; fire, wind, and stack pressures on a door; sprinkler and detector activation; and other values useful in evaluating fire hazards in building spaces.

Version 3.2 of FPEtool is now available. New features include smoke waves in a long corridor, reduction in burning rate under sprinkler spray, and tenability in areas of refuge. The new users' manual clearly describes the application, theory, limitations, input and output, and literature references for each calculation.

Researchers at the NIST Building and Fire Research Laboratory also developed HAZARD I, a fire hazard assessment method with associated computer software. HAZARD I is the most comprehensive integrated model for fire hazard assessment available today.

"Today's fire service officer has computerized communications opportunities that were virtually unknown 10 years ago," he says. "They include fax machines, electronic file transfer, electronic mail, and electronic bulletin boards. A variety of hardware platforms, from sophisticated local area networks (LANs) to lap-

To use HAZARD I, the computer operator specifies the fire and its growth, the building and its characteristics, and the occupants and their locations and characteristics as input variables. The software then calculates the development of fire effects— smoke, gases, thermal effects, oxygen depletion—throughout the building over time; the reactions and actions of the occupants, including their attempts to evacuate; the activation of detectors; and the predicted fatal injury or survival of every occupant. If the user's input is accurate and the real fire or fires of interest to the user involve situations, buildings, and occupants whose characteristics follow the assumptions of HAZARD I, the model's calculations will predict outcomes in real fires reasonably well, providing a wealth of information useful in decision-making.

The HAZARD I package consists of a two-volume report and a set of computer disks containing the program. Documentation of the underlying science used in the models, along with a detailed discussion of assumptions and their projected impact on results and a set of worked examples, is presented in the *HAZARD I Technical Reference Guide.* The accompanying *HAZARD I Software User's Guide* includes detailed instructions for using the software, the form of the data each module requires, and examples for using the software in a self-teaching format that incorporates pictures of the computer screens as they should appear. HAZARD I version 1.2 has been improved to include up to 15 rooms, 16 fires, and ceiling and floor venting. Specific applications depend on the user, but some include material/product performance evaluation, fire reconstruction and litigation, evaluation of code changes and variances, fire department preplanning, and extrapolation of fire test data to additional physical configurations.

Both FPEtool and HAZARD I are available from NFPA's One-Stop Data Shop. The cost of FPEtool, covering shipping and handling only, is $8.96 for NFPA members and $9.95 for nonmembers. The cost of HAZARD I is $225 for NFPA members and $250 for nonmembers. For more information on either package or to order, call (617) 984-7450.

top computers, can all provide the fire officer with electronic capabilities."

The addition of fax/modem hardware to computers elevates faxing to its next level, permitting instant document transmission directly from a computer without first printing the document.

Two basic types of software can be used with fax/modems. The first requires the conversion of a completed document into an ASCII format file. The second is built into other software programs, such as word processing programs. This allows for the immediate conversion of the document into a fax-compatible format, followed by transmission.

Faxed documents can be received either by a standard fax machine that prints the documents out or by another computer equipped with compatible fax/modem hardware. In this case, the transmission is paperless until the recipient prints the document.

Another method of transferring information involves the direct transfer of computer files from one computer to another. This requires four elements at both ends of the transfer: a computer, a modem, communications software, and a phone line. A call is placed by one computer to a second computer, and the communications software electronically connects the two. The software then selects and transfers the files, a process that can be controlled by those at the transmitting and receiving computers. A number of different file transfer protocols may be used.

The most recent processing software developments facilitate the conversion of transferred files into a compatible format, thus allowing the transfer of a DOS file to a Macintosh computer and vice versa. Electronic file transfer makes it possible to transfer large documents that include text, spreadsheets, graphics, and entire programs.

Another exciting development is electronic mail, or E-mail, which is rapidly becoming the medium of choice for both the office and the traveler. E-mail has all the features of ordinary mail. Copies can be sent to several recipients, a return receipt can be produced, files can be transferred, and so on. Mail can be filed, printed, forwarded, or deleted.

Several commercial electronic mail services are available today, including Compuserve, ICHIEFS (Connect, Inc.), America Online, Prodigy, and the Internet, and each can send electronic mail anywhere in the world. Mail is prepared in the appropriate software communications program, then sent to a recipient's electronic mailbox. Delivery times are usually measured in minutes—although certain services may take longer—so it is literally possible for two individuals at distant locations to exchange critical correspondence almost instantaneously.

Yet another form of communication is the electronic bulletin board on which a posted message can be read by anyone who happens to browse through it. This dramatically expands a document's audience, increasing the number of people who can request information, share information, or simply talk to each other. Two examples of electronic bulletin boards include ICHIEFS and the Safetynet, both of which provide message posting and exchange, electronic mail, file upload and download, and information databases called libraries.

Users of electronic bulletin boards are literally in contact with the entire world. Many of them post urgent federal, state, and local legislative information that will have an impact on emergency service operations. Or they conduct database searches of national resources such as the NFPA's Morgan Library or the National Fire Academy.

All this sounds simple, but users of electronic formats must be prepared for a significant investment of sweat equity. Once they've mastered the basic skills, they find the advanced capabilities of the electronic formats relatively simple. But, in an electronic world where there are no uniform file, protocol, hardware, or software standards, communicating across different systems requires some effort.

An additional consideration is cost: None of this is free. However, one can easily measure the benefits of a properly designed, administered, and used system in increased productivity, efficiency, and effectiveness.

Computers and emergency services

Also increasing productivity, efficiency, and effectiveness, at least in Monroe County, New York, are computer-based emergency service communications centers.

Recently, I had a call from Captain Ted Conners of the East Rochester, New York, Fire Department extolling Monroe County's brand-new, computer-based emergency service communications center, which dispatches most of the community's 2,800 volunteer and 800 career responders. The county, which covers 663 square miles and has 714,000 residents, is served by 41 fire departments that run out of 93 stations, including 16 in the City of Rochester, and use more than 300 emergency vehicles. Ted suggested that I check out the emergency service center, simply because it shows how the power of a computer-based system can be harnessed to serve a typical urban area served by a wide variety of emergency organizations.

According to Thomas Free, senior shift supervisor at the new center, "our community has used enhanced 911 and CAD systems since 1985, but recent innovations in technology now allow us to serve those in the fire suppression and EMS services more efficiently than ever before."

The state-of-the-art emergency service center, called the Office of Emergency Communications, or OEC, was opened on June

Computers and kids—a good fire safety mix

When I said that my youngest grandchild could use a computer, I was only stating what most of us already know: Kids find computers fun. They become proficient very quickly, and they learn from them—something the engineers and software designers at FPE Software, Inc. in Prince Frederick, Maryland, keep in mind as they produce fire safety programs and game software for children.

"Fire safety education is an ongoing process which we in the business take very seriously," says Kevin Kimmel, an engineer and software designer at FPE Software. "Over time, we've developed a number of methods of promoting fire safety education, including classroom visits, coloring and comic books, videos, and musical cassettes. With personal computers becoming more and more accessible in school and at home, it's only natural that fire safety education will progress into this new format."

Computer hardware significantly affects the type of computer games produced. Eight years ago, full-color interactive graphics

5, 1994 with a new CAD system, new telephone and radio systems, and ergonomically correct dispatcher work stations developed to provide a healthy, user-friendly work environment. The center's workflow was also designed to be user-friendly. For example, an interface between the CAD system and the CETRON tone encoding equipment now allows dispatchers to execute from their terminals a simple dispatch command to send tones. They no longer have to go to a keypad and look up a four-digit number before they can alert a department or agency.

New tower sites and microwave links were established throughout the county to support new transmitter and receiver sites, enhancing alerting coverage and portable operation in the area. Soon to be operational is equipment that will allow three different transmitter sites in the county to transmit simultaneously to provide effective paging alerting for the volunteer services. No matter where the volunteers are, they'll be able to hear a strong radio signal. Receiver sites are being upgraded, as well, to allow for effective talk-back coverage from portables to the OEC from all areas of the county. Installation of an 800-Mhz system that will support terminals and PCs in all area fire and EMS stations has also begun.

Computer interfaces with the OEC's CAD system will give fire fighters and EMS workers access to all the information that the 911 dispatcher has at the center's work station. The local re-

would have been difficult, if not impossible, to perform. Today, desktop computers use color, sound, music, and interaction to hold a child's attention long enough to establish an effective fire safety message.

The age of the audience is an important consideration in developing computer games, as well. To improve the likelihood of success, it is necessary to match the subject to the interests of the age group and to balance the game's entertainment and educational components. Without a good balance, a program, however well-intentioned, will not be successful.

"Fire safety is a vitally important message, one that should be discussed throughout the year," says Kimmel. "Computer games provide teachers, librarians, and fire safety educators with a fire safety education tool they can use year round, as long as the computer equipment is available. As more and more people have access to computers, more and more of our children will be able to learn about and understand fire safety."

sponding agency will now be able to access cross streets, hydrant locations, hazard files, call-back numbers, names, and locations on a system that also records the time of alarm, the amount of time spent en route, and the time responders arrive. This will help alleviate congestion on already over-crowded radio channels, since local agencies will no longer have to ask "Where did the call come from?" or "Can I have my time out?" All the information available to the local dispatchers will help officers and incident commanders to keep better records and to fill out the required state and local incident reports.

Computer-aided management of emergency operations, or CAMEO, is also available to all fire agencies in the area. CAMEO provides an exhaustive computer database of hazardous materials and chemical properties of hazardous materials, as well as mapping applications for response, planning, and local operational tasks (MARPLOT).

Monroe County also anticipates that it will eventually replace its tone/voice paging and alerting systems with digital paging. This will allow the dispatcher to alert responders without transmitting a long series of tones before the voice message, which may not be easily heard or understood. Responders carrying digital pagers will be able to read the location of the emergency, the box numbers, and the type of emergency in an alphanumeric format on their belt-carried pagers. This, too, will help decrease channel congestion and give the responders a clear, concise indication of where they must go and what they will find when they get there.

All these systems are just examples of the things computers can do for us now. Can you imagine what they'll be able to do for emergency services 20 years from now? Wow!

City Managers and the Fire Service: Survey Results

Ron Coleman and
Randy R. Bruegman

Editor's note: The following article reports the results of a survey asking city managers their views of the fire service. After summarizing the responses, the authors challenge their colleagues in the fire service to improve communication between their departments and the appointed and elected officials with whom they work.

Want to know what city managers really think about the fire service and fire chiefs' leadership ability? During an annual conference of the International City/County Management Association in Chicago, the authors and IAFC staff liaison Andrea Walter were able to ask the question. They presented a seminar entitled *New Challenges Facing Fire Departments.*

The session was divided into two parts. The first, *Fire Service 2000—The Forces of Change,* provided the managers an overview of some of the changes the fire service will face during the next decade. The second half of the program included an overview of the fire service accreditation program.

We had the managers complete a survey before the session started and one at the end of the day to determine their perspectives of the fire service, the role of the chief in meeting the challenges of the future, and their feelings about the fire service accreditation model.

Survey results appear on the following pages.

Adapted from "City Manager Survey Reveals Tough View of Fire Service and Chiefs," by Chief Ron Coleman and Chief Randy R. Bruegman, courtesy of *IAFC on Scene* (November 1, 1994).

What do you believe is the single biggest issue that you and your fire chief will face in the next five years?

- Staffing and equipment replacement
- Conversion from a three-tier to a single-tier system
- Unfunded mandates, confined space rescue, Title III, NFPA
- Establishing a permanent funding source to allow the expansion of a county fire service in developing areas
- Increased costs, increased union demands, higher public expectations and less income while state and federal mandates continue
- EMS
- Keeping cost of service at a reasonable level
- Staffing
- Female employees
- Limited financial resources and a work force with a poor work ethic—gone are the days when you could expect a fair day's work for a fair day's pay
- Increasing call volume, funding for more personnel
- Increase in work-related injuries and sickness due to more calls and exposure to infectious diseases
- Funding needed service or smaller department—per capita costs are high!
- Ability to gain political support for funding and resources when the city does not provide advanced EMS at this time
- EMS and hazardous materials
- Downsizing to meet budget constraints—whether a freestanding city of 30,000 without city EMS can continue to support a full-time paid department
- Need to manage a plan to be prepared for increasing hazardous materials entering the community
- Communication needs within the department resulting from change from a military-type organization to team and empowerment environments
- Changes in service needs in the community
- Change traditions in work schedule and work tasks and responsibilities become more involved in community issues
- Conversion to paid, full-time staff and integration with existing part-time and on-call volunteers
- Growth of the city in population and area coverage
- Meeting needs in the area of EMS and fire suppression while looking at the benefits of staffing differently for peak service rather than the traditional 24-hour shifts
- Aggressive annexation will cause us to consider a relocation of an existing station or adding a fire station

- Desire to consolidate services and reduce costs versus a desire to maintain the past
- Participating in cost-cutting requirements for entire organization—the fire department needs to stop politicking and become a team with the city
- Reduce personnel costs
- Fire service costs
- Public/private interface on EMS
- Reduced financial resources
- Problems in recruiting volunteers

Do you believe that your fire chief has a plan to meet the challenges ahead?
Yes—23%
No—77%

Is the fire department taking action to create opportunities for change?
Yes—63%
No—37%

Are the goals and objectives, policies and procedures of the fire department closely linked with your plan for the community at large?
Yes—52%
No—48%

If "No," why not?
- Traditional contractual arrangements with municipalities limits flexibility
- Now developing, integrating goals into municipal plan
- No advanced life support or medical transportation
- Lack of productivity within the fire service
- City officials need to review the needs and obligations of the fire service
- Goals not financed for implementation
- Overall plans/goals vague and constantly changing as the city grows at a rapid pace
- Volunteer fire department never established close links with city hall and vice versa
- They are looking for ways to expand services to justify existence; the city needs to examine the priorities
- The city has the support of the fire chief but not the department, i.e., the union

- Extremely resistant to change and defining the needs of department by developing objectives
- Resistance of personnel and unwillingness/inability of fire management to effectively lead them
- Lack of coordination and establishment of goals and objectives for community at large—will the fire department participate or protect its turf in this effort?
- Planning not integrated, but it will be soon

On a scale of one to ten, one being the highest and ten the lowest, how would you rank the fire department as being a participant on the overall management team in your community?

High   Low

1	2	3	4	5	6	7	8	9	10
7	7	7	19	22	4	7	15	7	4

Number of respondents

On a scale of one to ten, one being the highest and ten the lowest, how would you rank the fire department as being designed and managed in relationship to the risk level in the community and the needs of the elected body?

High   Low

1	2	3	4	5	6	7	8	9	10
0	11	7	29	11	4	19	15	4	0

Number of respondents

If fire service accreditation was available today, would you encourage your fire chief to participate?
Yes—98%
No—2%

What does it all mean?

One of the surprises that came out in the survey results is that 77 percent of the managers did not feel that the fire chief was planning to meet the challenges ahead. Also, there was a high percentage of negative response relating to the fire departments' goals and objectives being linked with the overall community plan and how the fire service (and fire chief in particular) are linked into the overall management team. This could be taken in two contexts:

The group of managers that attended this seminar could be having problems with their fire service and, therefore, have an overall negative impression of what fire departments do. However, in discussions and open dialogue throughout this whole seminar, that did not appear to be the case. What was clear was that the managers are looking for fire chiefs in the 90s to be less parochial and much more global in their perspective.

Many of the more lengthy discussions revolved around such things as productivity, work schedules, why fire departments have to have the largest and most expensive fire trucks, consolidations, territories, and the traditional aspects of not only the fire service but also the fire chief.

We should take this information and the perspectives offered and use them wisely.

The last question we asked the managers was if fire service accreditation was available today, would they encourage their chief officers to become part of the process. Ninety-eight percent indicated they would encourage their chiefs to become involved as another means to measure the effectiveness and efficiency of their organizations.

It is clear to us that we have a substantial amount of work that needs to be done to educate and enlighten those who we work for. For many communities, the public safety budget represents the largest percentage of expenditure. It was interesting to note, looking at the educational program and the exhibits, that the fire service was only given minimal attention.

One thing that is crystal clear is that we must continue to participate in sessions such as this with the ICMA, with the National League of Cities, and other regional and management association meetings. We must carry our message not only on fire service accreditation, but on the issues that are facing the fire service as a whole during the next decade.

There truly is an information gap as to what the managers perceive, their level of understanding as to the impact, and the solutions that exist for the issues we will face as chief officers during the next decade. Still, we are the only ones who can provide that information, so it is imperative that we become more active in their educational process.

Ask the right questions

This article provoked the following exchange in the January 15, 1995, issue of *IAFC On Scene:*
Letter to the editor from Chief Harry F. Diezel, Virginia Beach, Virginia:

Ron. Randy. You did not ask the right questions! Consequently, the responses were predictable, gloomy and completely within norms. The next time you get that group together, and before the fire chief bashing begins, try a few questions to establish the meeting framework!

- Does your elected body have a published vision with goals and objectives tied to it?
- Have you communicated this to your department heads in writing, outlining your expectations for their performance?
- Have you measured department outcomes against community vision?
- When was the first time (if ever) you discussed the current and future community issues with your fire chief, asking for action plans to integrate fire department resources for community solutions?

It's time for all of us to talk-the-talk and walk-the-walk. Using fire chiefs as a thumping post is convenient, perhaps, but silly in the context of effective leadership. When the fire chief fails, the question is not who, but why?

Ask the right question(s).

Response by Chief Randy Bruegman:

I think Harry brings up some good points. I assure you that the next time we can gather a group of city management types, we will pose some of the questions he brings up to see if their house is in as much order as they expect ours to be.